T0211088

Lecture Notes in Computer Science 13176

More information about this series at https://link.springer.com/bookseries/558

Simon Parkin · Luca Viganò (Eds.)

Socio-Technical Aspects in Security

11th International Workshop, STAST 2021
Virtual Event, October 8, 2021
Revised Selected Papers

Editors
Simon Parkin ⓘ
Delft University of Technology
Delft, The Netherlands

Luca Viganò ⓘ
King's College London
London, UK

ISSN 0302-9743   ISSN 1611-3349 (electronic)
Lecture Notes in Computer Science
ISBN 978-3-031-10182-3   ISBN 978-3-031-10183-0 (eBook)
https://doi.org/10.1007/978-3-031-10183-0

This Springer imprint is published by the registered company Springer Nature Switzerland AG
The registered company address is: Gewerbestrasse 11, 6330 Cham, Switzerland

Preface

The 11th International Workshop on Socio-Technical Aspects in Security (STAST 2021) aimed at creating an exchange of ideas and experiences on how to design systems that are secure in the real world where they interact with users. The term "socio-technical," in this context, means a reciprocal relationship between technology and people. The 2021 workshop focused especially on the interplay of technical, organizational, and human factors in achieving or breaking computer security, privacy, and trust.

As typical for STAST, the workshop received a wide range of inter-disciplinary submissions with a number of distinct methodologies.

The peer-review was organized as a double-blind process, with a strong conflict-of-interest management system. Each submission received a minimum of three reviews. Submissions with appreciable variance in review scores were assigned a fourth review as a tie-breaker. The peer-review process included an active discussion phase, facilitated by a designated discussion lead for each submission, who subsequently summarized the discussion outcome and, when needed, agreed conclusions in a meta-review.

All of the 25 papers initially submitted to the workshop were retained by the chairs for peer-review after an initial check against the stipulations of the call for papers. Eventually, we accepted 10 submissions for publication in this volume, yielding an acceptance rate of 40%.

We prepared this volume with the following three sections. First, the section 'Web and apps' includes investigations on social media and applications. Second, the section 'Context and modelling' considers how to model the context of socio-technical systems in order to reason about their security. Finally, the section 'From the present to the future' includes analyses of, and positions on, the past, the present, and the future of the field itself.

Ashwin Mathew was recognized with the STAST 2021 Best Paper Award for the paper 'Can Security be Decentralised? The Case of the PGP Web of Trust.'

Overall, we were very pleased with the quality of STAST's 11th anniversary volume. We are grateful for the high-quality work of the authors involved and for the invaluable contributions of the 30 Program Committee members and three additional reviewers, whose dedication and attention to detail enabled this volume. We thank Borce Stojkovski and Itzel Vazquez Sandoval for their help with the publicity for the workshop and the workshop's web site.

February 2022

Simon Parkin
Luca Viganò

Message from the Workshop Organizers

It has been eleven years since we had the idea of founding a workshop dedicated to socio-technical aspects of cyber-security. At that time, something was missing in the landscape of events in security research: a venue to discuss security in a broader manner, a manner that combined technical discussion with other topics traditionally linked to usability and human computer interaction research, yet much broader than just these. There was a need to discuss attacks that exploit technical hacking in combination with social engineering and, equally, there was a need to discuss user practices, organizational processes, and social culture as instruments to establish security or, by contrast, as possible vectors to break it.

Discussing such matters was, and still is, relevant since evidence shows that designing systems that are secure when analyzed from a merely technical perspective, regardless of the values and merits of the approach, does not guarantee that security works as expected once deployed. The common and arguable explanation is that the human, the "weakest link," did not comply. However, blaming users neither helps nor gives us instruments to design stronger systems. We have learned by experience that a better strategy is to holistically conceive systems whose security emerges by harmonizing the technical features with the modalities in which humans, organizations, and societies operate. The manifesto of addressing the security problem socio-technically means exactly that all those components are to be addressed as a whole. We have also learned that such a manifesto has a very wide impact, concerning virtually all application areas where human beings may play a role through the effectiveness of security measures, hence on virtually every ICT application that must be protected from criminals.

Looking at the proceedings of this year's edition of the workshop, the published contents clearly attest that the idea outlined above has rooted well. As a result, the Workshop on Socio-Technical Aspects in Security (STAST) is now fully mature. Its aims have come to a clear focus, while the affiliation with the European Symposium on Research in Computer Security (ESORICS) is naturally well principled and practically fruitful.

We would like to thank all the Program Chairs and Committee members that in this decade have helped STAST to become a successful series. And we are particularly grateful to this year's Program Chairs, Simon Parkin and Luca Viganò: they have done an impeccable job and brought, with a top-level Program Committee, this year's edition to a unmatched success with a great scientific program.

February 2022

Giampaolo Bella
Gabriele Lenzini

Organization

General Chairs

Giampolo Bella   University of Catania, Italy
Gabriele Lenzini   University of Luxembourg, Luxembourg

Program Committee Chairs

Simon Parkin   Delft University of Technology, The Netherlands
Luca Viganò   King's College London, UK

Program Committee

Panagiotis Andriotis   University of the West of England, UK
Ingolf Becker   University College London, UK
Giampaolo Bella   University of Catania, Italy
Zinaida Benenson   University of Erlangen-Nuremberg, Germany
Vladlena Benson   Aston University, UK
Jan-Willem Bullee   University of Twente, The Netherlands
Michael Carter   Queen's University, Canada
Lynne Coventry   Northumbria University, UK
Sarah Diesburg   University of Northern Iowa, USA
Rosario Giustolisi   IT University of Copenhagen, Denmark
Thomas Groß   Newcastle University, UK
Pieter Hartel   University of Twente, The Netherlands
Ulrike Hugl   Innsbruck University, Austria
Markus Jakobsson   ZapFraud, USA
Kat Krol   Google UK
Gabriele Lenzini   University of Luxembourg, Luxembourg
Shujun Li   University of Kent, UK
Alexandra Mai   SBA-Research, Austria
Jean Everson Martina   Universidade Federal de Santa Catarina, Brazil
Masakatsu Nishigaki   Shizuoka University, Japan
Norbert Nthala   Michigan State University, USA
Jason Nurse   University of Kent, UK
Simon Parkin   Delft University of Technology, The Netherlands
Saša Radomirović   Heriot-Watt University, UK
Karen Renaud   University of Strathclyde, UK

Peter Y. A. Ryan	University of Luxembourg, Luxembourg
Diego Sempreboni	King's College London, UK
Kerry-Lynn Thomson	Nelson Mandela University, South Africa
Luca Viganò	King's College London, UK
Konrad Wrona	NATO Communications and Information Agency, The Netherlands/Military University of Technology in Warsaw, Poland

Publicity and Web Site Chairs

| Borce Stojkovski | University of Luxembourg, Luxembourg |
| Itzel Vazquez Sandoval | University of Luxembourg, Luxembourg |

Additional Reviewers

Ehsan Estaji
Masoud Tabatabaei
Sarah Turner

Fonds National de la Recherche Luxembourg

securityandtrust.lu

UNIVERSITÀ degli STUDI di CATANIA

UNIVERSITÉ DU LUXEMBOURG

Contents

Web and Apps

Who Watches the Birdwatchers? Sociotechnical Vulnerabilities in Twitter's Content Contextualisation

Garfield Benjamin[✉]

Solent University, Southampton, UK
garfield.benjamin@solent.ac.uk

Abstract. At the start of 2021, Twitter launched a closed US pilot of Birdwatch, seeking to promote credible information online by giving users the opportunity to add context to misleading tweets. The pilot shows awareness of the importance of context, and the challenges, risks and vulnerabilities the system will face. But the mitigations against these vulnerabilities of Birdwatch can exacerbate wider societal vulnerabilities created by Birdwatch. This article examines how Twitter presents the Birdwatch system, outlines a taxonomy of potential sociotechnical vulnerabilities, and situates these risks within broader social issues. We highlight the importance of watching the watchers, not only in terms of those using and potentially manipulating Birdwatch, but also the way Twitter is developing the system and their wider decision-making processes that impact on public discourse.

Keywords: Twitter · Sociotechnical · Vulnerabilities · Online content

1 Background

Against the backdrop of ongoing problems with social media platforms and online content moderation, Twitter's Birdwatch system enables users to add 'notes' to tweets, in order to add context, fact-check or other explanation aimed at promoting more credible information online. At face value, the initiative seems positive, particularly following waves of not only political but also public health issues caused by misleading information circulating through social media, and the flurry of forthcoming regulatory changes in response [19]. If anything, the main criticism we could level is that it should have been introduced sooner.

It is reassuring - maybe even a little surprising - to see a social media platform introducing important concepts like context. Researchers have been emphasising the importance of context in issues of data, privacy and algorithms [7, 16, 22, 23, 44, 48, 50, 51]. Seeing a major platform embrace the nuances of context that surround all information is an important step, particularly if it involves users being able to contribute to that context.

But there are clear potential problems with Birdwatch: in its conceptualisation, in the design of the pilot, and in the planned path towards global rollout.

S. Parkin and L. Viganò (Eds.): STAST 2021, LNCS 13176, pp. 3–23, 2022.
https://doi.org/10.1007/978-3-031-10183-0_1

Any system engaging with complex sociotechnical issues will likely be riddled with bugs and vulnerabilities. Sociotechnical problems generally have no single concrete 'fix'. Controlling and moderating content online has competing arguments and interests that resist a final resolution to these issues.

Grimmelmann calls content moderation "the governance mechanisms that structure participation in a community to facilitate cooperation and prevent abuse" [31], including processes of designing and moderating. But moderation is a fiendishly difficult problem to tackle, riddled with issues of power and labour [54], and often involving competing interests, ideals and methods.

Content moderation, and the inadequate approaches by platforms thus far, have come under much scrutiny and criticism [54]. This includes issues of ghost work by exploited and undervalued moderators [30,46], hidden decision-making by corporate interests [26], and defining what constitutes the public sphere [66]. In practical terms, content moderation has been criticised for negative or contradictory user perceptions [9,49], inspiring practices of avoiding moderation techniques [25], and promoting further engagement (even if negative) with harmful or false content [67]. Content moderation demonstrates difficulties in regulation, in terms of defining harms and the hidden algorithmic back-end [13], the informal interactions between platforms [18] or with states and NGOs [27], and the need to support international human rights across legislative settings [41].

Birdwatch adds in further issues by inserting community-based mechanisms [40] within the organised processes of "commercial content moderation" [54] that form one of the key commodities provided by online platforms [26]. But how far is Birdwatch a community-based approach? It is certainly crowdsourced, and makes impressive claims for transparency. But it risks being at best a partial offloading of labour and responsibility to the community while the platform itself continues to benefit from providing user-generated content.

Given the "systemic vulnerabilities in our democracy" [35] created by social media platforms, we need to keep a careful watch over Birdwatch. We need to ask intersectional questions of "who" [16]: who benefits from the platform? Whose voice will be (further) amplified? Who will be (further) marginalised? Who is exploited to generate the data for the platform to function? Whose interests and biases are designing the system? We must also keep watch for other motives at work. Is Birdwatch's contextualisation even content moderation? Or is it another step towards promoting platform engagement to distract from outside regulation, leaving the underlying power of Twitter unchecked?

In her critique of racialised histories of surveillance, Browne [10] emphasises the need to watch the watchers: sousveillance, the surveillance *of* authorities rather than *by* them, is both a critique and a practice. Power comes not only from watching authority but by using insights into surveillance to find ways of resisting. With the fraught intertwining of platform, content and users, it is imperative that we build on these practices to watch the Birdwatchers. This involves not only users watching other users but challenging the platform and dominant voices who control the metricising narratives of online media.

This paper examines how Twitter is constructing and presenting the Birdwatch trials, including the stated values, challenges and mitigations. A taxonomy of potential sociotechnical attacks is outlined, including not only vulnerabilities of the Birdwatch system but also societal vulnerabilities created by Birdwatch. These vulnerabilities are situated in a discussion of broader societal impacts. The article concludes by questioning what role Birdwatch is trying to play, for society and for Twitter. It emphasises the need to not only watch the Birdwatchers, but to scrutinise platform priorities in controlling content and discourse online.

2   Birdwatch

Birdwatch operates as follows [61]:

- A user posts a tweet containing claims that may be false or taken out of context;
- Other users add 'notes' to these tweets to provide context or evidence to explain or counter the claims made in the tweet, including a reason selected from a list of options;
- Further users upvote or downvote notes, selecting a reason from a list of options;
- Notes are ranked according to votes, influencing their visibility in relation to the tweet.

The aim is that users can then assess the credibility of a source themselves, based in crowd-sourced and crowd-rated contextualisation.

Notes are very different from replies. Notes are not a thread following a tweet, but exist alongside, aimed at providing context in a more authoritative way. Compared to anti-abuse mechanisms like hiding or restricting replies, notes are less about direct communication between the tweeter and note writer. They are between a note writer and the audience, and so intervene between the tweet and its reception.

As already noted, there is a lot to be positive about here: emphasising context; emphasising evidence; shifting discussion to around tweets rather than in antagonistic or abusive replies; collective assessment of notes; differentiating reasons for a note and how a note is ranked. There is also an open channel for feedback to Birdwatch, including to highlight risks and express concerns [61], and they show a desire to respond and engage, at least to some degree [1]. This echoes positive moves in other departments, such as the responsible machine learning team [63]. But each of the positives of Birdwatch also brings risks of abuse and wider societal impact, and the design of the system raises further questions we must examine before it becomes normalised.

Visibility is an essential point to consider. Which tweets will register for potential notes? How are notes made visible? These are important questions. Tweets will need "100 total likes plus retweets" [61] in order to appear in the Birdwatch system. This opens up some avenues of avoiding scrutiny either through obscurity, or through more directed means. Iterating tweets across bots to lower like/retweet counts could reduce the likelihood of it triggering Birdwatch (or simply making the same misleading information more widely seen). Followers pasting (perhaps with minor changes) the same information rather than retweeting could achieve similar results. Images of text could also be used for this purpose. However, these attacks would not scale well to those with large numbers of followers or the hopes of "viral" attention, and would require a greater deal of coordination and participation.

The note ranking system has mechanisms to prevent abuse, but these often shift attacks to other forms. Notes initially register as "Needs more ratings" until 5 or more votes have been received, at which point it may be shifted in the ranking system and have "Currently rated helpful" or "Currently rated not helpful" labels added [61]. During the pilot, rankings are calculated at regular intervals rather than changing in real-time. This might prevent a misleading or malicious note jumping to the top of the feed, but it also introduces what amount to timing attacks. Once a note is added, followers, sockpuppet or bot accounts could upvote it, and then it will (for a certain time at least) be mislabelled as helpful. Even if these things can be rectified by further votes, it relies on numerous assumptions: that the community can and should be willing to take on this role; that further follower/bot coordination isn't going to counter legitimate votes; that even a short time attached to a viral tweet isn't enough to sow misinformation or abuse, particularly if it crosses to a different platform.

Notes and note votes have lists of reasons attached. This to some extent adds further context at a glance. But it also adds another form of context attack. By targeting less used (or even irrelevant) reasons, a note can be made to seem like a different opinion or "diverse perspective". The ranking system is designed to seek out such diversity - different reasons for context, and notes coming from users who have engaged with different accounts or tweets. But it could also promote misleading notes that game the categorisation system.

This highlights an underlying problem with algorithmically sorting notes, and demonstrates how Birdwatch is still trying to turn context into metrics in order to deal with the issues of content moderation at scale. The note ranking algorithm is less transparent, and will need particular scrutiny as the pilot and system develop.

The ability to sign up for the current pilot is restricted to the US [61]. This introduces the potential for data pollution attacks. If these are intentional, it feeds into broader concerns of disproportionate influence by certain actors (perhaps mobilising bots or large numbers of followers). But it also leads to unintentional data poisoning in Birdwatch's design. If the system is shaped too tightly by US linguistic, social, cultural, political and economic concerns, a context attack develops by imposing these norms on other geographical locations when the system is rolled out globally.

The US context is also applicable to the ability to download Birdwatch data for research and accountability purposes [61]. Twitter has long been considered a "model organism" [58] for its publicly available data for research. But given the intention to deploy the system globally, the US-only access excludes wider perspectives from the development of the system. The data itself risks adding only faux transparency, as the ranking algorithms themselves remain more opaque, as do the ultimate decision-making processes within Twitter. It seems they are seeking external validation and fixes of vulnerabilities within Birdwatch rather than full sociotechnical audit of the impact of the system itself.

Within the US, there are limited places on the pilot, prioritising again those "diverse voices" by selecting accounts that interact with different tweets or other users on Twitter [61]. This is an attempt to stop bot-based attacks and promote more diverse data. But to gain access, you also need to verify your phone and email, and not have any recent notice of Twitter rules violations.

While these measures may prevent bot and sockpuppet attacks, in mitigating these vulnerabilities they introduce exclusion of those who may need to remain anonymous (abuse victims or whistleblowers, for example), or those who don't have access to the levels of verification needed. The need to sign up with a trusted US-based phone carrier and enact 2-factor authentication may exclude those with less access to technology based on cost or sharing devices. It will therefore likely prioritise already dominant voices and those who have the privilege of being able to use their real names on Twitter without fear of abuse. This shapes the context with an escalation attack in which loud voices get even louder. Mitigating this will rely on the success of the diverse engagement measures.

How is Twitter designing these measures? What would register as success of the system? The company outlines the Birdwatch values as "contribute to build understanding", "act in good faith" and "be helpful, even to those who disagree" [61]. At first glance, these seem reasonable. But, firstly, these are largely expectations placed on users rather than expressing the values of Birdwatch as an initiative. And, secondly, there are holes.

Language use can be easily gamed. Abusive comments could be concealed beneath a veneer of clear or scientific authority, and even citing evidence does not certify the validity of the evidence cited. Bots could be easily trained to write just within the guidelines while still being varied enough to count as different perspectives. Similarly, "baiting" other users into using language that triggers automated toxicity filters has already been employed on gaming platforms [53], and these techniques could be used to game notes.

There are also assumptions and potential data bias about such language. Will the automated parts of the system continue to misunderstand the context? Would critically discussing hateful language lead to a note being itself considered hateful, even if the abusive tweet it discusses didn't? The data used to define these triggers will be important [6,17,55], particularly when it comes to context shifts.

There are fundamental tensions in Birdwatch managing contextualisation through a metricised system. And relying on good faith on social media is almost certainly naive when it comes to a global platform with stakes in preventing abuse and promoting public discourse.

Twitter is aware of many of these challenges [61], and some of the measures already outlined are there to try to mitigate potential attacks. They state that

Birdwatch will add to rather than replacing existing misinformation measures. The aim of the pilot process is to experiment with "new ways to address adversarial coordination" to prevent "coordinated mass attacks" [61]. While these may work in the sandboxed pilot stage, it remains to be seen whether any solutions scale to global rollout across different contexts.

There are issues with Twitter's responses to the acknowledged challenges. Though they may mitigate vulnerabilities within the Birdwatch system, in doing so they may also contribute to further societal risks caused by Birdwatch. Diverse engagement systems offer some potential, but metricising diversity will always be problematic.

Similarly, the parallel reputation system for helpful Birdwatchers (separate from number of followers on Twitter itself, for example), not only risks adding further burden to marginalised communities but simply shifts the gaming. It may create more work to initiate an effective attack, but it is not much beyond trivial for major actors - particularly authoritarian regimes outside the US-EU zone that (so far) receive much less attention from social media platforms. Again, context is key, and the work of critical journalists, researchers and rights advocates paying close attention to global contexts (such as [3, 21, 62, 64, 65]) is hugely important.

The sandboxed trial itself raises methodological questions. The aim of preventing bots from sabotaging the trial is admirable, but any wider implementation will inevitably have to deal with bots. Including bots in the trial would provide a far more realistic view of what challenges will arise. Twitter's choice to test in this way relies on a 'best-case' context of sorts. This sidesteps many of the potential problems in the realities of online platforms, and of course limits the narratives to the already dominant US context. An alternative approach would be an open global trial, but maintaining the Birdwatch platform sandbox so that notes and rankings do not appear on tweets until thorough testing, analysis and consultation have been conducted.

Twitter acknowledges the difficulties in global contexts for expanding Birdwatch, including cultural differences and the specificities of misleading information in different settings - and they have stated that they will take into account these considerations as they expand [1]. But the questions remain of who decides? When will the pilot be expanded, and what measures of success are required first? Where will it be expanded to - other Anglophone or North America-European settings? When will the pilot become local or global implementation, and will the same attention be paid to continuing development?

There is also the fundamental question of would they decide to stop? Twitter's responsible machine learning team shows further reassurance here, giving users the option to turn off image-cropping algorithms that have been proven to be biased [63]. But would they make the leap to abandoning Birdwatch if it fails? And who would it need to fail for in order for it to be stopped? This is likely more a matter of who is failed by Birdwatch, and it will likely be those that platforms such as Twitter have already failed.

3   Sociotechnical Vulnerabilities

Algorithmic content moderation is about people [54], and any discussion of its effects must be embedded in social as well as technical concerns. For example, [28] identify how algorithmic content moderation faces a series of not only technical but political challenges. We argue to go even further and not separate these two spaces.

The technical is political; the political is technical. This is shown in algorithms that discriminate based on race and/or gender [11,32,38] and the proposal that categories of marginalisation such as race are themselves constructed as technologies [8]. We argue for talking in interwoven sociotechnical terms, particularly when assessing vulnerabilities in the integrity of public discourse and control over social narratives.

This approach differs from, for example, social engineering in that it is not concerned with the use of human or social side-channels as alternative vectors to attack technical systems. And it goes beyond looking at the social effects of technological vulnerabilities. Instead, it focuses on the use of both social and technical channels in order to attack systems that are themselves social. It employs the languages of vulnerability analysis and critical theories in order to examine potential social and societal harms, whether that is abuse of individuals, marginalisation of specific groups, or risks to public discourse and democracy. Sociotechnical vulnerabilities are about the distribution of power, equity and justice.

Applying these social vulnerabilities to Birdwatch generates two broad categories. Firstly, there are vulnerabilities of the Birdwatch system. This includes all the ways that Birdwatch can be manipulated or abused, from avoiding the system to weaponising notes to gaming rankings. Secondly, there are vulnerabilities by Birdwatch. This includes the risks to public discourse and other areas of societal concern created by the use of the system, even as intended.

Figure 1 shows how these types of vulnerability interact, highlighting how the mitigations of the vulnerabilities of Birdwatch can exacerbate the vulnerabilities created by Birdwatch. It is important, therefore, to carefully review how Twitter acknowledges and mitigates the challenges of developing the Birdwatch system. This is not just examining how effective they might be, or further loopholes for attack, but how the mitigations themselves feed back into how Birdwatch creates vulnerabilities for society.

An initial response to these broad categories of vulnerabilities should include a requirement for continual external audit. This should be enforced by regulators and could be conducted using methods following, for example, the Platform Governance Observatory [56]. This process highlights the importance of wider access to the data downloads and the underlying algorithms. The stakes of the system being rolled out globally suggest a narrowing of access to within the US - matching the terms of the pilot - could have long term harmful effects or necessitate those with access 'leaking' it to researchers, activist and rights advocacy groups, and regulators, in other geographical contexts.

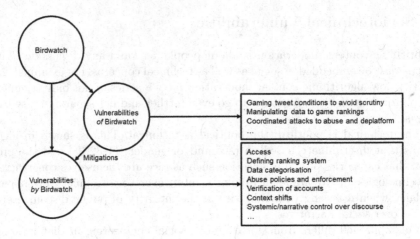

Fig. 1. Vulnerability structure of Birdwatch.

3.1 Taxonomy of Sociotechnical Vulnerabilities

Many of the vulnerabilities have been outlined in the analysis of Birdwatch above, but it is useful to consider how different vulnerabilities are related. Figure 2 shows a proposed taxonomy of the social vulnerabilities of and by Birdwatch. These are traced from the target area, through the various modes of attack, to the societal harms the attack creates or worsens. The taxonomy embodies the sociotechnical approach of this article, combining elements of, for example, the NIST adversarial machine learning taxonomy [57] as well as Citron and Solove's typology of privacy harms [12]. The taxonomy emerges from the reading of Birdwatch presented above, systematically analysing the parts of the system and Twitter's approach to developing and presenting it. The full description of these elements can be found in Appendix A.

3.2 Ranking Vulnerabilities

In technical settings, it is useful to rank attacks according to considerations such as likelihood or severity, particularly when taxonomising. However, in socially-embedded contexts such as online content moderation, this can prove impossible without introducing further assumptions and exclusions. Jiang et al. [37] show that "platform abuse and spam" ranked consistently low in user perceptions of severity of online harms. Even "mass scale harms" such as terrorism ranked lower than specific cases of harmful content, although they remained present as a concern. The study highlights the need to move beyond US-centric perspectives when moderating content, particularly when making assumptions about its severity. Any collapsing of complex social contexts into restrictive metrics will erase important details, and runs counter to the aim of examining the implications of online platforms. However, certain useful indicators can assist in the

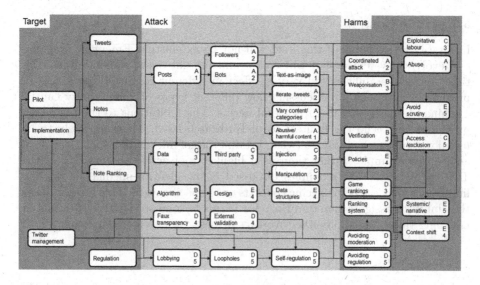

Fig. 2. Taxonomy of attacks.

examination of different types of attacks and harms, particularly against individuals. This tension exists within Birdwatch itself: mitigating individual harms while exacerbating systemic harms does little to resolve the narratives in which the individual harms are enabled. To this end, rather than the perceptual and evasive labels of severity or likelihood (which in any case are so unevenly distributed as to be of little use without further qualification), we instead rate attack and harm elements within the taxonomy according to the scale and timeframe of their effects. This is assigned based on the primary impact identified in the analysis above, and presents us with two values for each attack:

Scale

A Specific individual

B Specific types of individual (e.g. based on protected characteristics)

C Specific community

D Public discourse in a specific context (e.g. field or geographical area)

E Systemic/principles (e.g. democracy, discrimination, censorship)

Timeframe

1 Immediate (e.g. on posting)

2 Short term (e.g. sharing, including viral propagation before removal)

3 Mid term (e.g. posts over time)

4 Long term (e.g. impacting design iterations)

5 Persistent (e.g. ongoing narratives, systemic decision-making).

This allows us to further identify which vulnerabilities can be mitigated within Birdwatch, and which require external intervention (the potential vulnerabilities in society created by Birdwatch). It also highlights the different power relations at work, and the ways that harms are felt unevenly in society.

3.3   Limitations

Inevitably a taxonomy of this kind will not be exhaustive. Emergent practices and evolving system design will create and mitigate new vulnerabilities over time, and vulnerabilities will vary in effect in different contexts. The aim is to provide an approach for discussing how different types of vulnerability can be combined to cause social and societal harms. The limitations to the taxonomy presented here echo the limitations of Birdwatch itself. They are likely to be useful within specific contexts (with certain types of information such as medical advice, for example) rather than as a blanket tool across the entirety of the Twitter platform. The examples discussed below identify unequal harms and limitations that apply in specific contexts or to specific users. This further limits the ability to assign concrete ratings for harms beyond speculative potential or assigning values based on either averages or best-/worst-case scenarios.

4   Examples

We now examine one of the processes in which these social attacks might be mobilised. Consider the example of a scientist, who happens to identify as a Black woman, posting on Twitter about some new research findings or commenting on an issue of public concern well within her area of expertise. The example is familiar from throughout the Covid-19 pandemic in particular, but also applies more widely when minoritised groups (whether women, racialised people, trans or queer people, or disabled people, just to name a few) share their expertise and/or lived experience in fields from computer science to biology to politics to philosophy. Figure 3 shows a possible process of attack, which aligns with the outline of "The Abuse and Misogynoir Playbook" [60].

1. A *contribution* is made. This is the victim posting on Twitter.
2. This is met with *disbelief* by the abuser (which may be someone already in a position of power and/or platform, including senior academics, public officials/candidates, celebrities or other public figures) and their followers, leading the abuser to write a bad faith note containing falsehoods. The note itself, while based in opinion and falsehood, will likely be crafted to appear to follow the Birdwatch guidelines: no direct insult; appealing to a sense of commonly held knowledge, disputed or beside-the-point technicalities, or "whataboutism".
3. A combination of *dismissal, gaslighting* and *discrediting* emerges. This could be achieved by the abuser's followers piling on with further false or bad faith notes (many of which may get flagged as abusive), followed by the abuser's followers and/or bots upvoting the false notes while downvoting any notes written in support of the victim.
4. The result is the *erasure* of the victim through devaluing the original contribution and hijacking the narrative. Even if others support the original post with supportive notes, with enough negative engagement and conflicting false narratives, it will likely end up being downranked by the Twitter algorithm.

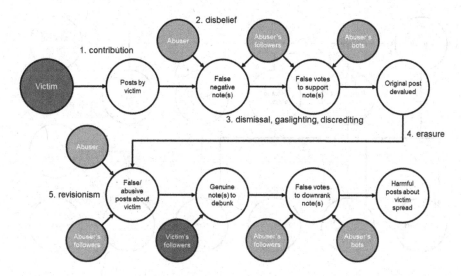

Fig. 3. Combining data poisoning, gaming the algorithm and coordinated attacks.

5. In the final misogynoir move - *revisionism* - the whole process happens in the negative: the abuser and their followers write false or abusive posts about the victim or their contribution; genuine notes by the victim's followers or others in the community are further gaslit and discredited by false downvotes by the abuser's followers, while continuing to upvote or add positive notes about the abusive content; and finally the harmful and abusive posts can be either spread further than the original contribution or entered into enough of a contested narrative that the lines between contribution and abuse become sufficiently blurred to devalue both.

Either way, data poisoning (false notes, false votes), gaming the algorithm (affecting the rankings), and coordinated attacks (whether by followers, bots or a combination) have led to abuse, weaponisation, exclusion and a perpetuation of oppressive narratives.

In this example, a number of different types of agent are mobilised. This includes: a human abuser, likely a public figure or other account with large numbers of followers; the human followers of that account, each with their own motives and patterns of behaviour; bots controlled by the abuser, their followers, or third parties seeking to capitalise on abuse, again for a variety of motives. There are also other different interactions and roles between agents to take into account. Figure 4 shows how different types of Twitter account could take on different roles as part of a coordinated mass attack.

This includes a range of bots and bot-human hybrids, building on Gorwa and Guilbeault's typology [29]. For example, sockpuppet accounts - additional and/or anonymous accounts often used specifically for trolling and abuse - could be used by abusers to try to avoid responsibility. Or, followers and bots could take on crowdturfing roles; the (often paid) fake reviewers that appear on online

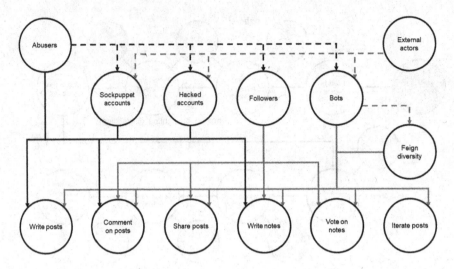

Fig. 4. Actors.

shopping or trust/review sites could be repurposed to write fake notes. Many existing forms of bots and collective human action could be mobilised in these different roles.

These roles could also manipulate Twitter's existing mitigations of the risks of Birdwatch. An automated or crowd-sourced trolling army could easily be created to spread across different engagement or community types. By establishing different patterns of interaction with different communities and types of content, a range of accounts could be created that the system would identify as coming from "diverse voices". Even a dedicated trolling sockpuppet that interacts solely with people from a specific marginalised group could appear to the system as belonging to or representing that group.

Particularly at scale, Twitter and Birdwatch's automated systems will not be able to tell genuine engagement as part of a community from a targeted harasser. Hijacked accounts can also be used for this purpose. These could then be brought into action as a supposedly representative set of opinions all saying the same thing for malicious and/or abusive ends.

Following existing social media information warfare techniques [39], it is easy to imagine a paid-for service using these different attacks on Birdwatch. Harassment and misinformation as a service is already a problem, and can be particularly damaging to political candidates, especially those from marginalised groups. The diverse voices Birdwatch aims to emphasise could be overridden in a hegemonising attack that collapses the aims of contextualisation.

The ability of different agents to target different aspects of the widening range of interactions - notes and votes as well as tweets - impacts on pathways of abuse. Birdwatch shifts not only where abuse can occur but also the responses to abuse. Because notes are intended for audiences of tweets, rather than being directed at the original tweeter as is the case with replies, they challenge existing methods of mitigation and recourse.

For example, note-writers may be able to operate outside of the blocking mechanisms that can be used to prevent malicious or abusive replies. This also reduces the effectiveness of tools like automated collective blocklists [24]. Removing tools developed by marginalised communities contributes to the harm of placing extra burden on those communities to rectify content moderation issues.

The wider sociotechnical vulnerabilities are evident in the risks of context shift. Despite being focused on contextualising individual tweets, Birdwatch runs the risk of imposing certain media and power structures onto other contexts. Figure 5 displays some of the aspects of this context shift vulnerability. Structural and cultural contexts often do not translate, and a major risk of Birdwatch is that the US pilot will entrench specific values and priorities. This has implications for imposing and erasing certain norms of public discourse on social media, and for removing agency from global communities.

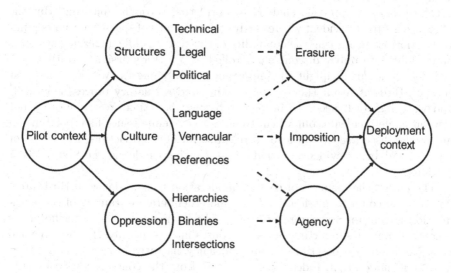

Fig. 5. Context shift.

We need to ask: whose context is Birdwatch adding? Without meaningful engagement with other communities during the development phases, it is likely to perpetuate the dominance of US-centric platforms. Public discourse in other geographical or international contexts is made vulnerable to further colonial (and other forms of) domination.

5 Discussion

Sociotechnical vulnerabilities - unlike many purely technical security vulnerabilities - often have no state of being "fixed", particularly for complex sociotechnical systems like content moderation. This is true both over time - contexts, norms and needs may change as society and platforms develop - and in terms of solutionism - there is no final finished state of content moderation, for example, it will always be an ongoing process. While these points may sometimes be true of technical vulnerabilities - cyber security is always to some extent a matter of constant "patching" or being "secure enough" for the given needs and context - a central tenet of finding solutions for social vulnerabilities is a resistance to seeing them as closable problems.

Indeed, the reading of Birdwatch and the subsequent taxonomy presented here suggests that closing vulnerabilities within Birdwatch tends to create further social vulnerabilities by Birdwatch. This is particularly the case with mitigations such as verification, which introduces issues of identification (leading to potential targeting and further abuse) previously not present on Twitter.

Citron and Solove [12] emphasise the differences between the goals of punishing harms - often compensation, deterrence and equity - and the remedies to the harms themselves. Contextualisation could be seen as focusing on remedies, such as the restorative approach enabled by correcting through educating. But the difference is further evident where Birdwatch sanctions of specific accounts punitively prioritise protecting the credibility of the system while increasing systemic vulnerabilities in public discourse controlled by Twitter's design narratives.

These concerns highlight the importance of watching the watchers, not just those on Birdwatch but the decision-making and regulatory process behind it. And watching itself needs to be one step towards action. Watching does not prevent single incidents, but when it comes to systemic issues like social media and public discourse, it can lead to recourse for specific victims, sanctions for abusers, and bring evidence to light that can help redefine the system as it develops.

There are other aspects of content moderation to consider with Birdwatch. Does it even count as moderation? The more deliberative framing of contextualisation is perhaps a separate process. It is not aimed at fixing specific pieces of content, but at supporting better discourse more generally. It moves beyond what Common [15] describes as an "efficiency narrative" in the enforcement of content moderation. Indeed, moving away from the concerns raised by [12], Birdwatch is not even really about enforcement. But does this different function detract from the need to address issues with specific pieces of content?

We could see Birdwatch as Twitter taking a longer, more constructive approach. The role of contextualisation could contribute to broader aims of improving public discourse on social media. It allows space for restorative justice approaches to moderation [34], as well as opportunities for other techniques such as digital juries [20]. Perhaps Birdwatch is a first step away from enforcement as a narrative, and a rejection of the idea that there is a quick fix for online content and online harms?

But what of the more immediate harms that will continue in the meantime? Responding to specific harmful tweets will still rely on tactics such as blocklists which have been shown to be problematic and inadequate [36]. Meanwhile, journalists and rights advocates may still have the visually shocking content they rely on blocked outright by content moderation before context can be added [4]. However, representation and narrative are important. There is a case that such posts should indeed be blocked to stop perpetuating victim or deficit narratives, like the calls to stop sharing footage of Black men in the US being shot by police as it not only desensitised but performs, perpetuates and normalises such acts. Contextualisation, moderation and refusal each have their place in making discourse on social media not just more credible but also more equitable. Power must be taken into account, not just authority.

This leads us back to key questions over what role contextualisation and community are playing on Birdwatch. The mechanisms seem more effective on fact-based issues, like their example of "whales are not actually mammals" [61], which can be readily countered with scientific context according to Birdwatch's guidelines. But the major risks and vulnerabilities have greater impact when it is social issues at stake. Hate speech and misrepresentation of gender (including trans), race, disability and other forms of discrimination require greater context but are more vulnerable to oppressive dominant narratives and attacks.

There are significant issues with relying on public fora as a marketplace of ideas [43], leading to further concerns with the more general gamification of social media discourse [45] and the individualising effects this is likely to have on Birdwatch [42]. Reducing context back to metrics could alienate the people and communities doing the work. Birdwatch claims to be community-based, but is this true? Twitter introduced Birdwatch as "community-based" [14], citing research on crowd-sourcing to tackle misinformation [2,47,52]. It is worth noting the overlap in authors of two of these papers, and the fact that [2] has not yet been peer-reviewed. But these papers present a significantly narrower scope than the aim of creating credible public discourse.

While it may to some extent avoid efficiency narratives, Birdwatch still feeds into the related and equally problematic narratives of scale [33]. Bell and Turkewitz highlight how "scale doesn't scale", or at least that "harms scale, solutions not so much" [59]. Whether misinformation or abuse, tackling such viral harms requires gargantuan efforts, likely entailing either more moderators than posters or error-prone automation which scales but not effectively. If information "with high civic value [...] is discriminated against by a system that favors scale and shareability" [5], is credible information simply incompatible with Twitter as a medium? Does Birdwatch signal a shift in this narrative? It at least attempts to reach the combination of human and algorithmic solutions that Bell and others propose, but the combination needs interrogating. Is it trying to humanise visibility algorithms? Or does it end up algorithmising human users?

Birdwatch may be crowd-sourced, but that is not the same thing as being community-based. Where is the agency for marginalised individuals or communities? Decision-making is still controlled centrally by Twitter, a private platform. It seems more like they are getting extra fact-checking done for free by users, rather than providing the service of moderation (which, as Gillespie [26] asserts, is a key function or commodity of a social media platform). The labour issues of content moderation [30,54] are displaced back onto users, and likely place further burden on already marginalised and abused people.

Contextualisation here appears as Twitter side-stepping moderation and accountability, shifting the focus onto misinformation. This is a current concern for many governments, and Twitter needs to be seen to be taking action. But that means that Birdwatch is also a tactical play against the imposition of further regulation. By giving tools to communities, Birdwatch has the potential to improve context, data literacy and representation. But the hidden and conflicting motives detract from this potential to tackle specific issues with online harms.

Birdwatch could be a thoughtful way of addressing some of the complex issues around online content and harms. Emphasising context is a key part of this. But it also introduces further sociotechnical vulnerabilities that we must pay attention to. This includes: weaponisation of the platform through potential gaming and gamification of rankings; the perpetuation of dominant harmful or hateful narratives; the continuation of control by opaque algorithms even as data is made more transparent; US-centrism in establishing online norms for global communities; exploitative labour through crowd-sourcing; and the veneer of community to avoid responsibility.

Birdwatch, and the watchers of Birdwatch, will need to keep the social effects of categorisation, individualisation, exploitation, inequity, constraining discourse and responsibility for moderation in mind as the system develops.

6   Conclusion

There is a lot of potential in Birdwatch. But the issue is complex and carries significant risk of generating further vulnerabilities for public discourse. In this article, we have examined the Birdwatch pilot scheme and plans for global rollout. We have identified sociotechnical vulnerabilities under two categories: vulnerabilities within the Birdwatch system; and vulnerabilities for public discourse created by the Birdwatch system. We have outlined a taxonomy of these interrelated vulnerabilities, and discussed how mitigations for the former can lead to an increase in the latter. We have then situated these concerns in wider social issues around online communication, including issues of power and agency.

The importance of watching the design of new sociotechnical systems - and the power structures and priorities behind them - cannot be overstated. We must continue to watch the Birdwatchers, as Twitter has made possible through transparent access to data on the pilot. But we must also continue to watch Birdwatch itself. This is a more difficult task as the decision-making and algorithmic systems remain much more opaque. But it is essential that Twitter is held accountable for deciding what and how information is shared and seen on its platform. We must continue watching Birdwatch closely.

A   Description of the Taxonomy

Key

> **Scale** [A] Individual, [B] Type of individual, [C] Community, [D] Public discourse, [E] Systemic/principles.
> **Timeframe** [1] Immediate, [2] Short, [3] Mid, [4] Long, [5] Persistent.

Targets

> **Pilot**: vulnerabilities during the US and subsequent pilots
> **Implementation**: the transition to global context;
> **Tweets**: user interactions and vectors for attacks;
> **Notes**: user interactions and vectors for attacks;
> **Note ranking**: user interactions and vectors for attacks;
> **Twitter management**: internal decisions create/mitigate vulnerabilities;
> **Regulation**: external (legislative) decisions prevent/permit vulnerabilities.

Attacks

A 1 **Posts**: tweets and notes, including many directly abusive tactics;
A 2 **Followers**: tools in extended abuse;
A 2 **Bots**: automating abuse to scale up coordinated attacks;
A 1 **Text-as-image**: an attack on whether the Birdwatch system is triggered;
A 2 **Iterating tweets**: as above;
A 1 **Varying content or categories**: as above;
A 1 **Abusive or harmful content**: as above;
C 3 **Data**: includes data poisoning of ranking system;
B 2 **Algorithm**: gives differential visibility or credibility to tweets/notes;
C 3 **Third party**: external attacks exploit vulnerabilities;
E 4 **Design**: internal flaws create vulnerabilities;
C 3 **Injection**: includes user interactions (likely) and breached security (less so);
C 3 **Manipulation**: includes user interactions and breached security;
E 4 **Data structures**: design flaws enable manipulation of data/the algorithm;
D 4 **Faux transparency**: data availability risks obscuring underlying structures;
D 4 **External validation**: public scrutiny and PR as tool for credibility;
D 5 **Lobbying**: pressure on regulators to prevent external constraints;
D 5 **Loopholes**: flaws in regulation (e.g. loose definitions) enable harmful design;
D 5 **Self-regulation**: Birdwatch is part of continued efforts to avoid regulation.

Harms

A 2 **Coordinated attacks**: combining attacks/accounts increases scale/impact;

B 3 **Weaponisation**: systematic targeting of certain groups/communities;

A 1 **Abuse**: effects (emotional, physical) against specific individuals(/groups);

B 3 **Verification**: shift for Twitter; harms marginalised groups with need for ID;

E 4 **Policies/enforcement**: precedent of unequal application/lack of context;

C 5 **Access/exclusion**: design, policies, implementation; method & type of harm;

D 3 **Game rankings**: vulnerabilities in practice and in credibility;

D 4 **Ranking system**: vulnerabilities to public discourse in Birdwatch design;

D 4 **Avoiding moderation**: not moderation; community not platform;

D 5 **Avoiding regulation**: visible action to placate regulators;

C 3 **Exploitative labour**: reliance on users; lack of protection; uneven burden;

E 5 **Avoid scrutiny**: systemic avoidance or deflection of external audit/criticism;

E 5 **Systemic/narrative**: structural impact on society; influence over debates;

E 4 **Context shift**: marginalisation of geospatial/cultural/etc. communities.

References

1. @Birdwatch: Private correspondence (Twitter DM), 29 March 2021 & 15 April 2021

2. Allen, J., Arechar, A.A., Pennycook G., Rand, D.G.: Scaling up fact-checking using the wisdom of crowds (2020). Preprint. Accessed 22 Apr 2021

3. Arun, C.: Rebalancing regulation of speech: hyper-local content on global web-based platforms (2018). Medium - Berkman Klein Center. Accessed 23 Apr 2021

4. Banchik, A.V.: Disappearing acts: content moderation and emergent practices to preserve at-risk human rights-related content. New Media Soc., 1–18 (2020)

5. Bell, E.J., Owen, T., Brown, P.D., Hauka, C., Rashidian, N.: The platform press: how silicon valley reengineered journalism. Tow Center Digit. J., 1–105 (2017)

6. Bender, E.M., Gebru, T., McMillan-Major, A., Shmitchell, S.: On the dangers of stochastic parrots: can language models be too big? In: FAccT 2021, pp. 610–623 (2021)

7. Benjamin, G.: From protecting to performing privacy. J. Sociotechnical Critique **1**(1), 1–30 (2020)

8. Benjamin, R.: Race After Technology: Abolitionist Tools for the New Jim Code. Polity (2019)

9. Binns, R., Veale, M., Van Kleek, M., Shadbolt, N.: Like trainer, like bot? Inheritance of bias in algorithmic content moderation. In: Ciampaglia, G.L., Mashhadi, A., Yasseri, T. (eds.) SocInfo 2017. LNCS, vol. 10540, pp. 405–415. Springer, Cham (2017). https://doi.org/10.1007/978-3-319-67256-4_32

10. Browne, S.: Dark Matters: On the Surveillance of Blackness. Duke UP (2015)

11. Buolamwini, J., Gebru, T.: Gender shades: intersectional accuracy disparities in commercial gender classification. In: FAT* 2018, pp. 77–91 (2018)

12. Citron, D.K., Solove, D.J.: Privacy harms. GWU Leg. Stud. **11**, 1–56 (2021)

13. Cobbe, J., Singh, J.: Regulating recommending: motivations, considerations, and principles. EJLT **10**(3), 1–49 (2019)
14. Coleman, K.: Introducing birdwatch, a community-based approach to misinformation (2021). Twitter Blog. Accessed 22 Apr 2021
15. Common, M.F.: Fear the reaper: how content moderation rules are enforced on social media. Int. Rev. Law, Comput. Technol. **34**(2), 126–152 (2020)
16. D'Ignazio, C., Klein, L.: Data Feminism. MIT Press (2020)
17. Davidson, T., Bhattacharya, D., Weber, I.: Racial bias in hate speech and abusive language detection datasets. In: ACL 2019 ALW3, pp. 1–11 (2019)
18. Douek, E.: The Rise of Content Cartels. Knight First Amendment Institute at Columbia, pp. 1–51 (2020)
19. Douek, E.: Governing online speech: from "Posts-As-Trumps" to proportionality and probability. Colum. L. Rev. **121**(1), 1–70 (2021)
20. Fan, J., Zhang A.X.: Digital juries: a civics-oriented approach to platform governance. In: CHI 2020, pp. 1–14 (2020)
21. Fisher, M.: Inside Facebook's secret rulebook for global political speech (2018). New York Times. Accessed 23 Apr 2021
22. Gangadharan, S.: Context, research, refusal: perspectives on abstract problem-solving (2020). Our Data Bodies. Accessed 21 Apr 2021
23. Gebru, T., et al.: Datasheets for Datasets. In: FAT* 2018, pp. 1–17 (2018)
24. Geiger, R.S.: Bot-based collective blocklists in Twitter: the counterpublic moderation of harassment in a networked public space. ICS **19**(6), 787–803 (2016)
25. Gerrard, Y.: Beyond the hashtag: circumventing content moderation on social media. New Media Soc. **20**(12), 4492–4511 (2018)
26. Gillespie, T.: Custodians of the Internet: Platforms, Content Moderation, and the Hidden Decisions That Shape Social Media. Yale University Press (2018)
27. Gorwa, R.: The platform governance triangle: conceptualising the informal regulation of online content. IPR **8**(2), 1–22 (2019)
28. Gorwa, R., Binns, R., Katzenbach, C.: Algorithmic content moderation: technical and political challenges in the automation of platform governance. BD&S **7**(1), 1–15 (2020)
29. Gorwa, R., Guilbeault, D.: Unpacking the social media bot: a typology to guide research and policy. P&I **12**(2), 225–248 (2020)
30. Gray, M., Suri, S.: Ghost Work: How to Stop Silicon Valley from Building a New Global Underclass. Houghton Mifflin Harcourt (2019)
31. Grimmelmann, J.: The virtues of moderation. YJoLT **17**(42), 42–109 (2015)
32. Hamidi, F., Scheuerman, M.K., Branham, S.M.: Gender recognition or gender reductionism? The social implications of embedded gender recognition systems. In: CHI 2018, pp. 1–13 (2018)
33. Hanna, A., Park, T.M.: Against scale: provocations and resistances to scale thinking. In: CSCW 2020, pp. 1–4 (2020)
34. Hasinoff, A.A., Gibson A.D., Salehi, N.: The promise of restorative justice in addressing online harm (2020). Brookings Institute. Accessed 22 Apr 2021
35. Information Commissioner's Office: Letter from the Information Commissioner ICO/O/ED/L/RTL/0181 (2020). ICO. Accessed 23 Apr 2021
36. Jhaver, S., Ghoshal, S., Bruckman, A., Gilbert, E.: Online harassment and content moderation: the case of blocklists. TOCHI **25**(2), 1–33 (2018)
37. Jiang, J.A., Scheuerman, M.K., Fiesler, C., Brubaker, J.R.: Understanding international perceptions of the severity of harmful content online. PLoS One **16**(8) (2021). e0256762

38. Keyes, O.: The misgendering machines: Trans/HCI implications of automatic gender recognition. In: CSCW 2018, pp. 1–22 (2018)
39. Krasodomski-Jones, A., Judson, E., Smith, J., Miller C., Jones, E.: Warring songs: information operations in the digital age (2019). Demos. Accessed 26 Apr 2021
40. Lampe C., Resnick, P.: Slash (dot) and burn: distributed moderation in a large online conversation space. In: CHI 2004, pp. 543–550 (2004)
41. Land, M.: Regulating private harms online: content regulation under human rights law. In: Jorgensen, R.F. (ed.) Human Rights in the Age of Platforms, pp. 285–315. MIT Press (2019)
42. Maddox, J.: Will the gamification of fact-checking work? Twitter seems to think so (2021). Medium - Start It Up. Accessed 22 Apr 2021
43. Maddox J., Malson, J.: Guidelines without lines, communities without borders: the marketplace of ideas and digital manifest destiny in social media platform policies. SM+S, 1–10 (2020)
44. Marwick, A.E., Boyd, D.: Networked privacy: how teenagers negotiate context in social media. NMS **16**(7), 1051–1067 (2014)
45. Massanari, A.: Playful participatory culture: learning from reddit. AoIR (2013)
46. Matias, J.N.: The civic labor of volunteer moderators online. SM+S **5**(2), 1–12 (2019)
47. Micallef, N., He, B., Kumar, S., Ahamad M., Memon, N.: The role of the crowd in countering misinformation: a case study of COVID-19 infodemic. IEEE BigData **2020**, 1–10 (2020)
48. Mitchell, M., et al.: Model cards for model reporting. In: FAT* 2019, pp. 220–229 (2019)
49. West, S.M.: Censored, suspended, shadowbanned: user interpretations of content moderation on social media platforms. NMS **20**(11), 4366–4383 (2018)
50. Nissenbaum, H.: A contextual approach to privacy online. Daedalus **140**(4), 32–48 (2011)
51. Noble, S.: Algorithms of Oppression. NYU Press (2018)
52. Pennycock, G., Rand, D.G.: Fighting misinformation on social media using crowdsourced judgments of news source quality. PNAS **116**(7), 2521–2526 (2019)
53. Reddit: Rainbow Six Siege players who use slurs are now getting instantly banned (2018). Reddit. Accessed 23 Apr 2021
54. Roberts, S.: Behind the Screen. Yale University Press (2019)
55. Sap, M., Card, D., Gabriel, S., Choi, Y., Smith, N.A.: The risk of racial bias in hate speech detection. ACL **57**, 1668–1678 (2019)
56. Suzor, N.: Understanding content moderation systems: new methods to understand internet governance at scale, over time, and across platforms. In: Whalen, R. (ed.) In Computational Legal Studies, pp. 166–189. Edward Elgar (2020)
57. Tabassi, E., Burns, K.J., Hadjimichael, M., Molina-Markham, A.D., Sexton, J.T.: A taxonomy and terminology of adversarial machine learning (draft) (2019). NIST IR 8269. Accessed 21 Apr 2021
58. Tufekci, Z.: Big questions for social media big data: representativeness, validity and other methodological pitfalls. ICWSM **8**(1), 505–514 (2014)
59. Turkewitz, N.: The week in tweets: the "Scale Doesn't Scale" Ition feat. Emily Bell (2020). Medium. Accessed 22 Apr 2021
60. Turner, K., Wood, D., D'Ignazio, C.: The abuse and misogynoir playbook. In: Gupta, A., et al. (ed.) The State of AI Ethics Report January 2021. Montreal AI Ethics Institute, pp. 15–34 (2021)
61. Twitter (2021). Birdwatch Guide. Accessed 7 Sept 2021

62. UN Human Rights Council: Report of the independent international fact-finding mission on Myanmar (2018). OHCHR/A/HRC/39/64. Accessed 23 Apr 2021
63. Williams, J., Chowdhury, R.: Introducing our responsible machine learning initiative (2021). Twitter Blog. Accessed 23 Apr 2021
64. Wong, J.C.: How Facebook let fake engagement distort global politics: a whistleblower's account (2021). The Guardian. Accessed 23 Apr 2021
65. York, J.C.: Syria's Twitter spambots (2011). The Guardian. Accessed 23 Apr 2021
66. York, J.C., Zuckerman, E.: Moderating the public sphere. In: Jorgensen, R.J. (ed.) Human Rights in the Age of Platforms, pp. 137–162. MIT Press (2019)
67. Zannettou, S.: "I Won the Election!": an empirical analysis of soft moderation interventions on Twitter. In: ICWSM 2021, pp. 1–13 (2021)

Provenance Navigator: Towards More Usable Privacy and Data Management Strategies for Smart Apps

Sandeep Gupta[1]([✉]), Matteo Camilli[1], and Maria Papaioannou[2]

[1] Free University of Bozen-Bolzano, Bolzano, Italy
{sgupta,mcamilli}@unibz.it
[2] Instituto de Telecomunicações, Aveiro, Portugal
m.papaioannou@av.it.pt

Abstract. Billions of people have embraced numerous smart apps (applications) for browsing, chatting, emailing, entertainment, fitness, navigation, shopping, social-networking, transportation, and many other activities, with a notion to make their day-to-day life easy and better. Smart apps like TikTok, Uber, Facebook, Google Maps, etc., simply direct users to accept their data policy if they are willing to get their services free of cost. Typically, these apps providers bank on data collected from the users for generating revenue, which is equivalent to a compulsive invasion of the users' privacy. Further, data usage policies are apps provider-centric therefore, user-friendly control mechanisms to restrict the collection and usage of sensitive data are highly demanded by end-users (*particularly, for the countries that have not enacted specific legislation for users' data protection*). In the paper, we present a study of users' data collected by popular smart apps along with the existing privacy and data management mechanisms provided by their app providers and conduct an online survey to collect public opinion towards the privacy policies and data collection done by smart apps providers. We propose a conceptual model of Provenance Navigator that can improve the transparency of data collection and usage by a smart app. Finally, we provide some recommendations based on the survey findings to improve the usability of smart apps' privacy and data management mechanisms to grow the awareness of the user.

Keywords: Smart apps · Privacy policies · Usability · Provenance graph

1 Introduction

The fundamental concept of regulating how a user's data can be stored, protected, and processed is not entirely new since the time first yellow book was published around 1879 [35]. From early inceptions such as Sweden's Data Act [24] of 1973 and Europe's Data Protection Directive of 1995 [25] to moving forward

© Springer Nature Switzerland AG 2022
S. Parkin and L. Viganò (Eds.): STAST 2021, LNCS 13176, pp. 24–42, 2022.
https://doi.org/10.1007/978-3-031-10183-0_2

to 2018 the European Union's General Data Privacy Regulation (GDPR) [18], and now the California Consumer Privacy Act (CCPA) [5] are laudable efforts towards the implementation of data privacy legislation. To comply with privacy laws [5–7], app-providers that *collect*, *process*, *use*, and *share* data of their users are required to guarantee that they have readily-accessible privacy policies to disclose how they will collect, store, use, or share their users' data along with the exact purpose.

Recently, India banned 59 apps, including TikTok, because they put the sensitive data and privacy of users at risk [32]. The reasons for banning these apps are 1) illegal users' data collection, and 2) hidden transmission of the data, in an unauthorized manner, to servers located outside India [3]. Typically, common users are unable to understand complex privacy policies and data management mechanisms provided by apps-providers. Thus, the requirement of usable privacy and data management strategies become more acute for countries that have not enacted specific legislation for users' data protection.

App-providers collect and share data of their users on the pretext of enhancing users' personal experience after taking consent from their users. Studies have shown that app-providers' take users' consents merely to adhere to privacy policies, however, they keep maneuvering privacy laws and policies in their self-interests [20]. Generally, users provide their consent simply by ticking a 'checkbox' or clicking the 'agree' button without thoroughly reading and understanding the privacy and data policies. Therefore, app-providers must provide user-friendly interfaces to inform the privacy and data policies to the users as well as facilitate usable mechanisms to access, delete, and opt-out of data that has been collected and shared.

In this paper, we present a case study of users' data collected by popular smart apps and analyze the privacy and data management mechanisms provided by them. Our study focuses on determining the shortcomings of existing privacy management mechanisms to enrich users' understanding to explore, perceive, and decide their data access and usage by app-providers. We propose a Provenance Navigator model that can provide transparency in the data collection and usage by a smart app. We also perform an online survey to know public opinion on the privacy policies and data collection strategies provided by smart apps providers. Based on the survey findings, we provide some recommendations for achieving usable privacy and data management strategies for the benefit of users.

Paper Organization: The rest of the paper is organized as follows: Section 2 presents important data privacy policies and standards. It gives an insight into data collected by some of the popular smart apps. Section 3 discusses privacy management mechanisms provided by popular app-providers. Section 4 presents the survey results and a discussion smart apps privacy policies. Section 5 proposed provenance navigator design and some recommendations to enhance usability. Finally, Sect. 6 concludes the paper.

2 Background

This section briefly discusses some of the important data privacy policies and standards. Then, we present the users' data collected by popular smart apps like Facebook, Chrome, Instagram, LinkedIn, YouTube, etc. We selected these apps based on the number of average active users and their popularity.

2.1 Data Privacy Policies and Standards

Recent privacy regulations, such as General Data Protection Regulation (GDPR), California Consumer Privacy Act (CCPA), Health Insurance Portability and Accountability Act (HIPAA), or Gramm-Leach-Bliley Act (GLBA), mandate an increase in responsibility and transparency around personal data use and storage.

GDPR Article 5(1) set out the six privacy principles for personal data handling: 1) lawfulness, fairness, and transparency, 2) purpose limitation, 3) data minimization, 4) accuracy, 5) storage limitation, and 6) integrity and confidentiality [16]. These six principles must be exercised together with the additional requirement, i.e., accountability, covered in Article 5 (2). Similarly, the CCPA gives consumers important new rights: i) a right to knowing (transparency) about how the data is being used, ii) a right to access, and iii) a right to opt-out of having their data sold (opt-in for minors) to third parties [5].

HIPAA applies to healthcare providers involved in transmitting health information in an electronic form [17]. They must ensure that individuals' health information is properly protected without affecting the flow of health information to maintain high-quality healthcare. The privacy rule calls any identifiable health information of an individual held or transmitted by a covered entity or its business associate, in any form or media, whether electronic, paper, or oral as protected health information (PHI). The purpose of the HIPAA act is to limit the use of PHI by covered entities or their business associate with a "need to know" and to penalize who do not adhere to confidentiality regulations.

GLBA applies to financial institutions or companies that offer consumers financial products or services such as loans, financial or investment advice, or insurance [10]. The purpose of this act is to safeguard customers' sensitive data and to communicate information-sharing practices to them. The institutions must inform customers about their information-sharing practices and customers' right to "opt-out" if they don't want their information shared with certain third parties.

2.2 Popular Smart Apps: User Data Collection

Table 1 shows the data collected by popular smart apps that are gathered by analyzing the privacy and data policies published by their providers. According to Patil et al. [28], apps like Facebook gain uninterrupted access to users' sensitive data including their social relationships and online interactions, etc., with

Table 1. User data collected by popular online apps.

App	Active users	Data collection
Facebook [8]	2.4 billion	Uploaded contents (image, video, audio), communications (text, audio-visual), contextual information (location, hashtag), online transactions (purchases, payments, billing, shipping), devices information (attributes, identifiers, network and connections)
YouTube [11]	2 billion	Audios and Videos (uploaded, watched), ads-viewed, search history, comments, devices attributes, personal data (age, address), authorization from a parent or guardian
Instagram [8]	1 billion	Uploaded contents (image, video, audio), communications (text, audio-visual), contextual information (location, hashtag), online transactions (purchases, payments, billing, shipping), devices information (attributes, identifiers, network and connections)
Chrome [11]	1 billion	Browsing history information, personal information and passwords, cookies, downloaded information, data saved by addons
TikTok [30]	700 million	Personal data and the used platform details, information shared related to third-party social network providers, technical and behavioral information (IP address, geolocation-related data, browsing and search history, messages, metadata, cookies)
LinkedIn [22]	610 million	Name, email address and/or mobile number, user data (work details, education details, recommendations, messages, articles, job postings, messages, mails, comments), device and location
Edge [26]	330 million	Browsing history, cookies, diagnostic data, device data, preferences, bookmarks, extensions, personal information and passwords
Twitter [33]	330 million	Email address, phone number, address book contacts, and public profile, contents (tweet, retweeted, read, likes, messages), miscellaneous information (age, languages a user speak)
Skype [26]	300 million	Personal data, device attributes, interaction data
Google Map [11]	155 million	Location data (favorite, want to go, labeled, reservations, visited), search history, device attributes, reviews, comments, photos,

(continued)

Table 1. (*continued*)

App	Active users	Data collection
Alexa [1]	100 million	Users' voice recordings, data like messages send or received, online searches, home maps, inventory of all connected smart devices' activities (like turn on and off timings)
Uber [34]	95 million	Data provided by users to Uber, such as during account creation, data created during use of our services, such as location, app usage, and device data, data from other sources, such as Uber partners and third parties that use Uber APIs
Safari [2]	-	Name, mailing address, phone number, email address, contact preferences, device identifiers, IP address, location information, credit card information, profile information, government issued ID, family and friends data such as name, mailing address, email address, and phone number

their consents. However, in reality, these apps get users' consent by bartering their desire to use free services offered.

Generally, app-providers claim to collect and share users' data to enhance the users' personal experience in using their products, services, platform functionality, support, and information for internal operations, including troubleshooting, data analysis, testing, research, statistical, and survey purposes.

3   Privacy Management Mechanisms by Popular Apps Providers

This section describes the existing privacy and data management mechanisms of popular smart apps. To comply with data privacy policies and standards, apps providers are bound to incorporate methods that can safeguard users' privacy interests. We provide readers with some of the privacy management dashboards adopted by popular app-providers, i.e., Facebook, Google, and Microsoft, for their popular apps.

3.1   Facebook

The Facebook app provides privacy settings, and tools for users to manage their future posts, comments and tags reviews, and limit the audience for the past posts [8]. Using more options, users can manage their future activities, access and down their information. Further, the Facebook privacy management dashboard allows users to keep some content completely private, whereas most of the contents can be restricted from public visibility but remain visible to friends or friends of a friend. This type of multi-level privacy settings adds complexity as well as reduces usability.

Instagram users can control who can follow them by making their accounts private [8]. However, business profiles can not be private, it can be private only by switching to a personal account. People can send photos or videos directly to a user even if they're not following her. But only followers can like or comment on a user's photos and videos. Sharing a photo or video to a social network like Twitter, Facebook will be publicly available irrespective of privacy settings on Instagram. Instagram users can use keyword filters to hide comments that contain specific words, phrases, numbers, or emoji that they prefer to avoid. Users can turn off commenting to prevent people from commenting on an individual post. The likes or comments of a user will be visible to anyone who can see the post.

A study by Fiesler et al. [9] revealed that the contents of most Facebook users are either all public or all non-public in their collected dataset. Han et al. [15] presented a case study on Instagram app users that include 18 privacy items. They determined that users' information (e.g., hometown, education, religion, political views, relationship status, profile photo, favorites/likes, emotions/sentiments, and sexual orientation) required attention to better preserve users' privacy. Furthermore, their study revealed that many users do not change the default privacy settings and approximately, 60 to 70% of user' personal (e.g., name, date of birth, phone number, and relationship status) or demographic information (e.g., city, workplace) are publicly available. Thus, it indicates that many such apps users are not able to use privacy settings, effectively. Also, there are no controls that can inform users about 1) who is browsing their profile, 2) how many times their profile is visible in a public search, 3) country-wise or region-wise profile restriction.

3.2   Google

Google Chrome users can control their privacy settings, delete their browsing history, passwords, auto-fill information, cookies, and browse in incognito mode [11]. The Manage Sync feature enables users to synchronize apps, Bookmarks, Extensions, History, Passwords, Personal Data, Payment methods across multiple devices, where they are using the same google account. Activity controls allow users to enable or disable information like Ad personalization, location history, browsing history of the web, and app.

Chrome sync panel allows users to view and reset or remove their Apps, Bookmarks, Extensions, History, and other settings. Likewise, YouTube and Google Map users can manage their information by deleting their browsing history, comments, ad preferences, locations, places that they visited, etc. YouTube users can review the potentially inappropriate comments posted on their public videos by visiting the "Held for review" tab. They can add create their own blocked words or phrases list. They can completely turn off comments to deny viewers to comment on their videos. Also, users can block or hide specific commenters across all videos on their channel.

Jevremovic et al. [19] described Google Chrome as a dangerous product from a user privacy aspect. Google uses a large number of background services to communicate with their servers. If users are logged in with their Google account their data, (e.g., browsing history, data entered in web forms, bookmarks, passwords, and currently opened tabs) get tracked and stored unless users specifically disabled those services. Google tracks user's geolocation with this they can find out their users' location and their movements. Google and Facebook need to be more transparent about what data is tracked and how it is obtained [36].

3.3   Microsoft

Microsoft provides a centralized privacy and data management dashboard that enables users to view and clear their browsing or search history, location, voice, media, product, and service activities [26]. They can connect or disconnect their apps, e.g., LinkedIn, Skype, and manage their shared data.

Users can manage their activity data for their Microsoft account. The "My Activity" panel provides the filters to choose the data type then select Clear activity to instruct for the removal from the systems. Users can change the data that Microsoft collects, adjust their privacy settings for their devices, and for the apps or services that they are using. The "Download My Data" panel allows users to download and archive a copy of the data that appears on their Activity history page.

Social networking apps, such as LinkedIn, Facebook, can easily be a target of data scraping. Highlighting the case of data scraper, hiQ, who asserted freedom of speech rights under California law to support their argument that they were entitled to collect and use publicly available information [21]. This raises a legal question regarding the control over the public information available on social networking platforms. Likewise, using tools like Skype for doctor-patient communication [23] raises the question if the HIPAA compliant will be able to protect the confidentiality of protected health information, unauthorized access, usage, or disclosure of such information.

4   Our Study

We conducted an online survey[1] to record public opinion on privacy concerning to smart apps usage. The survey was published on various social media platforms like Linkedin, Facebook, Twitter and distributed to specialize groups working in the field of privacy. We received 50 responses that were completely anonymous.

The reporting of the survey results is divided into four sections: 1) demographic statistics, 2) privacy-policies awareness, 3) user's response on existing smart apps privacy policies, and 4) user's response to usability requirements. Refer Appendix A for questionnaire, it overall consists of 18 questions.

---

[1] https://docs.google.com/forms/d/e/1FAIpQLSeiMoyDICyh_AwIys9-bRASwBjhTzokoUFg2fM1tC3Kmk-A1g/viewform.

4.1   Demographic Statistics

The survey contains 3 demographics questions related to the participant's gender, age group, and continent-wise location. Demographic statistics of 50 participants are displayed in Fig. 1.

Figure 1a exhibits gender-wise distribution having 52% male and 46% female participants. Figure 1b shows survey participants' age-wise distribution from 17 to 60 years that are most frequent users of smart apps. And, Fig. 1c shows the continent-wise participants distribution.

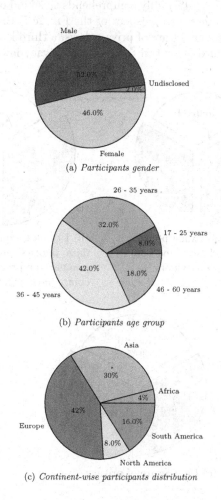

(a) *Participants gender*

(b) *Participants age group*

(c) *Continent-wise participants distribution*

Fig. 1. Demographic statistics

4.2 Privacy-Policies Awareness

The survey contains 3 questions related to participant's awareness of privacy policies, as illustrated in Figs. 2a–2c. Figure 2a indicates that only 30% of the participants reads the privacy policies thoroughly before giving consent to the app providers, while virtually 50% of them gives their consent without reading the privacy policies at all. Furthermore, it is clear that the consistently highest percentage of smart device users (i.e., 56%) finds that the privacy and data policies provided by popular app providers are not fully comprehensible, whereas only a small fraction (i.e., 14%) fully comprehends this kind of policies, as shown in Fig. 2b. Finally, the interesting aspect of the Fig. 2c is that approximately a third of the participants are aware of privacy laws, a third is not informed about them, while the last third is neutral towards the privacy laws.

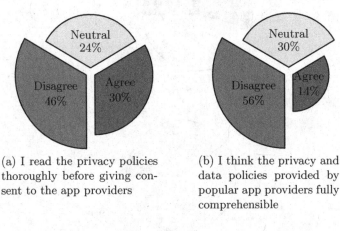

(a) I read the privacy policies thoroughly before giving consent to the app providers

(b) I think the privacy and data policies provided by popular app providers fully comprehensible

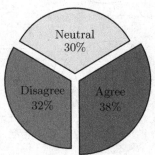

(c) I am aware of privacy laws

Fig. 2. Privacy-policies awareness

4.3   Users' Response on Existing Smart Apps Privacy Policies

Figure 3 illustrates the participant's response to current privacy policies provided by smart apps providers. A majority of survey participants either disagree or is neutral in response to the question - whether the current privacy policies and data management mechanisms provided by popular apps are not usable. Approximately 95% of the survey participants indicated that the lengthy privacy policies are one of the main demotivating factors to read and comprehend fully. Nonetheless, 80% of the survey participants think that multilevel privacy settings are too complex to understand.

1. I think current policy privacy and data management mechanisms provided by popular apps usable

2. I think the lengthy privacy policies is one of the main demotivating factors to read them fully

3. I think multilevel privacy settings is too complex to understand

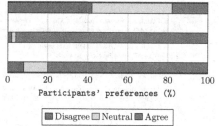

Fig. 3. Response on existing smart apps privacy policies

Participant's response suggests that the current privacy policies presentation and graphical interfaces provided by smart apps providers are not adequate, and thus, efforts must be put into the design and development of usable policy privacy and data management mechanisms that can enable users to be fully aware of smart apps' privacy policies.

4.4   Users' Response to Usability Requirements

Figure 4 illustrates the participant's response on usability improvements on current privacy policies provided by smart apps providers that consist of 9 questions. Approximately 85% of participants finds that short videos or pictures to explain privacy policies would be more intuitive, as well as that app-providers should include a mechanism that can generate a comprehensive report for how user's data are being used by them, while a half believes that voice commands to enable or disable privacy settings will be easier in contrast to the existing interfaces. In addition, approximately 70% of the participants agree that app-providers should integrate mechanisms that will be able to: (a) automatically hide user's public content in case of no-activity for a certain period of time, (b) help users to make their profile available region-wise or country-wise, and (c) monitor inappropriate comments, photos, or videos proactively, irrespective of users' review setting to rule-out any harassment, trolling, or untoward incidents. Nonetheless, the same percentage of participants consistently believes that permission for any type of data collection must be kept disabled by default, subscription-based data collection process might enable a more flexible data collection, as well as data traceability mechanisms, must be provided allowing users to trace their collected data and determine their usage.

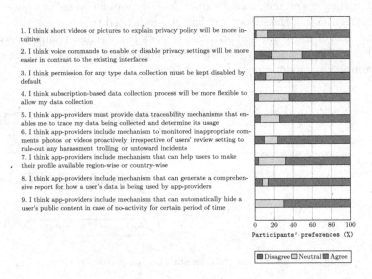

Fig. 4. Participant's response to improve usability

It is worthwhile to highlight that based on these survey results, Sect. 5 provides a foundation for organizing research efforts towards the design and development of effective and efficient usable privacy and data management strategies for smart apps.

4.5   Discussion on Smart Apps Privacy Policies

With the rapid rise of smart apps usage, the intent of new and recently revised data privacy laws is a commendable attempt to protect the privacy of apps users. However, yet many users do not thoroughly read the privacy and data policies, and comprehend them [20].

Our study findings demonstrate that users' privacy and data management mechanisms require more attention to make them more usable. Lengthy privacy policies hinder a thorough reading, which most users skip. Multilevel privacy settings add complexity as well as reduce usability. Typically, only a few users change the privacy settings to configure it as per their requirements, otherwise, most of the users do not care to adjust the default privacy settings and prone to higher chances of privacy violation and data abuse.

Smart apps run a large number of background services to communicate with their servers, continuously recording users' data. For example, users' location and their movements can be easily traced by geolocation tracking. A report [31] mentioned that Uber can now predict where you're going before you get in the car using Bayesian statistics based algorithm that exploits the history of the user, the behavior of other users, and the general popularity of specific places, which is a clear breach of users' privacy and would be frustrating for a user to rely on on-demand and ride-sharing platforms [12,14]. Social networking apps, such as LinkedIn, Facebook, can easily be a target of data scraping. These are some of the clear overreaches of such smart apps. Finally, our recommendations are an attempt towards more usable privacy and data management strategies for smart apps, both for enhancing the current privacy policies, as well as for establishing ones, particularly, for the countries that have not yet enacted specific legislation for users' data protection [4].

5   Our Proposal

5.1   Provenance Navigator Conceptual Model

Consumers' data overuse, misuse, or abuse in smart apps is a commonly occurring issue that motivates to investigate more usable privacy and data management strategies from the users' perspective [13]. Therefore, we propose Provenance Navigator to achieve transparency in data collection and usage that can be seamlessly integrated into smart apps, thus, enabling users to navigate the origin of and transformations applied to their collected data for better users' rights compliance and legal requirements coordination.

Pasquier et al. [27] described provenance data can be represented as a directed acyclic graph to establish a relationship between data entities, agents, and activities including contextual information and usage criteria. Provenance graphs are a more structured approach for establishing relationships between all the active elements over unstructured approaches like log files. With recent advances in graph theory, provenance graphs can provide a quick search mechanism, space optimization for storage, and interactive visual representation [29].

Figure 5 presents a simplified architecture of Provenance Navigator for smart apps. The server can be cloud-based that interacts with the Data Collection & Management (DCM) module to pull users' data and stores the data in the form of entities. On the Client-side, Directed Acyclic Graph (DAG) generator fetches the information from the DCM module to dynamically construct provenance graphs, which can be stored locally.

Figure 6 depicts a typical provenance graph creation process. DAG generator fetches information from the DCM module to construct a provenance graph by creating a new node for each data entity that a smart app is collecting, i.e., $DE_i \forall i = N$, where N total data entities and agents that use the data entities, i.e., $A_j \forall j = M$, where M total agents. When an A_j accesses a DE_i an edge $([DE_i, A_j])$ is established between them. Similarly, a new node can be created for each new activity (AC_k) performed by an agent (A_j) and a new edge $([A_j, AC_k])$ can be defined for linking them.

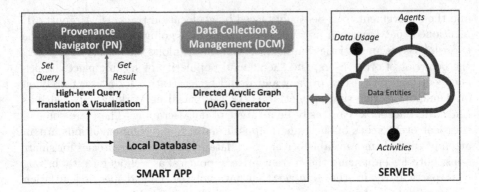

Fig. 5. Provenance navigator architecture

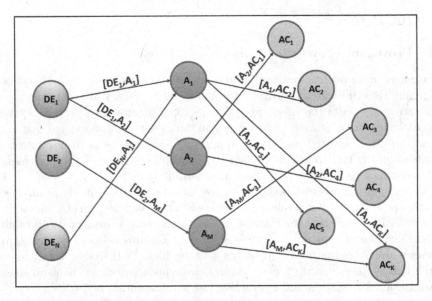

Fig. 6. Provenance graph creation process

Thus, Provenance Navigator (PN) can enable users to audit their data collection and usage by the app providers. Audits can reveal: 1) the state of data collected, 2) the agents accessing the data, and 3) the activities in which the data is used. Ultimately, users can utilize PN for a precise understanding of their sensitive data embarking into smart apps.

5.2 Recommendations

Finally, some recommendations based on our survey for data collection and privacy management mechanisms improvements are as follows.

I. Long and lengthy privacy policy texts can be replaced with short videos or pictures to add intuitiveness.

II. Voice commands can be introduced for easy interaction to deal with privacy settings.

III. Multi-level privacy settings introduce complexity that can be simplified to enhance usability.

IV. Opt-out options can be kept enabled by default. Users can opt-in for a particular data tracking or selective services as per their preferences or requirements.

V. The data collection process can be subscription-based. This will give flexibility to users to subscribe to the services for a desired amount of time, therefore, the data collection by app-providers can be restricted only for the selected period. Moreover, apps should start being fair in-hand before to say that they will collect the data indicating its purpose lucidly.

VI. Some data traceability mechanisms can be provided to users to link between the data collection permissions given by them and the purpose for which the data is being used by the app-providers.

VII. Any inappropriate comments, photos, or videos can be monitored proactively, irrespective of users' review setting to rule-out any harassment, trolling, or untoward incidents.

VIII. Controls can be introduced for users to make their profile available region-wise or country-wise.

IX. Controls can be provided to users to generate a comprehensive report about how their data is being used by app-providers over a period that they can select.

X. The automatic-hide feature can be introduced for users' to hide their public content. Users can set the no-activity period to enable this feature.

6   Conclusions

People get enthralled with unprecedented innovation, business opportunities, economic benefits, and the world-wide nexus offered by numerous smart apps, such as Facebook, Instagram, LinkedIn, and YouTube. Users get free services by fueling smart apps with their data that app-providers use for advertising, subscriptions, selling merchandise, in-app purchases, etc.

The epicenter of people's digital lives is the trust between consumers and app-providers. Customers' trust can be enhanced by providing fair privacy policies and ethical data collection practices to optimize data usage and to prevent any unforeseen incidents or corollaries, consequently, benefiting individuals' privacy and society as a whole. Our recommendations for privacy and data management strategies for free apps can enhance usability as well as can make their users more aware of their privacy and data usage.

In the future, we will design a Provenance Navigator prototype that can dynamically exhibit and explain the privacy policies and data management by smart apps to their users. Thus, users can be more aware of the consequences emanating from any violations of their privacy.

Acknowledgement. The authors would like to thanks Neha Gupta (ng@apachetechnology.in) and Wagner Santos (wagnersantos@copin.ufcg.edu.br) for their valuable contribution to the survey data collection.

Appendix A: Survey Questionnaire

1. I think I read the privacy policies thoroughly before giving consent to the app providers.
   - Agree
   - Neutral
   - Disagree
2. I think the privacy and data policies provided by popular app providers fully comprehensible.
   - Agree
   - Neutral
   - Disagree
3. I think I am aware of privacy laws, such as, General Data Privacy Regulation (GDPR), California Consumer Privacy Act (CCPA), Health Insurance Portability and Accountability Act (HIPAA), or Gramm-Leach-Bliley Act (GLBA).
   - Agree
   - Neutral
   - Disagree
4. I think current policy privacy and data management mechanisms provided by popular apps usable.
   - Agree
   - Neutral
   - Disagree
5. I think the lengthy privacy policies is one of the main demotivating factors to read them fully.
   - Agree
   - Neutral
   - Disagree
6. I think multilevel privacy settings is too complex to understand.
   - Agree
   - Neutral
   - Disagree
7. I think short videos or pictures to explain privacy policy will be more intuitive.
   - Agree
   - Neutral
   - Disagree
8. I think voice commands to enable or disable privacy settings will be more easier in contrast to the existing interfaces.
   - Agree
   - Neutral

- Disagree

9. I think permission for any type data collection must be kept disabled by default.
   - Agree
   - Neutral
   - Disagree

10. I think subscription-based data collection process will be more flexible to allow my data collection.
    - Agree
    - Neutral
    - Disagree

11. I think app-providers must provide data traceability mechanisms that enables me to trace my data being collected and determine its usage.
    - Agree
    - Neutral
    - Disagree

12. I think app-providers include mechanism to monitored inappropriate comments, photos, or videos proactively, irrespective of users' review setting to rule-out any harassment, trolling, or untoward incidents.
    - Agree
    - Neutral
    - Disagree

13. I think app-providers include mechanism that can help users to make their profile available region-wise or country-wise.
    - Agree
    - Neutral
    - Disagree

14. I think app-providers include mechanism that can generate a comprehensive report for how a user's data is being used by app-providers.
    - Agree
    - Neutral
    - Disagree

15. I think app-providers include mechanism that can automatically hide a user's public content in case of no-activity for certain period of time
    - Agree
    - Neutral
    - Disagree

16. Please select your gender
    - Female
    - Male
    - Prefer not to say

17. Please select your age category
    - 16 years and below
    - 17–25 years
    - 26–35 years
    - 36–45 years

  - 46–60 years
  - 60 years and above
18. Please select the continent where you are residing at present?
  - Africa
  - Asia
  - Australia
  - Europe
  - North America
  - South America

References

1. Amazon: Alexa internet privacy notice (2020). https://www.alexa.com/help/privacy. Accessed 20 Sept 2021. Online web resource
2. Apple: Privacy policy (2020). https://www.apple.com/privacy. Accessed 20 Sept 2021. Online web resource
3. BBC: why has TikTok been banned in India? (2020). https://www.bbc.co.uk/newsround/53266068. Accessed 20 Sept 2021. Online web resource
4. Burman, A.: Will India's proposed data protection law protect privacy and promote growth? (2020). https://carnegieendowment.org/files/Burman_Data_Privacy.pdf. Accessed 20 Sept 2021. Working Paper
5. Constitution, C.: Ab-375 privacy: personal information: businesses (2018). https://leginfo.legislature.ca.gov/faces/billTextClient.xhtml?bill_id=201720180AB375. Accessed 20 Sept 2021. Online web resource
6. Edemekong, P.F., Haydel, M.J.: Health Insurance Portability and Accountability Act (HIPAA). StatPearls Publishers (2019). Online web resource
7. EU: Principles of the GDPR. https://ec.europa.eu/info/law/law-topic/data-protection/reform/rules-business-and-organisations/principles-gdpr_en. Accessed 20 Sept 2021. Online web resource
8. Facebook: Data policy (2020). https://www.facebook.com/policy.php. Accessed 20 Sept 2021. Online web resource
9. Fiesler, C., et al.: What (or who) is public? Privacy settings and social media content sharing. In: Proceedings of the ACM Conference on Computer Supported Cooperative Work and Social Computing, pp. 567–580. ACM, Portland (2017)
10. FTC: Gramm-Leach-Bliley act (2020). https://www.ftc.gov/tips-advice/business-center/privacy-and-security/gramm-leach-bliley-act. Accessed 20 Sept 2021. Online web resource
11. Google: Google Chrome privacy notice (2020). https://www.google.com/chrome/privacy/. Accessed 20 Sept 2021. Online web resource
12. Gupta, S., Buriro, A., Crispo, B.: DriverAuth: a risk-based multi-modal biometric-based driver authentication scheme for ride-sharing platforms. Comput. Secur. **83**, 122–139 (2019)
13. Gupta, S., Buriro, A., Crispo, B.: A risk-driven model to minimize the effects of human factors on smart devices. In: Saracino, A., Mori, P. (eds.) ETAA 2019. LNCS, vol. 11967, pp. 156–170. Springer, Cham (2020). https://doi.org/10.1007/978-3-030-39749-4_10
14. Gupta, S., Crispo, B.: A perspective study towards biometric-based rider authentication schemes for driverless taxis. In: Proceedings of the International Conference on Innovation and Intelligence for Informatics, Computing, and Technologies (3ICT), pp. 1–6. IEEE, Bahrain (2019)

15. Han, K., Jung, H., Jang, J.Y., Lee, D.: Understanding users' privacy attitudes through subjective and objective assessments: an Instagram case study. Comput. Soc. **51**(6), 18–28 (2018)

16. Henriksen-Bulmer, J., Faily, S., Jeary, S.: Implementing GDPR in the charity sector: a case study. In: Kosta, E., Pierson, J., Slamanig, D., Fischer-Hübner, S., Krenn, S. (eds.) Privacy and Identity 2018. IAICT, vol. 547, pp. 173–188. Springer, Cham (2019). https://doi.org/10.1007/978-3-030-16744-8_12

17. HHS: Summary of the HIPAA privacy rule (2020). https://www.hhs.gov/hipaa/for-professionals/privacy/laws-regulations/index.html. Accessed 20 Sept 2021. Online web resource

18. ICO: Guide to the general data protection regulation: the principles (2020). https://ico.org.uk/for-organisations/guide-to-data-protection/guide-to-the-general-data-protection-regulation-gdpr/principles/. Accessed 20 Sept 2021. Online web resource

19. Jevremovic, A., Veinovic, M., Shimic, G.: An overview of current security and privacy issues in modern telecommunications. In: Proceeding of the 13th International Conference on Advanced Technologies. Systems and Services in Telecommunications (TELSIKS), pp. 119–123. IEEE, Nis (2017)

20. Koohikamali, M., Kim, D.J.: Do mobile app providers try enough to protect users' privacy?-A content analysis of mobile app privacy policies. In: Proceedings of the International Conference Information Systems. Association for Information Systems, Dublin (2016)

21. Lawrence, J.A., Ehle, K.: Combatting unauthorized webscraping-the remaining options in the United States for owners of public websites despite the recent hiQ labs v. LinkedIn decision. Comput. Law Rev. Int. **20**(6), 171–174 (2019)

22. LinkedIn: User agreement (2020). https://www.linkedin.com/legal/user-agreement. Accessed 20 Sept 2021. Online web resource

23. Macias, M., Hess, C.: Hey doc, wanna skype? An explorative study on rural telemedicine (2019). https://digscholarship.unco.edu/cgi/viewcontent.cgi?article=1007&context=cess. Accessed 20 Sept 2021. Online web resource

24. Mayer-Schonberger, V.: Generational development of data protection in Europe. Technol. Priv. New Landscape **219**, 232–35 (1998)

25. Mayer-Schonberger, V., Padova, Y.: Regime change: enabling big data through Europe's new data protection regulation. Colum. Sci. Tech. L. Rev. **17**, 315 (2015)

26. Microsoft: Microsoft privacy statement (2020). https://privacy.microsoft.com/en-US/privacystatement. Accessed 20 Sept 2021. Online web resource

27. Pasquier, T., Singh, J., Powles, J., Eyers, D., Seltzer, M., Bacon, J.: Data provenance to audit compliance with privacy policy in the internet of things. Pers. Ubiquit. Comput. **22**(2), 333–344 (2018)

28. Patil, V.T., Shyamasundar, R.K.: Efficacy of GDPR's right-to-be-forgotten on Facebook. In: Ganapathy, V., Jaeger, T., Shyamasundar, R.K. (eds.) ICISS 2018. LNCS, vol. 11281, pp. 364–385. Springer, Cham (2018). https://doi.org/10.1007/978-3-030-05171-6_19

29. Pimentel, J.F., Freire, J., Murta, L., Braganholo, V.: A survey on collecting, managing, and analyzing provenance from scripts. ACM Comput. Surv. (CSUR) **52**(3), 1–38 (2019)

30. Tiktok: Privacy policy (2020). https://www.tiktok.com/legal/privacy-policy?lang=en. Online web resource

31. Titlow, J.: Uber can now predict where you're going before you get in the car (2014). https://www.fastcompany.com/3035350/uber-can-now-predict-where-youre-going-before-you-get-in-the-car. Accessed 20 Sept 2021. Online web resource

32. Today, I.: Why is India banning and blocking TikTok, ShareIt and other apps (2020). https://www.indiatoday.in/technology/news/story/why-is-india-banning-and-blocking-tiktok-shareit-and-other-apps-1695296-2020-06-29. Accessed 20 Sept 2021. Online web resource
33. Twitter: Privacy policy - Twitter (2020). https://twitter.com/en/privacy. Accessed 20 Sept 2021. Online web resource
34. Uber: Data collections and uses (2020). https://www.uber.com/global/en/privacy/notice. Accessed 20 Sept 2021. Online web resource
35. Vitaliev, V.: My phone phobia-after all...-[time out telephone]. Eng. Technol. 4(11), 88 (2009)
36. Williams, E., Yerby, J.: Google and facebook data retention and location tracking through forensic cloud analysis. In: SAIS 2019 Proceedings (2019)

Bringing Crypto Knowledge to School: Examining and Improving Junior High School Students' Security Assumptions About Encrypted Chat Apps

Leonie Schaewitz⬡, Cedric A. Lohmann⬡, Konstantin Fischer,
and M. Angela Sasse$^{(\boxtimes)}$⬡

Ruhr-Universität Bochum, Universitätsstraße 150, 44780 Bochum, Germany
{leonie.schaewitz,konstantin.fischer,cedric.lohmann,martina.sasse}@rub.de

Abstract. End-to-end encryption (E2EE) of everyday communication plays an essential role in protecting citizens from mass surveillance. The especially vulnerable group of children and young adolescents move quickly between chat apps and use them frequently and intensively. Yet they have had the least time to learn about online security compared to other age groups. In a two-part study conducted with four classes at a junior high school ($N = 86$ students, ages 12–16), we examined perceptions of security and privacy threats related to chat apps and understanding of E2EE using a questionnaire. A pre-post measure allowed us to examine how a short instruction video shown in class to explain the concept of E2EE and how it works in chat apps affected students' security understanding and threat perceptions. Our results show that students are aware of a variety of online threats but they are not familiar with the term E2EE. After the instruction, students gained confidence in explaining the concept of encryption and their understanding of the security features of E2EE improved. Our results also show that explanation of threats and E2EE can shift the intention of some participants towards tools that offer more protection.

Keywords: End-to-end encryption · Secure communication · Secure messaging · Security knowledge · Threat perceptions

1 Introduction

Digital communication tools such as chat apps and social networking sites play an important role in teenagers' everyday lives. A PEW research study from 2018 [4] has shown that already then 95% of U.S. teens ages 13 to 17 owned a smartphone or had access to one and regularly used various communication services such as Facebook, Snapchat, and Instagram. These tools help them build and maintain relationships by facilitating communication with friends and family and contact with new people. However, there are also risks associated with using chat apps.

S. Parkin and L. Viganò (Eds.): STAST 2021, LNCS 13176, pp. 43–64, 2022.
https://doi.org/10.1007/978-3-031-10183-0_3

Although most digital communication today is encrypted in some way, many popular chat apps do not employ End-to-End-Encryption (E2EE) by default – and some do not offer it at all. Well implemented E2EE removes the provider's capability to passively eavesdrop on any messages sent between users. This greatly helps preventing undesired breaches of confidentiality for purposes like mass surveillance in the setting of a compromised provider, or for gathering data for targeted advertising in the setting of the "honest-but-curious" threat model [20].

For these reasons, security advocates have long been promoting E2E encrypted communication tools. There are many different tools available, with quite different security models, and understanding their security properties, and how they protect against specific risks is challenging. Previous research with adult users of chat apps has shown that many users do not understand the security properties of (E2E)encryption and different communication tools [1, 7, 8, 21].

In 2020, Lindmeier and Mühling investigated K-12 students' understanding of cryptography and proposed that "students first and foremost lack a clear understanding of networked communication [which] may subsequently prevent them from forming correct mental models about cybersecurity" [18, p. 1]. We argue that trying to get students to develop a sufficiently complex mental model of networked communication would not be the most efficient, or even the most effective way of increasing their day-to-day security. Instead, building on existing mental models and transforming them into functional understanding of E2EE seems more promising.

Hence, to designing effective interventions and education programs, we consider it important to investigate students' beliefs about threats and protections in secure communications as a first step. We therefore report an attempt to capture and improve this type of knowledge. In this paper, we elicited from a group of students (12–16 years old) their perceptions of secure communications in general, and message encryption in particular. The students then got to watch an instructional video about E2EE in chat apps, and their security perceptions and understanding of threats was elicited again.

With this study, we want to explore whether conveying intentionally simplified functional mental models [10] – as simple as "If a chat app uses E2EE, the provider cannot read along" – can pose a feasible solution to our overarching goal of improving students' online security.

This paper addresses the following research questions:

RQ1 What risks do teenagers perceive when using chat apps, and what are their security needs?
RQ2 How do teenagers judge the security of chat apps?
RQ3 What are teenagers' threat models when using chat apps?
RQ4 What do they know about (end-to-end) encryption (in chat apps)?
RQ5 Can an instruction video about E2EE change teenagers' perceptions about security threats and their understanding of secure communication?

Our results show that most students did have intuitive knowledge about security goals like confidentiality when using chat apps – for most students a secure chat app is one that does not allow third parties to read along. Even though most students have heard of the term E2EE before, they struggled to pinpoint the actual security benefits it offers and were understandably unsure about its effectiveness. We see similar assumptions about E2EE, such as that E2EE cannot protect against messages being read along by the app provider, suggesting that misconceptions may form quite early. Our results also show that explanation of threats and E2EE can shift the intention of some participants towards tools that offer more protection.

2   Background and Related Work

2.1   The Effectiveness of E2EE in Chat Apps

Chat apps that implement E2EE like to claim that they protect their users from a range of threats, even a malicious operator. This is not strictly true. Users still rely on the chat app operator's honesty to distribute the correct encryption keys for their contacts. When Alice wants to chat with Bob, she has to query the chat app operator for Bob's encryption keys. A malicious or compromised operator would simply return Mallory's key material, and reroute all of Alice's messages intended for Bob to Mallory, who then re-encrypts the messages for Bob.

If this is done both ways, Alice and Bob will think they are chatting end-to-end encrypted – unknowing that Mallory can happily read along, or manipulate message content. To prevent such key-swapping attacks, multiple modern chat apps support *authentication ceremonies*: Users can check whether they are using the correct encryption secret for a given contact by scanning a QR-Code, or by comparing key fingerprints by hand. However, research has shown that most users struggle to understand the need for authenticated encryption, and are not able to use it correctly [15, 21, 23].

In the "honest-but-curious" attacker threat model, we assume that the chat app operator does not actively try to compromise message security. Paverd et al. [20, p. 2] define the "honest-but-curious" adversary as follows: "The honest-but-curious adversary is a legitimate participant in a communication protocol who will not deviate from the defined protocol but will attempt to learn all possible information from legitimately received messages."

This threat model translates to the reality of chat apps quite well: The authors, in the context of smart grid energy suppliers, list various factors limiting an operator's capability to mount active attacks – factors that also apply to chat app operators: Regulatory oversight, external audits, and the desire to maintain reputation. We thus argue that even opportunistic[1] E2EE in chat apps can offer desirable security benefits for users, and is something they should look for.

Correctly implemented, E2EE removes the provider's capability to passively eavesdrop on any messages sent between users. This goes a long way towards

---

[1] Opportunistic E2EE: A system where users do not verify the correctness of their encryption keys for a given contact. The key server has to be trusted by users.

preventing undesired breaches of confidentiality for purposes like mass surveillance in the case of a compromised provider, or for data-gathering for targeted advertising in the case of the "honest-but-curious" threat model.

2.2   Security Perceptions and Understanding of E2EE

Previous research has shown that users' understanding of E2EE is limited [1,2,8]. In 2018, Abu-Salma et al. [1, p. 2] asked adults to evaluate the security of the hypothetical E2E encrypted chat app *Soteria*, based on a short textual description: "Soteria communications (messages, phone calls, and video calls) are E2E encrypted." They found that only few participants felt confident explaining E2EE, and that many rated the E2E encrypted chat app's security lower than SMS or phone calls. Participants believed that the provider, government employees, and people with technical knowledge could access the messages sent via the app. Several studies have identified similar worries about E2EE, like the belief that encryption is futile because any encryption could be broken by capable attackers, such as hackers or governmental organizations [2,7,17,26]. While it might be possible that these attackers find ways to circumvent encryption, e.g., by compromising the endpoints where the messages are stored, it is a misconception that modern encryption can be broken and would thus be futile.

Gerber et al. [14] and Dechand et al. [7] found that WhatsApp users were unaware of E2EE, did not understand its associated security features, or did not trust the protection offered. Moreover, the mental models that users have of encryption are generally quite sparse. Wu and Zappala found that users' mental models of encryption can often be described as "a functional abstraction of restrictive access control" [26, p. 395] and Lindmeier and Mühling [18] identified similar models in K-12 students.

2.3   Communicating Threat Models to End Users

Successfully conveying the nuanced differences between a malicious operator and an "honest-but-curious" operator to all chat app users is not feasible – only a dedicated amateur would invest the effort required to acquire expert knowledge in form of a structural mental model [10] and maintaining it (knowledge stored in memory that is not frequently accessed fades). In this paper, we start from the position that E2E encrypted chat apps overall offer security benefits to our target group (junior high school students), because using them reduces the potential risk of a privacy breach at the operator's servers, and that a brief, simplified, but convincing explanation of those benefits can shift at least some of them to consider adoption.

A small number of studies have tested interventions to help users gain a functional understanding of the concept of E2EE. Demjaha et al. [8] tested a metaphor-based approach to convey functional understanding of E2EE but found that none of the different metaphors tested were able to evoke a correct mental model of E2EE in participants. Bai et al. [5] found that a tutorial to teach "high-level" information about E2EE was able to improve users' understanding of E2EE. However, some misconceptions remained, e.g., several users remained unconvinced that encryption cannot be broken, and still found concepts like integrity and authenticity difficult to grasp. Akgul et al. [3] designed brief educational messages that informed readers about the key principles of E2EE and demonstrated their effectiveness in improving users' understanding of E2EE, using an online questionnaire study. However, when the same messages were tested in a realistic use case, embedded in an actual messaging app, no improvement in comprehension was observed.

One study that examined approaches to teach cryptography to school children used a virtual reality setting that built on a medieval love story where letters are encrypted and decrypted using magic potions [9]. This setting provided the opportunity to use metaphorical descriptions for explaining the complex concept of asymmetric encryption in an immersive way. The study found that presence was a key predictor of learning outcomes. However, the VR environment also poses challenges for the teacher and does not necessarily lead to better learning outcomes than other forms of instruction.

In this paper, we test whether a relatively easy-to-implement 20-minute instruction video explaining the basic security features of E2EE in chat apps can have an impact on students' security perceptions and self-reported behaviors.

3   Method

To answer the research questions, we conducted a two-part study with 86 high school students (ages 12–16). The study consisted of a pre- and post-test design and a teaching unit in the form of an instruction video. The preliminary questionnaire was used to obtain baseline measurements against which the results from the second questionnaire could be compared to gauge whether the students' understanding of E2EE had improved, and what changes they intended to make as a result of the intervention.

3.1   Procedure

The study was conducted during the students' normal classroom time on two days, with a one-day break between questionnaires. On the first day, the students first completed the pre-questionnaire with 8–10 open and 12 closed questions (depending on filter questions) about their security and privacy perceptions in the context of chat apps (see Subsect. 3.3). Following this, they were shown an instruction video explaining the concept of E2EE in chat apps (see Subsect. 3.2). Two days later, the students filled out the post-video questionnaire, which included mainly the same questions plus some additional questions about behavioral intentions (see Subsect. 3.3). Both questionnaires were completed online. The grades 7–9 were in online distance learning at the time of the study due to the COVID-19 pandemic and, hence, filled out the questionnaires from their homes while connected to their teacher and classmates remotely. The 10th grade students had on-site lessons.

3.2 Instruction Video

The instruction video was developed in an iterative procedure. An initial version was created by one of the authors, which was discussed with the other authors as well as additional researchers and refined multiple times. We also consulted other web resources on how to explain E2EE to non-experts, such as the Surveillance Self-defense website by the EFF [11].

The final video was about 20 min long. In the first part (ca. 3 min.), the basic concept of encryption was explained by the example of the Caesar Cipher, which was already taught in history lessons and known to the students. The second part (ca. 11 min.) focused on secure communication with chat apps and explained the concept of E2EE by means of a fictional narrative in which Bob wants to confess his love to Alice via a chat app without anyone else reading along. The concepts of public and private keys were introduced and a simplified key exchange between Bob and Alice was illustrated. The video then gave an overview about which chat apps currently provide E2EE by default, which allow users to opt-in to E2EE, and which do not offer E2EE at all. The video also instructed viewers on how to check whether the E2EE operates correctly by explaining the meaning of the security number and QR code. The third part (ca. 6 min) summarized why encryption is important (i.e., to keep personal data, such as calls, messages, or pictures private) and explained which types of data are typically not protected by E2EE (e.g., different types of metadata) and which types of attackers E2EE can and cannot protect against.

3.3 Measures

The survey included the following measures, which were used in both the pre- (t1) and post-questionnaire (t2) unless otherwise noted.

Frequency of Chat App Use (only asked at t1). For each of the following chat apps, we asked participants how frequently they use it on a 5-point scale (1 = never, 2 = less than once a week, 3 = once a week, 4 = multiple times a week, 5 = multiple times a day): Snapchat, Facetime/iMessage, Telegram, Instagram Messenger, Facebook Messenger, Skype, Signal, WhatsApp, Threema. We also asked via free-text field which chat app they use most frequently.

Perception of Secure Communication, Security Needs, and Perceived Risks. We used free-text fields to receive free-text answers to the following questions: "What does secure communication with the smartphone mean to you?", "If you were to communicate with others over the Internet, what would you like to protect in your communication?", "What are the risks of using a chat app to communicate with other people?"

Perceived Security of Chat Apps. For each chat app, we asked: "How secure do you think it is to send a private message using this service?" Answers were rated on a 7-point scale from 1 = very insecure to 7 = very secure; optional answer: "I do not know the app."

Perception of Threats. We then asked the participants to imagine sending a private message to a friend using the chat app they used most frequently and asked if they thought anyone other than their friend could read this message (yes/no). If answered "yes", we asked to specify who might read the messages and how (free-text responses). If answered "no," we asked why they thought no one else could read the messages. Moreover, we asked them to describe how they can make sure they are communicating with the right person.

Understanding of Encryption and E2EE. Participants indicated on a 5-point scale (1 = very unsure to 5 = very sure) how sure they felt explaining the term "encryption", and to describe what it means to them (free-text response). Then, we asked if the term E2EE means anything to them (yes/no; filter question, only at t1) and if so, to provide a brief free-text description. To determine whether participants understood that E2EE protects the content of their messages from third-party access (correct response option from the list), but that other metadata are typically not protected, we asked participants to select from the following list all data that is protected by E2EE (time and duration of conversation; message content; location; how data was transmitted; sender and receiver). In addition, we presented a list of attacks, three with physical access to the phone that E2EE does not protect against (mobile phone theft, friends or parents with access to the phone) and four without physical access and protected by E2EE (blackmail by hackers, government surveillance, messaging app provider, advertising companies). Participants were asked to tick all those that E2EE can protect against.

Knowledge About Which Chat App Uses E2EE and Perception of Security Notifications. For each chat app, participants indicated whether they thought it uses E2EE by default or not. Since WhatsApp is the most popular and frequently used chat app in Germany, we also asked (at t1) if they ever saw WhatsApp's notifications about using E2EE or the change of a security number (yes/no), what these messages mean (free-text response), and how helpful they are (1 = not helpful at all to 7 = very helpful). At t2, we asked how they handle the notification informing them of a security number change.

Behavioral Intentions (only at t2). Participants indicated how likely they are to pay attention to whether a chat app encrypts their messages E2E when writing messages in the future (1 = not at all likely to 7 = very likely). We also asked if they will activate E2EE whenever possible (yes/no), how important it is to them that their chats are E2E encrypted (1 = not at all important to 7 = very important), which chat apps they are going to use in the future, and whether they intend to change anything about their messaging behavior. Moreover, we asked whether they told their parents, friends, or relatives about what they have learned about encryption, whether they feel to have a better understanding of what to look for to communicate securely via chat apps, whether they have checked the security number of a contact by scanning the QR code, and to evaluate the video.

3.4 Data Analysis

Qualitative Data. We coded participants' free-text answers in a data-driven and iterative procedure using the software MAXQDA. The coding was performed by two researchers – one with a background in IT security, one with a background in cognitive science and psychology. In a first step, both researchers coded the open responses independently from a randomly selected sub-sample of 30 participants to create an initial codebook for each question. Then, the coders discussed and refined their codes and established a final codebook, which was validated by both coders independently coding answers of another set of 20 participants (ca. 23% of the data, which is in the typical range for determining coder agreement [19]). As a measure for intercoder reliability, ReCal2 [13] was used to compute Cohen's Kappa for each code, of which we report a weighted mean for each question that takes into account the frequency of each code. Codes that did not occur in the subsample for which intercoder reliability was calculated were not included in this calculation. The remaining sets of answers were then coded by one coder. An overview of all codes, frequencies, and intercoder reliability is provided in Table 3 in the Appendix.

Quantitative Data. To test for significant effects of the video, we conducted repeated-measures analyses, such as the paired-samples t-test to compare differences in means for a single dependent variable at two time points, the repeated-measures multivariate analysis of variance (MANOVA) to detect differences in multiple dependent variables over time, and the McNemar test for paired nominal data. We use $p = 0.05\%$ as the significance level for the statistical tests.

3.5 Research Ethics

Our university department where the study was conducted did not have an institutional review board that time. Instead, our study followed best practices in human subjects research and data protection policies that were reviewed and approved by our institution's data protection authority. The procedure of the study was developed in close consultation with the school's administration and was carried out in the presence of the class teachers. Students' participation was voluntary, without negative consequences. The school informed the students' parents or guardians about our study, and only students who brought a consent form signed by both the student and a parent or guardian, were allowed to take part in our study. We did not collect personal identifiable information about our participants. Participant IDs were distributed randomly among students by their teachers, and at no point did we know which student had given which answer.

3.6 Sample

A total of four classes (one class each from grades 7 to 10) from a German junior high school took part in the study. 100 students took part in the first questionnaire. Of these, 86 also completed the second questionnaire. We suspect that the drop-out of 14 students can be explained by the pandemic situation and distance learning, as only students who attended school lessons from home dropped out. Our final sample consists of 86 students who completed both questionnaires ($n = 36$ female, $n = 45$ male, 2 "diverse", 3 did not want to indicate their gender). These were distributed among the four classes as follows: $n = 22$ class 7, $n = 13$ class 8, $n = 22$ class 9, $n = 29$ class 10. 16 students had practical experience in IT (e.g., internship in IT or computer science) and 17 had a family member or someone close to them who works in IT.

4   Results

4.1   Perception of Secure Communication, Perceived Risks, and Security Needs (RQ1)

For most participants, secure communication means that the messages they exchange with others are private and not accessible to others outside the communication ($n_{t1} = 31$; $n_{t2} = 56$) or that their personal data is protected (e.g., not accessibly by third parties, not forwarded, securely stored, protected from hacking etc.; $n_{t1} = 24$; $n_{t2} = 15$).

The risks most frequently mentioned by participants were that their messages could be read by others ($n_{t1} = 38$; $n_{t2} = 54$), that they could be hacked ($n_{t1} = 8$; $n_{t2} = 12$), that the other person forwards their messages ($n_{t1} = 9$; $n_{t2} = 7$), data misuse (e.g., that data is sold, $n_{t1} = 9$; $n_{t2} = 2$), that personal information about them was publicly revealed ($n_{t1} = 6$; $n_{t2} = 4$), or that the person they communicate with was pretending to be someone else ($n_{t1} = 5$; $n_{t2} = 5$).

When asked what they want to protect when communicating online, most respondents mentioned their messages ($n_{t1} = 27$; $n_{t2} = 39$), general private data ($n_{t1} = 29$; $n_{t2} = 33$), photos/videos ($n_{t1} = 17$; $n_{t2} = 21$), location data ($n_{t1} = 11$; $n_{t2} = 9$), contacts and numbers ($n_{t1} = 4$; $n_{t2} = 8$), account information/passwords ($n_{t1} = 7$; $n_{t2} = 1$), or everything ($n_{t1} = 5$; $n_{t2} = 6$).

4.2   Perceived Security of Chat Apps (RQ2)

The three most often used chat apps in our sample are WhatsApp (multiple times a day: 87.2%; never: 1.2%), Snapchat (multiple times a day: 66.3%; never: 18.6%) and the Instagram Messenger (multiple times a day: 45.3%; never: 22.1%). All other chat apps were only used by a small proportion of participants or very infrequently, thus, we focus on these three chat apps when presenting the results.

When we asked students to rate the security of the different chat apps they use (on a 7-point scale) at baseline (t1), the perceived security of sending private messages via the chat apps was at a medium level for WhatsApp ($M = 4.35$, $SD = 1.70$, $n = 86$), Snapchat ($M = 3.91$, $SD = 1,55$, $n = 80$), and Instagram Messenger ($M = 3.56$, $SD = 1.51$, $n = 80$). The Facebook Messenger was rated as least secure ($M = 2.81$, $SD = 1.44$; $n = 52$) and Threema as most secure

($M = 5.20$, $SD = 2.68$; however, only $n = 5$ people rated Threema, the rest did not know the service). All means and standard deviations of students' security ratings of the different apps can be seen in Subsect. 4.2 (Table 1).

Table 1. Means (M) and standard deviations (SD) of students' assessments of the security of chat apps from 1(very insecure) to 7(very secure) before (t1) and after (t2) watching the video. N: Number of students that knew the app and gave an answer.

Perceived security of chat apps						
	Before video ($t1$)			After video ($t2$)		
	N	M	SD	N	M	SD
WhatsApp	86	4.35	1.700	85	5.24	1.593
Snapchat	80	3.91	1.552	81	3.06	1.495
Instagram Messenger	80	3.56	1.508	82	3.00	1.491
Skype	63	4.21	1.427	68	4.38	1.446
iMessage	58	4.62	1.705	66	4.79	1.524
Facebook Messenger	52	2.81	1.442	67	3.39	1.487
Telegram	26	3.65	1.810	45	4.27	1.514
Signal	6	4.83	1.472	32	5.53	1.545
Threema	5	5.20	2.683	29	5.17	1.416

$N = 74$ of our participants (all WhatsApp users except one) knew or suspected that WhatsApp offers E2EE by default, $n = 52$ correctly indicated that Snapchat does not have E2EE by default (37 Snapchat users, 15 non-users), and $n = 44$ correctly indicated that the Instagram Messenger does not have E2EE by default (32 Instagram users, 12 non-users).

$N = 75$ have seen the information message provided in WhatsApp to explain E2EE, which was rated rather helpful ($M = 5.11$, $SD = 1.97$; $n = 76$; scale: 1 = not very helpful, 7 = very helpful).

Moreover, $N = 54$ saw the information message about the change of a security number in WhatsApp. The perceived helpfulness of this message was on a medium level ($M = 4.30$, $SD = 2.28$; $n = 63$). Most participants guessed that the message meant that their contact's number ($n = 27$), security number ($n = 14$), or cell phone ($n = 7$) had changed. $N = 3$ said that the app had been reinstalled, 4 associated security with the message, 16 did not know, and 21 gave other responses, including three claiming the chat was now no longer secure.

4.3 Perception of Threats: Attackers, Methods, and Protections (RQ3)

Prior to the lecture, the majority of participants ($n = 63$) believed that if they sent a private message to a friend via the chat app service they used most often, someone other than their friend could also read this message ($n = 53$ used an E2E encrypted chat app, such as WhatsApp, $n = 10$ used chat apps without E2EE, such as Snapchat or Instagram most frequently). Most of them believed that the provider of the app ($n = 35$), hackers ($n = 17$), friends ($n = 7$), government or intelligence ($n = 7$), family members ($n = 4$), or others ($n = 12$; e.g., persons to whom the message is forwarded or shown, others with access to the account, companies who buy this data) could read their messages.

When asked how others could read their messages, they mention hacking ($n = 13$), access via the receiver ($n = 10$; e.g., that the friend forwards/shows the message to someone else), that the provider has access ($n = 9$), via physical access to the device ($n = 6$), via logging into the chat ($n = 6$), or via access to the server ($n = 5$) as potential methods.

$N = 23$ did not believe that a person other than the receiver could read their messages ($n = 22$ of them used E2E encrypted chat apps). As reasons, they mentioned (E2E)-encryption of their messages ($n = 5$), their perceptions about the protection of their data (by the app; $n = 7$), or other, such as that their messages were not interesting, or that they send the message only to a specific person or number.

When asked how they could check if they were writing to the right person, only one person mentioned to verify the person by scanning the QR code. Most participants answered with different strategies, such as asking about something personal ($n = 22$), talking to or calling the person ($n = 16$), checking the name ($n = 11$) or number ($n = 10$), asking them to send a photo of themselves ($n = 7$), checking the profile picture ($n = 3$) or writing style ($n = 5$). 14 people were not sure, and 24 mentioned other aspects, such as knowing or trusting the person, or gave unclear answers.

4.4   Assumptions About Encryption and E2EE (RQ4)

When asked at t1 what the term "encryption" means, $n = 32$ referred to the protection of their messages, which are protected from being read by people outside the communication. $N = 14$ had associations with access control, describing encryption as a barrier that protects or keeps something secret, or as a password or mechanism for locking accounts, messages, or devices, and $n = 12$ described it as converting data into another form, such as a (secret) code or something that makes it unreadable. Some described that encryption means that their data is protected ($n = 11$), that their messages are secure ($n = 4$), or they simply explained the term with the term ($n = 5$; e.g., that something is encrypted), mentioned other/unclear aspects ($n = 3$), or to not know the answer ($n = 9$).

Only $n = 25$ indicated that the term E2EE meant anything to them. 13 described E2EE meaning that their messages are not readable by third parties, while the remainder did not refer to the non-readability of their messages but simply recited the term ($n = 5$; e.g., "messages are encrypted from beginning to end"), described that E2EE means that their messages ($n = 2$) or data are secure ($n = 1$), or that they did not know how to explain E2EE ($n = 3$).

Figure 1 shows that, when asked what data E2EE protects when communicating via a chat app, most participants ($n = 67$) correctly selected "message content." However, $n = 60$ also selected "sender and receiver", $n = 49$ "location", $n = 31$ "way of data transmission", and $n = 23$ "time and duration of conversation" – indicating great uncertainty about whether the metadata is protected by E2EE. In terms of potential attackers (see Fig. 2), participants seemed to assume that E2EE mainly protects them from hackers ($n = 62$). Only half of the participants ($n = 43$) stated that E2EE can protect their private communications from the app provider.

Does E2EE protect the following information when sending messages?

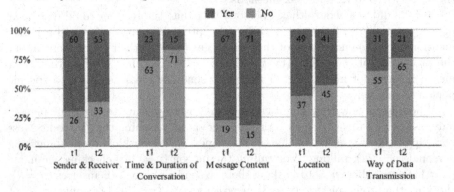

Fig. 1. Students' answers on what data is protected by E2EE. Before the video ($t1$) and after ($t2$).

4.5   Effects of the Video (RQ5)

Perception of Security, Threats, and Protections. To investigate whether the perceived security of the three most used chat apps, WhatsApp, Snapchat, and Instagram (dependent variables), had changed after the video (from t1 to t2), we ran a repeated measures MANOVA (using $n = 76$ data sets of participants who rated all three apps at t1 and t2). The analysis revealed a significant difference in the perceived security of the chat apps over time, Wilks's $\lambda = 0.56$, $F(3,73) = 19.09$, $p < .001$, $\eta_p^2 = .44$. While the perceived security of WhatsApp increased significantly, $F(1,75) = 19.23$, $p < .001$, $\eta_p^2 = .20$, the perceived security of Snapchat, $F(1,75) = 26.75$, $p < .001$, $\eta_p^2 = .26$, and the Instagram Messenger, $F(1,75) = 14.94$, $p < .001$, $\eta_p^2 = .17$, decreased. Converted to r as an effect size (see [12, p. 538]), these findings reflect a medium-sized effect for WhatsApp ($r = 0.45$) and Instagram ($r = 0.41$), and a large effect for Snapchat ($r = 0.51$). See Subsect. 4.2 for means and standard deviations.

The number of participants who correctly stated that WhatsApp uses E2EE by default increased from 74 to 79, and the number of participants who correctly stated that Snapchat [Instagram Messenger] has no E2EE by default increased from 52 to 68 [44 to 64]. See Table 2 for an overview of participants' ratings.

With regard to perceived threats, the number of participants who believed that someone else can read their messages was reduced from $n = 63$ to $n = 46$. Of those, $n = 20$ still mentioned the app provider (with $n = 11$ stating to use only E2E encrypted chat apps most frequently; $n = 6$ mentioned a mixture of apps with and without E2EE; $n = 3$ used apps without E2EE). On a positive note, the number of participants who mentioned E2E(encryption) as the reason they did not think it was possible for others to read their messages increased from 5 to 26.

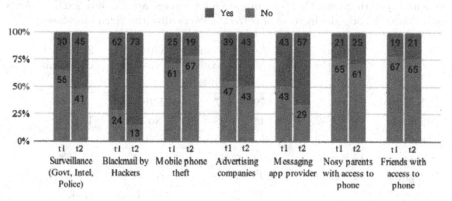

Fig. 2. Students' answers on who E2EE protects them from. Before the video ($t1$) and after ($t2$).

Moreover, ca. 40% of participants ($n = 34$) in t2 indicated that they had to check the security number or QR code of their contact to determine if they were writing with the correct person. In t1 only one person suggested this strategy.

Overall, participants' confidence in being able to explain the term encryption increased significantly from $M = 2.99$ ($SD = 1.02$) to $M = 3.47$ ($SD = 0.97$). A paired-samples t-test showed that this difference was statistically significant, $t(85) = -4.96, p < .001$, and represented a medium-sized effect, $d_z = -0.54$. And the number of participants who described that encryption means that no one else can read their messages increased from $n = 32$ to $n = 52$.

Figure 1 and Fig. 2 show the prevalence of participants' assumptions about what protection E2EE does and does not provide (before and after the video). An exact McNemar's test determined that there was a statistically significant difference in the proportion of participants assuming protection against state surveillance by E2EE before ($n = 30$) and after the instruction video ($n = 45$), $p = .017$. There was also a significant increase in the proportion of participants assuming protection against the app provider, $p = .029$ ($t1 : n = 43; t2 : n = 57$), and hackers, $p = .035$ ($t1 : n = 62; t2 : n = 73$), after the video. All other comparisons were not significant. Although these changes represent some improvement, many participants still had misconceptions after the video about what threats E2EE can and cannot protect against, and that metadata (e.g., sender and recipient) is not protected by E2EE.

Intentions and Actions. $N = 40$ participants indicated an intention to change something about their chat app use, $n = 33$ did not, and $n = 13$ were not yet sure. The likelihood that they will check whether a chat app used E2EE in the future was rated on a medium level ($M = 4.12$, $SD = 1.84$), but the majority ($n = 65$) want to activate E2EE in chat apps whenever possible.

Table 2. Students' answers on whether the listed chat apps use E2EE by default, before and after the video. Ground truth given for all chat apps in July 2021. *Students Improvement* denotes the increase of correct answers after the video was shown.

	Students' answers before the video		Students' answers after the video		Ground truth	Students' improvement
	E2EE	No E2EE	E2EE	No E2EE		
WhatsApp	74	12	79	7	E2EE	5.81%
Snapchat	34	52	18	68	No E2EE[a]	18.60%
iMessage	49	37	51	35	E2EE[b]	2.33%
Skype	43	43	42	44	opt-in[c]	1.16%
Telegram	32	54	38	48	opt-in[c]	−6.98%
Threema	32	54	40	46	E2EE	9.30%
Signal	26	60	44	42	E2EE	20.93%
Facebook Messenger	25	61	22	64	opt-in[c]	3.49%
Instagram Messenger	42	44	22	64	No E2EE	23.26%

[a] Snapchat uses E2EE encryption for Images, but not for text messages.
[b] iMessage offers E2EE when texting with other iMessage users (replaces SMS).
[c] E2EE has to be enabled by the user for each chat individually.

Overall, participants stated that it is rather important to them that their chats are E2E encrypted ($M = 5.19$, $SD = 1.74$). Moreover, $n = 18$ said they had tried to verified the security number of one of their contacts by scanning the QR code after the instruction video, n = 35 talked with their parents, friends, or relatives about what they had learned about encryption, and most of them ($n = 73$) had the feeling to know better what to look for when using a chat app to communicate securely.

5   Discussion

5.1   Perceived Security of Chat Apps

Interestingly, participants rated WhatsApps' security only at a medium level, even though most knew it offers E2EE by default, and had seen the notification from WhatsApp stating that E2EE was being used to secure their messages. One explanation is that participants do not consider WhatsApp secure due to negative experiences unrelated to E2EE, such as cyberbullying or exposure to harmful content, or because it is owned by Faceboook, which monetizes its users' data, and is therefore not trusted – which is in line with prior findings, such as [2,7,14]. Another explanation, supported by our data, is that many participants saw, but did not understand the notification about E2EE in their chats and did not associate E2EE with an effective increase in security. This is likely since the majority of our participants did not know what the term E2EE meant prior to the instruction video.

Users' stance of "not trusting WhatsApp" is understandable, and arguably "safer" than assuming WhatsApp will under no circumstances be able to read chat messages because it says it uses E2EE. If one does not trust WhatsApp, which belongs to Facebook, a company publicly associated with mishandling user data rather than protecting it [22], it is very hard to convince them that WhatsApp would implement E2EE correctly, not add backdoors, or stray from the role of an "honest-but-curious" provider. As security researchers, we have to agree that it comes down to how much you trust the company not to do this – when our participants do not, that skepticism should be seen as healthy.

That said, we wanted understand that it is not a reason to chose a chat app that doesn't offer E2EE over one that does. While E2EE cannot protect from resourceful targeted attack, current E2EE implementations in chat apps are likely to offer protection against passive eavesdroppers with access to the provider's systems. In the real world, E2EE can hinder mass surveillance and make app operators less tempted to collect private message contents for mischief.

5.2   Understanding of E2EE and Perception of Threats

Prior to the video, most participants were unsure about the concept of encryption and reported associations similar to those found in previous research [18,26]: Encryption was described as access control, or as transformation of data into (secret) code.

They intuitively knew that confidentiality is a key security goal when using chat apps, as for most students a secure chat app is one that does not allow third parties to read along. However, many participants believed that their communications with chat apps were not confidential, but that their messages could be read by others outside the communication. They named a number of different actors they suspected of being able to read the messages, most notably the provider of the communication tool – even if they claimed to use E2E encrypted chat apps like WhatsApp.

This clearly shows that our participants – similar to what previous research on adults has shown – did not connect E2EE to the protection of their messages' content from the provider of the chat apps [7,14]. This might have been the case because they connected encryption to the easily breakable Caesar Cipher, which they had learned about previously.

After seeing the instruction video, they seem to have learned to associate E2EE with increased security: They assessed chat apps which do not provide E2EE by default as significantly less secure than before. Moreover, WhatsApp, offering E2EE by default, was assessed as more secure than before. Because we measured these effects not immediately, but two days after showing the video, we assume that these effects can be considered long-term. Moreover, our findings also show that a short instruction video explaining threats and E2EE can shift the intention of some participants towards chat tools that offer more protection.

5.3   Limitations

The study was conducted at a single German junior high school. Although we were able to include classes from four different grades, the sample's diversity is limited. Due to the COVID-19 pandemic, the students from grades 7–9 were in online distance learning and hence, did not receive the lecture in presence as originally planned. Instead, we used a pre-recorded video for all students. Because we used only one version of the video in the study, the results may not be generalizable. An advantage of using a pre-recorded video, however, is that every class had received exactly the same information, which enhances the comparability of results between students.

5.4   Future Work

Future research could extend the intervention to include different versions of the instruction video or even different educational approaches. A between-subjects design could be used to compare the effectiveness of different approaches, for example, our narrative-based approach against a more fact-based approach, or an approach that works with metaphorical explanations. Moreover, future work could examine differences across age groups and test whether the effects of different educational approaches differ for students of different ages.

Finally, future research should also examine teachers' security perceptions and understanding of E2EE. This was out of scope for our research, but teachers are not IT security specialists, so it is important to develop appropriate training for them as well.

6   Conclusion

Our results show that an educational intervention explaining what E2EE is, and what protection a chat app that includes it can offer, had an effect with a good portion of our participants. After the instruction video, more students understood that – while it does not protect from all threats – choosing a chat app with E2EE offers protection against specific ones. We conclude that including threat models and security attributes of different technologies, such as E2EE, in the school curriculum would be beneficial – especially when it is directly related to the digital communication tools the students use.

Increasing students' general awareness of threats to digital technology and the benefits of different protection mechanisms is of course beneficial. But using concrete examples of how threats apply to their day-to-day activities, and that there are choices they can make to protect them, increases motivation and facilitates learning. After all, we know from mental models research that reasoning about concrete, familiar constructs significantly increases the chances of reaching correct conclusions [16]. Discussing them with their peers and applying the knowledge to their communication with each other should lead to repeated use, creating new habits and normalizing the use of security [25]. Our participants gained confidence in explaining the concept of encryption. This is a positive finding, because it could lead to an increase in self-efficacy [6], which in turn is a key predictor of secure behavioral practices. And increasing confidence in their ability to use IT security at a young age, is vital. From adults, security researchers today still hear the futility argument, "Hackers can always find a way in," first reported by Weirich and Sasse [24, p. 139].

We think that conveying the strength of modern encryption is important to fight negative consequences that come with the futility mindset. School is a promising place to instill this mindset. Educational interventions should not try to impart structural knowledge about encryption, but convey simple functional models that help students make the right decisions. Knowing that E2EE is not futile, and gaining confidence, provide a basis for secure habits they can build on as they progress through life.

Acknowledgment. Funded by the Deutsche Forschungsgemeinschaft (DFG, German Research Foundation) under Germany's Excellence Strategy - EXC 2092 CASA - 390781972.

Appendix

Code Frequencies for Free-Text Answers Before (t1) and After (t2) the Instruction Video

Table 3. Code frequencies for free-text answers before (t1) and after (t2) the instruction video. κ denotes Cohen's Kappa for each code group, weighted by code frequency.

Def. Secure Communication ($\kappa = 0.92$)		
Code	**t1**	**t2**
Messages not accessible by 3rd parties	31	56
Data protection	24	15
Communication with friends/familiy	7	2
Encryption	3	6
Important	8	2
Not (very) important	2	0
Dont know	1	0
Other/unclear	16	16
Security Needs ($\kappa = 0.92$)		
Code	**t1**	**t2**
General (private) data	29	33
Accounts and passwords	7	1
Location data	11	9
Contacts and numbers	4	8
Messages	27	39
Pictures	17	21
Everything	5	6
Nothing	3	2
Don't know	2	0
Other/unclear	9	4
Risks and Threats ($\kappa = 0.77$)		
Code	**t1**	**t2**
Messages readable by third parties	38	54
Hacking	8	12
Other person forwards messages	9	7
Data misuse	9	2
Personal information revealed	6	4
Person pretends to be someone else	5	5
Miscommunication	4	2
Unwanted sceenshots	3	2
Data stored on servers	2	3
Surveillance	2	1
None	1	1
Dont know	7	2
Other/unclear	4	10

(*continued*)

Table 3. (*continued*)

Who can read your messages ($\kappa = 0.93$)		
Code	**t1**	**t2**
Developer/provider	35	20
Hacker	17	16
Government/Intelligence	7	8
Friends	7	6
Family	4	7
Other/unclear	13	11
How can they read messages ($\kappa = 0.86$)		
Code	**t1**	**t2**
Hacking	13	13
Access via person	10	6
Provider has access	9	4
Physical access to device	6	3
Login to chat	6	3
Access via server	5	3
Not encrypted	1	4
Dont know	9	6
Other/unclear	10	14
Why can't they read messages ($\kappa = 0.82$)		
Code	**t1**	**t2**
Encryption/E2EE	5	26
Data protection	7	9
Dont know	1	1
Other/unclear	10	5
Authentication Strategy ($\kappa = 0.84$)		
Code	**t1**	**t2**
Check security number	1	34
Ask something personal	22	12
Call/talk to the person	16	13
Check name	11	8
Check number	10	7
Send photo	7	3
Check profile/ profile picture	3	5
Writing style	5	4
Encryption/E2EE	0	5
Dont know	14	7
Other/unclear	24	7

(*continued*)

Table 3. (*continued*)

Encryption Meaning ($\kappa = 0.84$)		
Code	**t1**	**t2**
Messages not readable by third parties	32	52
Transformation into (secret) code	12	14
Access control	13	7
Data protection	11	3
Messages are secure	4	5
Something is encrypted	5	3
Dont know	9	2
Other/unclear	3	5
E2EE Meaning ($\kappa = 0.89$)		
Code	**t1**	**t2**
Messages not readable by third parties	13	52
Messages are secure	2	5
Data protection	1	2
From start to end encrypted	5	3
Transformation into (secret) code	0	6
Dont know	3	9
Other/unclear	1	17
WhatsApp notification: E2EE ($\kappa = 0.94$)		
Code	**t1**	
Messages not readable by third parties	49	
Messages/data are secure	18	
Dont know	6	
Other/unclear	14	
WhatsApp notification: Security Number ($\kappa = 0.94$)		
Code	**t1**	**t2**
Change of number	27	32
Security number changed	14	15
Change of phone/device	7	15
App was reinstalled	3	4
Offers protection/security	4	4
Dont know	16	9
Other/unclear	21	24
Behavioral Change (self report)	($\kappa = 1.00$)	
Code	**t2**	
No	40	
Yes	33	
Maybe	13	

References

1. Abu-Salma, R., Redmiles, E.M., Ur, B., Wei, M.: Exploring user mental models of end-to-end encrypted communication tools. In: 8th USENIX Workshop on Free and Open Communications on the Internet (FOCI 18) (2018)
2. Abu-Salma, R., Sasse, M.A., Bonneau, J., Danilova, A., Naiakshina, A., Smith, M.: Obstacles to the adoption of secure communication tools. In: 2017 IEEE Symposium on Security and Privacy (SP), pp. 137–153. IEEE (2017)
3. Akgul, O., Bai, W., Das, S., Mazurek, M.L.: Evaluating in-workflow messages for improving mental models of end-to-end encryption. In: 30th USENIX Security Symposium (USENIX Security 21). USENIX Association, August 2021
4. Anderson, M., Jiang, J.: Teens, social media and technology 2018. Pew Research Center **31**, 2018 (2018)
5. Bai, W., Pearson, M., Kelley, P.G., Mazurek, M.L.: Improving non-experts' understanding of end-to-end encryption: an exploratory study. In: 2020 IEEE European Symposium on Security and Privacy Workshops (EuroS&P), pp. 210–219 (2020). https://doi.org/10.1109/EuroSPW51379.2020.00036
6. Bandura, A.: Self-efficacy: toward a unifying theory of behavioral change. Psychol. Rev. **84**, 191–215 (1977). https://doi.org/10.1037//0033-295x.84.2.191
7. Dechand, S., Naiakshina, A., Danilova, A., Smith, M.: In encryption we don't trust: the effect of end-to-end encryption to the masses on user perception. In: 2019 IEEE European Symposium on Security and Privacy (EuroS&P), pp. 401–415. IEEE (2019)
8. Demjaha, A., Spring, J.M., Becker, I., Parkin, S., Sasse, M.A.: Metaphors considered harmful? An exploratory study of the effectiveness of functional metaphors for end-to-end encryption. In: Proceedings 2018 Workshop on Usable Security, vol. 2018. Internet Society (2018)
9. Dengel, A.: Public-private-key encryption in virtual reality: predictors of students' learning outcomes for teaching the idea of asymmetric encryption. CoolThink@ JC, p. 41 (2020)
10. diSessa, A.: Models of computation. In: Norman, D.A., Draper, S.W. (eds.) User Centered System Design: New Perspectives on Human-Computer Interaction, pp. 201–218. Lawrence Erlbaum Associates, Hillsdale (1986)
11. Electronic Frontier Foundation: Surveillance self-defense: tips, tools and how-tos for safer online communications. https://ssd.eff.org/en
12. Field, A.: Discovering Statistics Using IBM SPSS Statistics, 4th edn. Sage, London (2013)
13. Freelon, D.G.: ReCal: intercoder reliability calculation as a web service. Int. J. Internet Sci. **5**(1), 20–33 (2010)
14. Gerber, N., Zimmermann, V., Henhapl, B., Emeröz, S., Volkamer, M.: Finally Johnny can encrypt: but does this make him feel more secure? In: Proceedings of the 13th International Conference on Availability, Reliability and Security, pp. 1–10 (2018)
15. Herzberg, A., Leibowitz, H.: Can Johnny finally encrypt? Evaluating E2E-encryption in popular IM applications. In: Proceedings of the 6th Workshop on Socio-Technical Aspects in Security and Trust, pp. 17–28 (2016)
16. Johnson-Laird, P.N.: Mental Models: Towards a Cognitive Science of Language, Inference, and Consciousness. Harvard University Press (1983)

17. Krombholz, K., Busse, K., Pfeffer, K., Smith, M., von Zezschwitz, E.: "If HTTPS were secure, I wouldn't need 2FA"- End user and administrator mental models of HTTPS. In: 2019 IEEE Symposium on Security and Privacy (SP), pp. 246–263. IEEE (2019)

18. Lindmeier, A., Mühling, A.: Keeping secrets: K-12 students' understanding of cryptography. In: Proceedings of the 15th Workshop on Primary and Secondary Computing Education. WiPSCE 2020. Association for Computing Machinery, New York (2020). https://doi.org/10.1145/3421590.3421630

19. O'Connor, C., Joffe, H.: Intercoder reliability in qualitative research: debates and practical guidelines. Int. J. Qual. Methods **19**, 1–13 (2020). https://doi.org/10.1177/1609406919899220

20. Paverd, A., Martin, A., Brown, I.: Modelling and automatically analysing privacy properties for honest-but-curious adversaries. Technical report (2014)

21. Schröder, S., Huber, M., Wind, D., Rottermanner, C.: When signal hits the fan: on the usability and security of state-of-the-art secure mobile messaging. In: European Workshop on Usable Security, pp. 1–7. IEEE (2016)

22. Team Guild: A timeline of trouble: Facebook's privacy record, August 2021. https://guild.co/blog/complete-list-timeline-of-facebook-scandals/. Posted 04 Aug 2012

23. Vaziripour, E., et al.: Is that you, Alice? A usability study of the authentication ceremony of secure messaging applications. In: Thirteenth Symposium on Usable Privacy and Security (SOUPS 2017), pp. 29–47 (2017)

24. Weirich, D., Sasse, M.A.: Pretty good persuasion: a first step towards effective password security in the real world. In: Proceedings of the 2001 Workshop on New Security Paradigms, pp. 137–143 (2001)

25. Wenger, E.: Communities of practice and social learning systems: the career of a concept. In: Blackmore, C. (ed.) Social Learning Systems and Communities of Practice, pp. 179–198. Springer, London (2010). https://doi.org/10.1007/978-1-84996-133-2_11

26. Wu, J., Zappala, D.: When is a tree really a truck? Exploring mental models of encryption. In: Fourteenth Symposium on Usable Privacy and Security (SOUPS 2018), pp. 395–409. USENIX Association, Baltimore (2018)

Context and Modelling

Can Security Be Decentralised?
The Case of the PGP Web of Trust

Ashwin J. Mathew(✉) [ID]

King's College London, London, UK
ashwin.mathew@kcl.ac.uk

Abstract. The PGP Web of Trust was intended to provide a decentralised trust model for digital security, an alternative to centralised security models that might be subject to government control. Drawing from five years of ethnographic research among cybersecurity engineers into the everyday practice of using the Web of Trust, I critically examine the relationship between security and trust in distributed computing systems. I employ sociological perspectives on trust to examine the distinct roles that decentralised interpersonal trust and centralised assurance structures play in ensuring security in the Web of Trust. I illustrate how the Web of Trust, although designed to evade government control, paradoxically relies upon assurances provided by government-issued documents to validate identity, even while also relying upon interpersonal trust for this purpose. Through my analysis, I offer a framework for thinking about the relationship between centralisation and decentralisation, and between trust and assurance, to ensure security in the design and operation of distributed computing systems.

Keywords: Trust · Security · Assurance · Decentralisation · PGP · Web of Trust

1 Introduction

Security and trust have been linked concerns throughout the history of the development of distributed computing systems. From being driving factors in the development of early Internet technologies - as with initial military investments [1] - to becoming critical issues in the operation and use of the public Internet [42], security and trust are regarded as essential for the provision of distributed computing. However, while these terms are often used together, their individual conceptions are often treated as being interchangeable. After all, secure technologies must surely by definition be trustworthy, just as trustworthy technologies must surely be secure.

But how do we go from trust to security, and from security to trust? It is essential to address this question if we are to design secure computing systems. In this paper, I critically examine conceptions of, and relationships between, security and trust. I draw from five years of ethnographic fieldwork in operational cybersecurity communities for my analysis, focusing on the social relationships

ⓒ Springer Nature Switzerland AG 2022
S. Parkin and L. Viganò (Eds.): STAST 2021, LNCS 13176, pp. 67–85, 2022.
https://doi.org/10.1007/978-3-031-10183-0_4

of trust necessary for security in the PGP Web of Trust. Through my research, I found how security and trust in distributed computing systems are enmeshed in social and political questions, just as much as they are in questions of technology.

PGP (Pretty Good Privacy) is an encryption technology, widely used to enable secure communications in operational cybersecurity communities around the world. The PGP Web of Trust (WoT) is the decentralised social network enabled by PGP, through which users employ cryptographic signatures to attest to the trustworthiness of their contacts' PGP encryption keys. As of this writing, there are over 6 million publicly observable keys in the PGP WoT.[1] The extended period over which the PGP WoT has been in use, as well as the scale of its use, make it an ideal case through which to examine the relationship between trust and security in the design and operation of secure distributed computing systems.

As perhaps the earliest publicly available encryption program in the world, it is unsurprising - likely even inevitable - that PGP was born of politics. The original developer of PGP, Phil Zimmerman, was a peace activist, working in anti-nuclear movements in the USA during the 1980s. He released PGP as open source software in 1991, in response to concerns about the US government promulgating laws that might force telecommunications companies to ensure that the contents of communications - whether text, voice, or video - should be made available in unencrypted form to law enforcement agencies on request [19]. Zimmerman's public release of PGP was intended to allow a broad public to communicate securely among themselves, while evading the perceived oppression of government surveillance.

At the heart of Zimmerman's concerns lie issues of trust grounded in politics. Should we trust governments to provide security for our societies, and in doing so, make allowances for surveillance of communications, in support of law enforcement? Or should we trust only in the communities and relationships with which we are most closely connected, treating government as an oppressive force to be held in check?

This remains a familiar debate, as governments, corporations, and societies today argue about if and how law enforcement should be granted back door access to the end-to-end encryption provided by secure messaging platforms such as WhatsApp or Signal. Understanding how these issues play out in the context of PGP provides important insights for current policy debates, as well as for the analysis and design of security in distributed computing systems.

I argue that the conception of trust conventionally employed in understandings of secure distributed computing systems - readily apparent in the PGP WoT - reduces complex social understandings of trust to calculated technological and psychological models. In contrast, I offer a sociological perspective on the relationship between trust and security which emphasises the distinction between trust and assurance. Although the PGP WoT was designed to be decentralised, I show how it relies for its operation upon centralised assurance structures, as much as upon decentralised trust.

---

[1] I draw this statistic from the Ubuntu keyserver: https://keyserver.ubuntu.com/pks/lookup?op=stats.

2   Methodology

I studied the PGP WoT through using ethnographic methods across a variety of research sites. My methods included interviews with cybersecurity engineers, and participant observation in a work setting and at cybersecurity conferences. I adopted a multi-sited approach to my research [35], following people, technologies, and narratives across different locations and levels of analysis to understand how the PGP WoT is constructed and maintained.

From 2014 to 2019, I was employed at a non-profit organisation involved in supporting the development of global Internet infrastructure. Working with cybersecurity communities around the world was integral to the organisation's mandate. We employed PGP to secure internal communications within the organisation, as well as external communications our with partners. As such, we were active participants in the PGP WoT. I build on this experience to provide an account of ordinary PGP use in a work setting.

The cybersecurity conferences I attended included the 2016 conference of the Forum of Incident Response and Security Teams (FIRST), and 2017 and 2019 conferences of the Messaging, Mobile, and Malware Anti-Abuse Working Group (M3AAWG).[2] These conferences were useful as sites for understanding attitudes towards security within major operational cybersecurity communities, especially through the experiences of PGP key signing events at these conferences that I draw on for this paper.

Throughout my work, I constructed a range of primary research materials for subsequent analysis, including field notes to document my experiences, and recordings and transcriptions of interviews. I also maintained a corpus of textual materials to support my analysis, including operational and standards documents related to PGP, and the PGP WoT. The range of evidence and experience that I draw from offers insight into trust and security in the ordinary usage of the PGP WoT across tightly knit intra-organisational trust relationships, and the broader networks of trust relationships in operational cybersecurity that span organisational and territorial boundaries.

To account for my active participation in the social worlds that I studied in this research, I adopt autoethnographic methods [3,9,16] to analyse and describe my experiences. In particular, I employ analytic autoethnography [4], using my experiences as means to study and illustrate the broader social and technological relationships that make up the PGP WoT. By the standards of much research in computer science, this may appear to be a "subjective" methodology, rooted as it is in my own personal experience. However, ethnography demands close attention to the ways in which the researcher is implicated in their field site, as the researcher is themself the research instrument. Effective ethnography must account for the ways in which the knowledge gained is situated [26] in the relationships between researcher and subject of research, as the researcher learns

---

[2] FIRST and M3AAWG are key global cybersecurity organisations with distinct, but overlapping, missions that facilitate coordination among government and private sector cybersecurity incident response and security teams. For more information, see https://www.first.org/ and https://www.m3aawg.org/.

through the process of becoming a participant in their field site [31]. The deep and extended engagement demanded by this kind of ethnographic work provides rich insights into social worlds that cannot easily be acquired through other methods.

3   Trust, Assurance, and Security

There are a range of substantially different conceptualisations used to make sense of trust across different disciplines. Psychological understandings evaluate how and why we trust others [6,36], interpersonal analyses focus on trust as a relationship between individuals [27,32], institutional perspectives focus on how trust functions in relation to institutions like government [17,21,33], and cultural perspectives engage with the idea that particular societies may be more or less willing to trust [13,18,40].

However, across these diverse perspectives, there is an agreement that trust is the social phenomenon that allows cooperation in the presence of risk, when there are no further assurances available to mitigate risk. Trust is fundamentally a leap of faith, which cannot be evaluated rationally [6,33]. In this view, trust manifests dynamically at moments of action, rather than a static attitude or state of mind. If we could perfectly determine future expectations in risky interactions, then there would be no need for trust, as any risk could be calculated away. But this is not the world we live in, especially when considering complex interdependent systems such as the PGP WoT.

In computer science, trust has historically been treated as a problem of management in security [8], with a view that computing systems are trusted when they are secure [30]. These perspectives have been developed to focus on *computational trust* as a means to calculate whether or not a person or component in a distributed system should be trusted [44,49], employing trust engineering to create secure systems [24].

These approaches have yielded valuable insights for the design of secure computing systems. However, in treating trust as a computational problem, their aim is to calculate away risk, providing trust through security. In doing so, the leap of faith essential to sociological understandings of trust is overlooked. From a sociological perspective, computational trust may be characterised as providing signals of trustworthiness, offering information for the choice to trust, but not determining whether or not the action of trusting is undertaken [27].

As my discussion suggests, the nature of trust in any technological system must be analysed in terms of sociotechnical relations, in the social bases of trust through which a system may be judged to be trustworthy [38]. Prior work has addressed this in large part by focusing on the psychological aspects of trust, whether through studies of user perceptions of trust online [14,46], or in the design of tools to support users' trust decisions [11,29]. In contrast, I adopt a relational perspective on trust. This requires attention to the social relations of trust enacted in the practice of operating secure sociotechnical systems, as well as to the assumptions of trust - and related conceptualisations of risk - that inform the technological design of these systems.

A relational perspective treats trust as dyadic and interpersonal [32], a three part relation in which a trustor places trust in a trustee only in regard to specific expectations, in a specific social context [27]. For example, while I might trust a colleague to sign PGP keys, I may not trust them to perform repairs on my bicycle. Trust requires choice: if PGP users cannot choose who to trust (and who not to trust) to sign keys, or which keys to trust, then they can hardly be said to be engaging in trust [34].

A trustor's choice to trust relies upon markers of trustworthiness linked to a trustee. These may include histories of interaction between the trustor and trustee in which the trustee has proved themselves reliable, recommendations from trusted acquaintances, reputation within a social group, or shared cultural markers (such as class, race, or gender) that incline a trustor to find a trustee trustworthy. Trustworthiness is evaluated from prior knowledge, located in qualities of a trustee, and a trustor's perspective on these qualities. In contrast, trust takes place in the moment of action, when a trustor is faced with the decision to trust [27]. Trustworthiness may be signalled through sociotechnical features - such as the design of user interfaces - but the act of trusting is always social, occurring in the moment. For example, the signatures on a PGP key act as markers of trustworthiness, but it is left to the trustee to make a choice as to whether or not to trust a PGP key (and it's owner) in a particular social context, for a specific purpose.

As I have discussed, choice is integral to trust. In the absence of choice, trust is better construed as confidence [34]. Confidence is fundamentally a matter of providing assurances - whether through institutional [21,33] or cultural means [48] - that allow risk and uncertainty to be overcome to support cooperative behaviour. For example, central banks provide assurances for the value of money, necessary for the function of economies. Most people have no choice in these matters, but they must have confidence in their central bank and currency for the economy to function.

Assurance structures offer an important means for enabling cooperation at scale, but only under conditions in which confidence is maintained. If confidence fails in an assurance structure, then the assurance structure becomes ineffective, as does the cooperation that it enabled. This can potentially be calamitous, especially when considering critical institutions such as central banks, as it takes substantial work to create and sustain confidence in an assurance structure, which cannot be easily recovered when lost. In contrast, when trust fails, the individuals involved may suffer emotional harm [32], but they have the choice as to whether to repair their trust, or to choose others to trust for similar purposes. Systems based upon interpersonal trust are resilient to individual failures of trust, but typically enable cooperation at smaller scales, while systems based upon assurance structures typically enable cooperation at larger scales, but are at risk of catastrophic failure when confidence is lost.

Both of these mechanisms - interpersonal trust between individuals, and confidence in assurance structures - can ensure the trustworthiness necessary for cooperation [12]. However, the political arrangements envisaged by each of these mechanisms are radically different, and are at the heart of the opposition between the anarchic decentralised organisation of the PGP WoT, and the desire for centralised oversight of communications by governments and security agencies. Within this opposition lies the trust paradox: the observation that effective assurance structures (like strong central banks) that enable cooperation without trust, destroy the need for trust within society; while it is anarchy (such as that found in decentralised systems like the WoT) that requires and encourages trust to maintain cooperative social order [20]. This is not to say that effective assurance structures destroy trust in general. As we will see, assurance structures may sometimes support the development of trust. Remembering that trust is always tied to a specific social context [27], I am concerned with specific social activities in which an effective assurance structure substitutes for trust. This was exactly the concern that Zimmerman had when he created PGP, in the worry that effective government security agencies might diminish the ability of individual citizens to trust each other in their communications. The trust paradox gives us the contradictory insight that to enable trust to flourish, we must allow for risk - rather than trying to engineer risk away with security.

The trust paradox flies in the face of conventional understandings of security as being a source of trust. Instead, security may be seen to actively impede the development of trust, even while providing the assurances necessary for the operation of reliable systems. If we mitigate risk in secure computing systems by removing choice in the design of technologies (by relying purely upon technological methods for security), or by removing choice in the operation of technologies (through reliance on centralised authorities), then we are building security based upon assurance structures, rather than trust [39]. The resulting systems may well be secure, but they encode political arrangements that inhibit trust, by substituting assurance structures for trust. There is an important role for these kinds of systems on the Internet (DNS and SSL certificate authorities are obvious examples). Understanding these as assurance structures offers a clearer perspective through which to analyse the relationship between trust and security in the political arrangements embedded in these systems. Indeed, the modern world is characterised by reliance upon assurance structures rather than trust, which scholars have variously termed *system trust* [33] or *trust in abstract systems* [21].

Yet the PGP WoT envisages a possibility for decentralised security based upon trust, in direct opposition to the political arrangements of security based upon assurance structures. This raises critical questions: Can security be provided through trust, rather than through assurance structures? In doing so, can security be a source of trust?

While it is analytically useful to separate trust and assurance structures - and related political choices - it is important to consider how these conceptually distinct means for cooperation almost always rely upon each other to ensure trustworthiness. Trust and assurance structures within any sociotechnical system interact in complex ways, sometimes reinforcing each other, sometimes acting in direct opposition. To comprehend a system in its totality, these must be studied both in the everyday usage of the system, as well as in the technologies that enable the system to function. I undertake this analysis in the following sections, as I first examine the technology behind PGP, and then investigate the everyday usage of PGP in the WoT. Throughout my analysis, I emphasise issues of risk and choice that are foundational to understanding trust and assurance structures.

4   An Introduction to PGP and the Web of Trust

4.1   PGP and Public Key Cryptography

PGP was the first widely available non-commercial implementation of public key cryptography. Until public key cryptography was conceived of in 1975 [15], encryption relied on shared keys.[3] Shared key encryption faces a fundamental problem in the key distribution process, to ensure that the shared key can itself be securely transmitted among all those who need to use it. This left shared key encryption open to being compromised by third parties, such as government security agencies - the very situation PGP was intended to avoid. Public key encryption functions through the fundamental innovation of creating two keys for each user, which satisfy two conditions: (1) anything encrypted with one key can only be decrypted with the other, and (2) neither key can be derived from the other.

Users maintain a private key which they must maintain securely, never sharing it with anyone; and a public key which they make publicly available. If anyone wishes to send a user a secure message, they need only look up the recipient's public key, and encrypt a message using that key. The message can only be decrypted using the private key, to which only the recipient has access. No-one can discover the private key merely by examining the public key, making communications as secure as the care with which a user manages their private key. This solves the key distribution problem, as keys do not need to be securely distributed: the private key is always private, and the public key always public.

In addition to encryption, public key cryptography offers facilities for authentication. A user may "sign" a message to attest that it came from them, and allow others to authenticate this attestation. Signing a message involves encrypting the message with the user's private key, and attaching the encrypted form of the message - the signature - to the original message. Anyone receiving the message may then decrypt the signature with the user's public key, and compare the decrypted message to the original message. If both messages match, then the attestation holds that message was signed by the user.[4] As we will see, signatures are an essential element in the construction of the WoT.

In order to ensure that it remained non-commercial and patent-free [25], PGP was submitted in 1996 to the standards process at the Internet Engineering Task

---

[3] An alternative history suggests that public key cryptography was invented earlier at the UK's GCHQ, but remained classified [43].

[4] In practice, a shortened version of the message - a unique fingerprint or "hash" - is used in signatures to save on the computation required to encrypt and decrypt large messages for the purposes of authentication.

Force (IETF), the principal standards body for the Internet [5]. The resulting OpenPGP standard has been implemented to provide public key cryptography in a range of software and services.[5]

4.2   Building a Social Network with PGP

PGP differs crucially from modern secure messaging platforms like Signal or WhatsApp in that it functions as a general purpose encryption mechanism. Even though it was initially intended for use with email, it is not tied to any particular platform or technology. PGP can be used to encrypt email for secure communications, encrypt files for secure storage, securely authenticate users for access to online services, and much more. The general purpose nature of PGP does, however, place a greater burden on users. Unlike modern secure messaging platforms which automatically generate and store encryption keys for users tied to their services, PGP requires users to generate encryption keys themselves, and take responsibility for secure storage of these keys. In addition, where modern secure messaging platforms take care of the mechanics of key exchange - sharing your public key with your contacts, and vice versa - PGP requires users to validate keys of contacts themselves. This is where the PGP WoT comes in, functioning as a social network for PGP users, constructed through the mechanisms of PGP itself.

Modern secure messaging platforms are closed social networks, requiring anyone who wishes to communicate over them to be a member of the platform. These platforms maintain encryption keys in integrated contact lists for each user, providing the means for users to discover and securely communicate with contacts within the platform. These platforms offer users the facilities to validate their contacts' keys (for example, using numeric codes or QR codes in messaging apps), but do not require them to do so. In contrast, when PGP users validate keys of their contacts - checking that a key actually belongs to a contact - they store these keys locally on their personal devices in a *keyring*, which is the equivalent of a contact list. Crucially, they may cryptographically sign their contacts' keys, to indicate that they have validated that the key belongs to the contact. It is through this mechanism that the PGP WoT is formed, as a social network of relationships between users is formed through signatures on each others' keys.

The contact lists maintained by modern secure messaging platforms - and by social network platforms more generally - provide the means to construct centralised representations of the social networks of users, along with the tools to traverse these social networks. Since PGP was designed to be decentralised, it places no such requirement upon the WoT. As a result, mechanisms must be provided to allow users to share the connections that they have each constructed, in the form of signatures, with each other. This may be done in a decentralised manner, with users emailing keys to each other once they have signed them. It is also possible to do this using PGP keyservers, which provide the means to publish and share public keys, along with associated signatures and other data.

---

[5] For more information, see https://www.openpgp.org/.

PGP allows users to embed additional information with their keys, in PGP certificates that include full names, email addresses, photographs, and so on, as well as signatures from other users. These effectively function as social network profiles for each user, containing identity information, as well as links to PGP certificates for those who have verified and signed the user's key. PGP certificates also contain technical information about a user's PGP keys, such as the cryptographic algorithm used to generate the key, and the length of the key. This information is important, as certain cryptographic algorithms and shorter key lengths are known to be insecure [37].[6]

Prospective contacts will evaluate the trustworthiness of a key based upon how secure it is, on whether they are able to reliably validate the identity tied to the key, and by examining how trustworthy they find those who have signed the key. These markers of trustworthiness do not in themselves guarantee that a user will trust a key. They merely provide information that a user may employ to decide whether or not to trust a key (and it's owner) in a particular moment and context of action.

Once connected in the PGP WoT, users may discover validated keys of new potential contacts. Given that the WoT is constructed in a decentralised manner by participants with varying levels of expertise and attitudes towards security, PGP allows users to specify how much trust they have in each of their contacts to be responsible in validating and signing others' keys. Users may specify these trust levels to be: (1) *unknown*, indicating that nothing is known about the contact's judgement in signing keys; (2) *none*, indicating that the user does not trust the contact, even though they have validated the contact's key; (3) *marginal*, indicating that the user considers the contact to be responsible in key validation and signing; and (4) *full*, indicating that the contact is trusted as much as user themselves.[7]

Unlike conventional social networks, since the WoT is constructed and maintained by users themselves (rather than a third party platform) users can specify the rules by which it should be traversed to discover new contacts [2]. For example, one of the most widely used OpenPGP implementations, the Gnu Privacy Guard (GnuPG) defaults to considering keys to be trusted if a user has signed them directly, or if they have been signed by one fully trusted key, or if they have been signed by three marginally trusted keys; while limiting traversal to a maximum path length of five.[8] Validation of keys is only half the story - we equally need to consider how users frame their social perspectives on the technical definitions of trust provided by the PGP WoT.

By sharing the signatures they've attached to their contacts' keys, PGP users can create an open decentralised social network: the PGP Web of Trust. Instead

---

[6] For a broader survey of attacks against PGP, see [25].

[7] The OpenPGP standard provides for finer grained trust levels, from 0 to 255 [10]. However, the levels indicated here are those used in practice in OpenPGP implementations.

[8] See the GnuPG manual for a more detailed explanation: https://gnupg.org/gph/en/manual.html#AEN335.

of relying on a centralised platform to maintain and discover contacts and keys, PGP users instead follow trusted connections across the WoT to discover trust-worthy keys for new contacts.

5   The Social Practices of Key Validation

PGP signatures provide the technological mechanisms to verify that a given pub-lic key and private key are related to each other as part of a key pair tied to the same identity. However, the question remains of how to validate that a PGP key actually belongs to the identity it claims to represent. Since the PGP WoT is intentionally decentralised, anyone can generate a PGP key purporting to rep-resent any identity they choose. There is no authority that can offer assurances to verify that a given key represents a given identity. It is through the social practices of validating identities against keys, and the technological process of signing keys to indicate that the identities connected to those keys have been validated, that new connections are forged to grow the PGP WoT.

To analyse the social processes of identity validation and key signing in the PGP WoT, I draw on the distinction between strong and weak ties in social net-works, which are useful as an analogy to the trust levels used to specify rules for traversing the PGP WoT. Strong ties mark those with whom we have deep social relationships, often based upon extended personal histories and trust. Weak ties indicate a looser network of acquaintances who we do not know as well. Strong ties are often densely knit (as with families, or close groups of friends), while weak ties comprise a low density network (for example, in extended professional communities). We might imagine strong ties to be the most important relation-ships in our social networks, as these connect us to the people who we know we can depend upon, providing essential solidarity and assistance in our everyday lives. However, weak ties are crucially important for finding opportunities, and building connections and understanding across the cliques formed by strong ties, which may otherwise remain isolated from each other [22, 23].

I employ this contrast to examine the distinct utility and social conceptions of trust across strong and weak ties in the process of forming connections in the PGP WoT. In the following sections, I discuss the social practices involved in validating keys, and in deciding what trust level to configure for a contact when traversing the PGP WoT, whether full trust (for strong ties), or marginal trust (for weak ties). Although weak ties may remain at unknown trust when a contact is only known in passing, it is in the interests of anyone wanting to leverage the PGP WoT to explicitly set trust levels, as they will otherwise be unable to access a contact's connections.[9] The associations that I draw between strong ties and full trust, and between weak ties and marginal or unknown trust, are by no means a given - what matters are the social practices involved in bridging social and technical conceptions of trust in the PGP WoT.

---

[9] I do not discuss the case of contacts with trust level none, regarded as untrust-worthy to sign keys. While this exceptional condition is important, my focus is on mechanisms through which connections are created, rather than explicitly rejected.

Studies of the PGP WoT have found that the vast majority of keys are connected in isolated groups of relatively small size (about 100 keys or less), with the sole exception being a group with almost 60,000 keys (as of 2015) termed the *strong set* [7,45]. The strong set very likely depends to a great degree upon weak ties, as it is unlikely that such a large number of keys could be connected purely through strong ties among their owners. To ensure it's continued growth, the WoT relies upon social practices that aid the formation of both strong and weak ties, which I discuss in the sections that follow.

5.1 Strong Ties

I created my PGP key in 2014. I'd just joined a non-profit organisation that supported the development and operation of Internet infrastructure around the world. All employees of the organisation were expected to have PGP keys to ensure security for our internal communications, and for communications with partners in the global cybersecurity community.

Although I already knew about PGP, and understood the basics of public key cryptography, I'd never had a PGP key before, nor had I heard of the WoT. Determining how to manage and use my key responsibly was a task in itself, much of which I learned through conversation with colleagues. The documentation for GnuPG, and the PGP email extension I used - Enigmail - were initially quite confusing, as the distinctions between key signing and trust levels were puzzling. I assumed that key signing implied trust, so the utility of setting trust levels for contacts' keys was unclear, as were the meanings of the trust levels available to assign to contacts' keys.[10]

Given the context of use, my confusion was perhaps unsurprising. The small size of the organisation (about 20 employees) created an environment for the formation of strong ties. As with any organisation, our ongoing and repeated engagement with one another offered the opportunity to build rich, multi-faceted social relationships, spanning both professional and personal lives. In addition, the technological focus of the organisation, and its engagement with the global cybersecurity community, provided assurances that colleagues were careful in their use of PGP.

I typically received keys from colleagues - and sent my key to colleagues - via email, as all of our various email clients were configured to sign outgoing messages to confirm authenticity. These signatures included the public key for the sender, to allow a receiver to decrypt the signature, proving that it was created with the sender's private key. When my email client received a message with a public key it hadn't seen before, it offered the option to import it to my keychain. While the signature on the email message verified that the sender held the private key corresponding to the public key attached to the message, it remained my responsibility to verify that this PGP key pair in fact belonged to the sender. After all, email systems can be compromised, and it was entirely

---

[10] As usability studies of PGP tools have indicated [41,47], I was far from alone in my confusion.

possible for an attacker to spoof a colleague's email address to manipulate or eavesdrop on our communications.

For the first few keys I imported, I was careful to confirm with colleagues that the key I'd received was in fact theirs, by physically showing them their public key on my computer. However, this was an onerous process, which required us to be in the office at the same time (many colleagues worked remotely), and interrupted our work days. Over time, I followed many of my colleagues in relying upon the security of our email server, and evaluations of the content of email I received, to ensure that the keys I received were in fact from the colleagues who sent them. While this approach doesn't follow the expectations of security practices in PGP, it reflects pragmatic decisions to fit PGP into our daily practices.

In essence, the organisation functioned as an assurance structure, providing basic guarantees against risk in everyday professional interactions with colleagues. With the support of these basic guarantees, a disparate group of people - not all of whom worked in the same location - primarily connected only through employment by the same organisation, were provided with a secure social space within which to build mutual trust in the context of working together. I do not mean to idealise the organisation through this account, but instead to show how assurance structures, trust, and technological systems need to work together to create secure and trustworthy computing environments.

It was only the first communication from a colleague that I needed to be careful about, as subsequent communications were secured by the colleague's key that I had imported to my keychain. I signed colleagues' keys as I received them, with the signatures automatically placed in my keychain, providing a record that I had verified the keys. While all signatures are equivalent technologically, my social conception of signing colleagues' keys carried with it many intertwined social and technological meanings: that the key belonged to a particular email address; that the email address belonged to a particular individual; that I knew the individual and found them trustworthy; and that our email server was secure, as it was managed by trustworthy colleagues. There are different senses of trust embedded across these meanings, that go well beyond the technological expression of "trust" in the PGP WoT. In making this observation I am not suggesting that PGP should be redesigned to support richer social expressions of trust. Rather, I am illustrating how technological expressions of trust by necessity collapse social context, especially when considered in relation to strong tie relationships.

I typically marked colleagues' keys as having full trust, even though this had limited utility within the organisation. Since we all held each other's keys, we had no need to traverse the WoT to find each other's keys. However, marking my colleagues' keys as having full trust offered the opportunity to access new contacts through colleagues' connections in the WoT. For the WoT to have utility within our organisation, we each needed to form external ties of our own, building wider inter-organisational and international relationships expressed in the WoT.

5.2   Weak Ties

As I prepared to attend the FIRST conference in 2016, my manager had two pieces of advice for me: that I should network widely to make as many connections as possible; and that I should by no means miss the PGP key signing party. FIRST is an international association of cybersecurity incident response and security teams, drawn from government and the private sector. It was formed in 1990 to coordinate international responses to early cybersecurity incidents, and has today grown to over 500 member organisations around the world. As such, the FIRST conference offered me the opportunity to build relationships with senior members of the global cybersecurity community, benefiting my organisation's ability to participate in international cybersecurity coordination activity.

PGP key signing is part of the conference activities, providing the means to extend the WoT in the FIRST community. This is organised with a dedicated session at the conference, the key signing party. Many other security conferences organise similar events to help connect their attendees in the WoT. I was interested in the key signing party to receive signatures on my key from members of the FIRST community, as well as to build social relationships in the process of key signing.

I was emailed instructions on how to participate in the key signing party well ahead of the conference, although there were also reminders of the key signing party during the conference opening. Apart from specifying when and where the key signing party was to take place, the instructions indicated that I should bring a government-issued identity document (such as a passport) to the event, and that I should upload my public key to a shared keyring hosted on biglumber.com in advance of the event. This shared keyring listed essential information about each uploaded key: a unique fingerprint identifying the key, the cryptographic algorithm used to generate the key, the key length, creation and expiry dates for the key, and email addresses associated with the key.

When I arrived at the key signing party, I found a hall with a handful of small tables, and a few dozen people in attendance. The organiser supplied us with printed copies of the information from the shared keyring, and walked us through the process we would follow. We were to circulate around the tables in the room, checking each other's identity documents, marking off keys as verified on our printouts if we were satisfied with the documents presented to us. We would go through the process of actually signing keys after the event, and then email the signed keys back to their owners, or upload our signatures to a keyserver if the owner of the key was willing (as some people prefer not to publish their keys).

I walked over a table, introducing myself to the group I met there, with people from Austria, Cote d'Ivoire, Germany, India, and the USA. We quickly got down to the business of verifying identities, one at a time. I showed my Indian passport to everyone at the table, some of whom took it from me, and checked it carefully, comparing the photograph in my passport against me, and comparing my name in the passport against that on their printout. Eventually satisfied, the passport was returned to me, and I was asked to verify the fingerprint identifying my key, at which point everyone marked my key as verified on their printouts. The next person to be verified had two identity documents, an Austrian ID card, as well as a US driver's licence. Several of the group were vocal in their distrust of the Austrian ID card, as it was simply a laminated piece of paper, but the US driver's licence was considered satisfactory. Before moving on to the next table, I joked that it might be more efficient to run the event like a beauty contest, having people take turns to stand up in front of the room, perhaps with their identity documents projected on a large screen. One of the members of our group remarked that he's seen key signing parties run in a manner similar to that which I proposed, especially when larger numbers of people are involved. He added that he preferred the more intimate process we're engaged in, which gave him the opportunity to have conversations and network.[11]

As I left the key signing party, I reflected on how uncomfortable I'd felt in having my passport scrutinised by a group of strangers. While passports, driving licenses, and other government-issued identity documents may be used for non-government purposes - such as proving identity when renting accommodation - they are primarily examined by police, immigration officers, and other state security personnel, with such interactions often fraught with concern. As a person of colour from the Global South, who has spent the last 15 years in the USA and the UK, this is a social dynamic that is only too familiar. During the conference, new acquaintances would often look at my name badge to check my affiliation, but they were hardly going to ask me for further proof of identity. The need for government identity documents at the key signing party illustrates how technical requirements may drive social practice, and in doing so, potentially carry over social perceptions of the broader security contexts within which these documents are ordinarily used. Since identity in the WoT is self-declared in PGP certificates, and warranted by contacts in a decentralised manner through signatures, the only recourse is to leave it to potential contacts to independently evaluate as best as they can whether or not an individual's identity is valid; and for individuals to prove their identity as best as they can. There are few forms of evidence better suited for this purpose than government identity documents.

Later that evening, I imported the keys that I'd checked off on my printout to my personal keyring, signed them, and uploaded them to a keyserver, as everyone present was comfortable with that option. I left the trust levels for these new contacts as unknown. Marking them at the marginal trust level would have given me access to their contacts in the WoT, but I was uncomfortable with doing that, as I had no knowledge of how responsible they were with key signing. When I checked my public key on a keyserver the following week, I found just 3 new signatures. Not everyone who had verified my identity had signed my key. If they had, they hadn't shared the signature with me, nor uploaded it to a keyserver. Perhaps they simply didn't get around to signing my key. Perhaps they didn't find my passport trustworthy. After all, it's hardly reasonable to expect cybersecurity engineers to be able to evaluate the veracity of identity

---

[11] The organiser of the FIRST key signing party recommended this document for guidance on different ways in key signing parties may be run: https://www.cryptnet.net/ fdp/crypto/keysigning_party/en/keysigning_party.html.

documents from around the world. Regardless, I had become just a little more connected in the WoT through this process.

Although PGP was originally created as a decentralised system, meant to oppose the perceived tyranny of governments, identity verification at key signing parties paradoxically relies upon identity documents issued by governments. In the absence of trust possible with strong ties, the assurance structures of government-provided identity are required to form weak ties in the PGP WoT. As I have discussed, weak ties are essential for their ability to bridge strong tie cliques - but the utility of weak ties in the PGP WoT depends upon assurance structures, rather than trust.

6   Security Through Trust, or Assurance?

My research shows how a purportedly decentralised system for security - the PGP WoT - is constructed in practice through a combination of decentralised trust relationships, and centralised assurance structures. While different analyses and designs may focus on one or the other, both trust and assurance are always present in the practice of security. The danger lies in assuming that either one can be focused upon in itself, to the detriment of missing out on how the other plays an essential role. Following my analysis, there is no such thing as a purely decentralised secure computing system, nor are there purely centralised secure computing systems. All secure distributed computing systems employ aspects of both centralisation and decentralisation, of trust and assurance, in their operation.

This is not only a matter of technological design. PGP was created for a political purpose, to create a decentralised system in opposition to centralised government power. More recently, various conceptions of trust have been employed to make similar political arguments about the advantages of decentralisation in blockchain projects [28]. I believe that our understandings of these systems will benefit from a careful analysis of trust following the framework of relationships between trust, trustworthiness, and security which I have outlined here. The problem lies in assuming that centralised political power, grounded in government, can be resisted and substituted for by decentralised political power designed and operated through only technological means.

The complex relationships between trust and assurance that I analyse is readily apparent in the distinction between strong tie and weak tie relationships in the PGP WoT. Although both of these are expressed identically in PGP signatures, they are produced through distinctive social mechanisms which are entirely external to the WoT, and which were not anticipated by the WoT. The strong tie relationships I described relied upon the assurance of shared organisational membership, which provided an environment for trust relationships to emerge. The weak tie relationships I described relied upon the assurance provided by government identity documents, which (following the trust paradox) militate against the functionally equivalent need for trust to verify identity. In both cases, the WoT was constructed in relation to pre-existing social formations

- a non-profit organisation, and government - rather than creating an alternative decentralised social formation through only technological means.

The relationship between trust and assurance is by no means simple, although the framework I have offered may be helpful for analysis. When considering technological systems, strong ties are produced through mutually reinforcing trust and assurance, while weak ties are produced through assurance which opposes the need for trust. This is especially true in cases where complex social contexts are necessarily collapsed into undifferentiated technological expressions, as is the case when considering how both strong and weak ties are expressed as identical forms in PGP signatures.

In focusing on the social practices of the WoT, I do not mean to suggest that the technology of the WoT has no effects upon the world. It does, after all, provide a decentralised means for secure communications that would not have otherwise been possible. In addition, it provides the means for a larger community to emerge through a shared commitment to the social practices of the WoT, whether within organisations, or among cybersecurity professionals at key signing parties.

We may analyse the implications of specific design choices in the technology of PGP by returning to the fundamental social phenomenon of risk, to which security, trust, and assurance are all responses. As I have discussed, risk cannot be calculated away with technology. Rather, technology *creates*, *modifies*, and *relocates* risk. New risks are created for users in traversing the WoT to find new contacts, as this relies upon the risks they accept in their choices for the trust levels they set for contacts in their keyrings, and the policies they select for traversal. Risks are modified for communications, which may be made secure with PGP, although users must now be aware of risks due to keys that are insecure due to length or algorithm. Risks are relocated for the verification of identity, from centralised identity authorities to decentralised PGP signatures. By anticipating how choices in the design of technology create, modify, and relocate risk, we can arrive at a more complete understanding of the articulations of trust and assurance required to ensure security.

If trust and assurance are essential responses to risk, then it is critical that we have a clear comprehension of the implications of relying on them to ensure security. A system that relies upon trust requires support for social spaces to enable the formation and maintenance of interpersonal trust relationships. In contrast, a system that relies upon assurances needs to build social mechanisms to ensure confidence in assurance structures. As I have shown, trust and assurance never function in isolation, as they always coexist in practice. It is through consciously combining trust, assurance, and technology that effective security can be provided for distributed computing systems.

References

1. Abbate, J.: Inventing the Internet. MIT Press, Cambridge (1999)
2. Abdul-Rahman, A.: The PGP trust model. EDI-Forum J. Electron. Commerce **10**(3), 27–31 (1997). https://ldlus.org/college/WOT/The_PGP_Trust_Model.pdf

3. Adams, T.E., Ellis, C., Jones, S.H.: Autoethnography. In: The International Encyclopedia of Communication Research Methods, pp. 1–11. Wiley (2017). https://onlinelibrary.wiley.com/doi/abs/10.1002/9781118901731.iecrm0011

4. Anderson, L.: Analytic autoethnography. J. Contemp. Ethnogr. **35**(4), 373–395 (2006). https://doi.org/10.1177/0891241605280449

5. Atkins, D., Stallings, W., Zimmerman, P.: RFC 1991: PGP Message Exchange Formats (1996). https://datatracker.ietf.org/doc/html/rfc1991

6. Barbalet, J.: A characterization of trust, and its consequences. Theory Soc. **38**(4), 367–382 (2009). https://doi.org/10.1007/s11186-009-9087-3

7. Barenghi, A., Di Federico, A., Pelosi, G., Sanfilippo, S.: Challenging the trustworthiness of PGP: is the web-of-trust tear-proof? In: Pernul, G., Ryan, P.Y.A., Weippl, E. (eds.) ESORICS 2015. LNCS, vol. 9326, pp. 429–446. Springer, Cham (2015). https://doi.org/10.1007/978-3-319-24174-6_22

8. Blaze, M., Feigenbaum, J., Lacy, J.: Decentralized trust management. In: Proceedings of the 1996 IEEE Symposium on Security and Privacy, pp. 164–173, May 1996. https://doi.org/10.1109/SECPRI.1996.502679. iSSN: 1081-6011

9. Butz, D., Besio, K.: Autoethnography. Geogr. Compass **3**(5), 1660–1674 (2009). https://doi.org/10.1111/j.1749-8198.2009.00279.x

10. Callas, J., Donnerhacke, L., Finney, H., Shaw, D., Thayer, R.: RFC 4880: OpenPGP Message Format (2007). https://datatracker.ietf.org/doc/html/rfc4880

11. Camp, L.J.: Designing for trust. In: Falcone, R., Barber, S., Korba, L., Singh, M. (eds.) TRUST 2002. LNCS, vol. 2631, pp. 15–29. Springer, Heidelberg (2003). https://doi.org/10.1007/3-540-36609-1_3

12. Cheshire, C.: Online trust, trustworthiness, or assurance? Daedalus **140**(4), 49–58 (2011). https://doi.org/10.1162/DAED_a_00114

13. Cook, K.S., Yamagishi, T., Cheshire, C., Cooper, R., Matsuda, M., Mashima, R.: Trust building via risk taking: a cross-societal experiment. Soc. Psychol. Q. **68**(2), 121–142 (2005). https://doi.org/10.1177/019027250506800202

14. Costante, E., den Hartog, J., Petkovic, M.: On-line trust perception: what really matters. In: 2011 1st Workshop on Socio-Technical Aspects in Security and Trust (STAST), pp. 52–59, September 2011. https://doi.org/10.1109/STAST.2011.6059256. iSSN: 2325-1697

15. Diffie, W.: The first ten years of public-key cryptography. Proc. IEEE **76**(5), 560–577 (1988). https://doi.org/10.1109/5.4442

16. Ellis, C., Adams, T.E., Bochner, A.P.: Autoethnography: an overview. Hist. Soc. Res./Historische Sozialforschung **36**(4), 273–290 (2011). https://www.jstor.org/stable/23032294

17. Farrell, H.: Constructing mid-range theories of trust: the role of institutions. In: Cook, K.S., Hardin, R., Levi, M. (eds.) Whom Can We Trust? How Groups, Networks, and Institutions Make Trust Possible. Russell Sage Foundation, New York (2009)

18. Fukuyama, F.: Trust: The Social Virtues and the Creation of Prosperity. The Free Press, New York (1996)

19. Garfinkel, S.: PGP: Pretty Good Privacy. O'Reilly Media (1995)

20. Gellner, E.: Trust, cohesion, and the social order. In: Gambetta, D. (ed.) Trust: Making and Breaking Cooperative Relations, pp. 142–157. Basil Blackwell (1988)

21. Giddens, A.: The Consequences of Modernity. Stanford University Press (1990)

22. Granovetter, M.: The strength of weak ties: a network theory revisited. Sociol. Theory **1**(1983), 201–233 (1983). https://doi.org/10.2307/202051

23. Granovetter, M.S.: The strength of weak ties. Am. J. Soc. **78**(6), 1360–1380 (1973). http://www.jstor.org/stable/2776392

24. Guttman, J.D.: Trust engineering via security protocols. In: 2012 Workshop on Socio-Technical Aspects in Security and Trust, pp. 1–2, June 2012. https://doi.org/10.1109/STAST.2012.15. iSSN: 2325-1697

25. Halpin, H.: SoK: why Johnny can't fix PGP standardization. In: Proceedings of the 15th International Conference on Availability, Reliability and Security, ARES 2020, pp. 1–6. Association for Computing Machinery, New York, August 2020. https://doi.org/10.1145/3407023.3407083

26. Haraway, D.: Situated knowledges: the science question in feminism and the privilege of partial perspective. Feminist Stud. **14**(3), 575–599 (1988). http://www.jstor.org/stable/3178066

27. Hardin, R.: Trust and Trustworthiness. Russell Sage Foundation Publications (2002)

28. Jacobs, M.: How implicit assumptions on the nature of trust shape the understanding of the blockchain technology. Philosophy Technol. **34**(3), 573–587 (2020). https://doi.org/10.1007/s13347-020-00410-x

29. Jakobsson, M.: User trust assessment: a new approach to combat deception. In: Proceedings of the 6th Workshop on Socio-Technical Aspects in Security and Trust, pp. 73–78. Association for Computing Machinery, New York, December 2016. https://doi.org/10.1145/3046055.3046063

30. Jøsang, A.: The right type of trust for distributed systems. In: Proceedings of the 1996 Workshop on New Security Paradigms, NSPW 1996, pp. 119–131. Association for Computing Machinery, New York, September 1996. https://doi.org/10.1145/304851.304877

31. Lave, J.: Apprenticeship in Critical Ethnographic Practice. University of Chicago Press (2011)

32. Lewis, J.D., Weigert, A.: Trust as a social reality. Soc. Forces **63**(4), 967–985 (1985). https://doi.org/10.2307/2578601

33. Luhmann, N.: Trust and Power. Wiley (1979)

34. Luhmann, N.: Familiarity, confidence, trust: problems and alternatives. In: Gambetta, D. (ed.) Trust: Making and Breaking Cooperative Relations, pp. 94–107. Basil Blackwell (1988)

35. Marcus, G.E.: Ethnography in/of the world system: the emergence of multi-sited ethnography. Ann. Rev. Anthropol. **24**, 95–117 (1995). http://arjournals.annualreviews.org/doi/abs/10.1146/annurev.an.24.100195.000523

36. Möllering, G.: The nature of trust: from Georg Simmel to a theory of expectation, interpretation and suspension. Sociology **35**(2), 403–420 (2001)

37. Nemec, M., Sys, M., Svenda, P., Klinec, D., Matyas, V.: The return of coppersmith's attack: practical factorization of widely used RSA moduli. In: Proceedings of the 2017 ACM SIGSAC Conference on Computer and Communications Security, CCS 2017, pp. 1631–1648. Association for Computing Machinery, New York, October 2017. https://doi.org/10.1145/3133956.3133969

38. Nickel, P.J., Franssen, M., Kroes, P.: Can we make sense of the notion of trustworthy technology? Knowl. Technol. Policy **23**(3–4), 429–444 (2010). https://doi.org/10.1007/s12130-010-9124-6

39. Nissenbaum, H.: Will security enhance trust online, or supplant it? In: Roderick, K.M., Cook, K.S. (eds.) Trust and Distrust in Organizations: Dilemmas and Approaches, pp. 155–188. Russell Sage Foundation Publications (2004). http://www.nyu.edu/projects/nissenbaum/papers/trust.pdf

40. Putnam, R.: The prosperous community: social capital and public life. Am. Prospect (2001). https://prospect.org/api/content/27753724-6757-5e80-925d-9542fc7ad4cb/

41. Ruoti, S., Andersen, J., Zappala, D., Seamons, K.: Why Johnny still, still can't encrypt: evaluating the usability of a modern PGP client. arXiv:1510.08555 [cs], January 2016. http://arxiv.org/abs/1510.08555. arXiv: 1510.08555

42. Schneider, F.B. (ed.): Trust in Cyberspace. The National Academies Press, Washington, D.C. (1999)

43. Singh, S.: The Code Book: The Science of Secrecy from Ancient Egypt to Quantum Cryptography. Anchor Books, New York (2000)

44. Twigg, A., Dimmock, N.: Attack-resistance of computational trust models. In: WET ICE 2003. Proceedings. Twelfth IEEE International Workshops on Enabling Technologies: Infrastructure for Collaborative Enterprises, pp. 275–280, June 2003. https://doi.org/10.1109/ENABL.2003.1231420. iSSN: 1080-1383

45. Ulrich, A., Holz, R., Hauck, P., Carle, G.: Investigating the OpenPGP web of trust. In: Atluri, V., Diaz, C. (eds.) ESORICS 2011. LNCS, vol. 6879, pp. 489–507. Springer, Heidelberg (2011). https://doi.org/10.1007/978-3-642-23822-2_27

46. Vidiasova, L., Kabanov, Y.: Online trust and ICTs usage: findings from St. Petersburg, Russia. In: Proceedings of the 13th International Conference on Theory and Practice of Electronic Governance, ICEGOV 2020, pp. 847–850. Association for Computing Machinery, New York, September 2020. https://doi.org/10.1145/3428502.3428637

47. Whitten, A., Tygar, J.D.: Why Johnny can't encrypt: a usability evaluation of PGP 5.0. In: Proceedings of the 8th USENIX Security Symposium, pp. 169–183 (1999)

48. Yamagishi, T., Yamagishi, M.: Trust and commitment in the United States and Japan. Motiv. Emot. 18(2), 129–166 (1994)

49. Ziegler, C.N., Lausen, G.: Spreading activation models for trust propagation. In: IEEE International Conference on e-Technology, e-Commerce and e-Service, EEE 2004, pp. 83–97, March 2004. https://doi.org/10.1109/EEE.2004.1287293

"I'm Doing the Best I Can."
Understanding Technology Literate Older Adults' Account Management Strategies

Melvin Abraham[1]([envelope]), Michael Crabb[2]([envelope]), and Saša Radomirović[3]([envelope])

[1] University of Glasgow, Glasgow, UK
m.abraham.1@research.gla.ac.uk
[2] University of Dundee, Dundee, UK
m.z.crabb@dundee.ac.uk
[3] Heriot-Watt University, Edinburgh, UK
sradomirovic@acm.org

Abstract. Older adults are becoming more technologically proficient and use the internet to participate actively in society. However, current best security practices can be seen as unusable by this population group as these practices do not consider the needs of an older adult.

Aim. We aim to develop a better understanding of digitally literate, older adults' online account management strategies and the reasons leading to their adoption.

Method. We carry out two user studies (n = 7, n = 5). The first of these gathered information on older adults' account ecosystems and their current online security practice. In the second, we presented security advice to the same group of older adults facilitated by a bespoke web application. We used this to learn more about the reasons behind older adults' security practices by allowing them to reflect on the reported security vulnerabilities in account ecosystems.

Results. Our participants are aware of some online security practices, such as not to reuse passwords. Lack of trust in their own memory is a critical factor in their password management and device access control strategies. All consider finance-related accounts as their most important accounts, but few identified the secondary accounts (e.g. emails for account recovery) or devices that provide access to these as very important.

Conclusions. Older adults make a conscious choice to implement specific practices based on their understanding of security, their trust in their own abilities and third-parties, and the usability of a given security practice. While they are well-aware of some best security practices, their choices will be different if the best security practice does not work in their personal context.

1 Introduction

Older adults (70+) are an underrepresented demographic in cyberspace and can unconsciously be ignored when designing secure cyber-systems [46]. An increasing number of older adults use the internet and smart devices [33]. Some actively

© Springer Nature Switzerland AG 2022
S. Parkin and L. Viganò (Eds.): STAST 2021, LNCS 13176, pp. 86–107, 2022.
https://doi.org/10.1007/978-3-031-10183-0_5

seek to improve their technological literacy through training [1] and university programmes [7]. However, older adults, as a demographic, are also regularly targets of cybercrime [2,42] and they have traditionally been seen as less technologically literate [6,16].

For more than a decade a considerable effort has been invested in understanding the strategies used by end-users when securing their online accounts. We call a user's online accounts and the physical and digital means that provide access to them an *account ecosystem*. Keeping a secure account ecosystem is becoming increasingly difficult due to the number of online accounts that each individual owns and the multitude of methods used to secure a growing number of systems. It is unclear whether the problems associated with managing multiple accounts are compounded for older adults due to technology literacy and age-related decline.

In this work, we attempt to understand the methods used by older adults when securing online accounts, and why their chosen strategies are adopted. We carried out semi-structured interviews to gain information regarding online account structures within a group of 7 older adults. We then developed a system that can highlight security issues within an individual's online account graph and used this as a conversation aid to conduct secondary interviews with the same group. We used this second set of interviews to uncover the reasons behind current security practice adoption.

This research contributes an understanding of account security strategies that are used by older adults. The demographic that we include in this work can be classed as digitally literate and yet still at a high risk of being targeted for cyber-attacks. We see this work as developing a niche understanding of the current security strategies that are used by this group which can inform future development of security tools.

2   Related Work

Older adults are more at risk of attacks aimed at their online security compared to other age demographics [16]. This increase risk of attack is, in part, due to older adults having better financial stability [27], and also being more trusting towards advice given [25] due to aspects such as social isolation [3]. Older adults are particularly vulnerable to social engineering attacks [3,17], likely caused by high levels of trust and a low ability to gauge accuracy of advice that is received [44]. The impact of attacks is amplified for older adults as they have fewer digital strategies in place to protect themselves against spam and phishing attacks, as compared to younger adults [17].

Older adults face technical uncertainty when implementing security best practices online [13] and are likely to prioritise security advice based on the availability of advice rather than advice expertise [32]. Being overly trusting and taking information at face value creates challenges in gauging the accuracy of such advice. Following bad security advice can lead to accepting and believing fake news [26], an increased risk of social engineering [26], and a potentially false sense of security by entrusting others, such as family members [22,36].

2.1   Securing Online Accounts

Many strategies are used to secure accounts including password creation, password management, and additional security tools such as multi-factor authentication. Password based authentication continues to be the dominant authentication method for online accounts.

Guidance exists to assist in creating passwords that are secure for online usage [15,30]. However, it is recognised that password reuse is a common method used by people when securing their online accounts [8], with this likely due to the challenges associated with remembering multiple complex pieces of information [47]. Password reuse creates an account security vulnerability which an attacker can exploit [8]. When one shared password is discovered for a user through methods such as a password database breach [8], dictionary attack [20] or just guessing, every account that shares the same password is also at risk of compromise [23].

One method that can be used to remove password reuse is for users to rely on software such as password managers. Password Managers are essential tools that facilitate the use of distinct, strong passwords by assisting with their generation and removing the need to remember them. Despite the clear benefits, adoption rates for password managers with built in password generation features are poor [35,43]. Adoption is even lower for older adults with suggested reasons for this being a lack of independence, trust and usability [38]. Reasons for not using password managers can include suspicion of the software, and a belief that there is not a current need to adopt this tool [10,35].

There are many authentication methods that are employed in addition to or instead of standard password authentication. One of the simplest is single sign-on, whereby an account with one service provider is used to authenticate to another service provider. Other authentication methods rely on out-of-band communication, such as the sending of a code to a mobile device the user has access to and is the sole owner of. A related and frequently used authentication method to recover access to an account is by proving ownership of a particular email address. More recent authentication methods employ authenticator apps on smart devices or dedicated authentication devices such as U2F security keys. End-user devices also employ biometric authentication. Finally, two ore more authentication methods that all rely on different authentication principles, such as biometrics, secret information or physical artefacts, can be chained to yield a stronger authentication method. These are known as multi-factor authentication methods. A typical two-factor authentication method is the combination of password authentication with a code sent to a mobile device.

2.2   Understanding Links Between Accounts

With each account, authentication method or artefact that is added into the security practice of an individual, their account ecosystem grows. This growth can occur, for example, due to an online account's additional requirement for 2-factor authentication. The new authentication method may require both the user's password and a code sent to the user's phone. A look at the bigger picture outside the blinders of individual accounts brings to light critical security issues and lack of best practices which cannot be identified when accounts are considered individually [19].

Account access graphs [19] are a convenient tool to represent an account ecosystem and examine it for security issues. An account access graph is an edge-colored, directed graph whose edges represent a "gives access to" relation between the graph's nodes which represent accounts, devices, sensitive information, or physical objects. Equally coloured edges pointing to the same target node indicate that access to all source nodes is necessary to gain access to the target node. Edges of different colours thus represent alternative access methods.

As with all demographic groups, older adults are increasing the length of time that they use technology for, and the types of services that they engage with online [33]. This increase bring additional challenges in maintaining secure practices for a growing number of online accounts. In order to understand this area and to develop an insight into the challenges that may be present, we ask *RQ: What are the account management strategies used by older adults, and why are these strategies adopted?*

3 Older Adults' Account Ecosystems

Recall that an *account ecosystem* is the collection of a user's online accounts and all the physical and digital means that provide access to the accounts. The typical means to obtain access to an online account are credentials such as (cryptographic) private keys and passwords, physical devices such as smart phones, and other accounts such as email recovery and single sign-on accounts.

In order to understand an older adult's personal account management strategy, we must first elicit information on their account ecosystem. To achieve this, we carried out semi-structured interviews with 7 older adults. Each interview was conducted by the same person to ensure coherence and consistency between all the interviews and each interview lasted between 60–90 min. The participant's personal account ecosystem was modelled as an account access graph [19] (see Sect. 2.2) which we annotated with additional information gathered during the interview.

3.1 Study Setup

Demographic Information: We recruited 7 participants, all living in North East Scotland. From our 7 participants, 5 were female and 2 were male. The ages ranged from 70–90 years old (mean = 75.4). All participants are retired and none were from an IT or related field. All 7 participants stated they have a reasonable competency when using technology for day to day tasks such as communication, information retrieval and online shopping. 3 participants previously worked in the medical sector, 2 in educational teaching/advising, and 1 in economic development. All participants consented that their responses could be quoted and used. We refer to the participants of this study as P1, ..., P7.

Interview Setup: The semi-structured interview took place using video conferencing software. When the account access graph was being created the interviewer's screen was shared with the participant to allow them to see the account access interview tool. This was done to aid the participants memory and lower mental strain that could be caused from remembering the answers they gave throughout the process.

Interview Script: An interview script (see Appendix A) based on a script of Hammann [18] was used to maintain a high level of consistency and coherence between all of the interviews. The script was designed specifically to follow a semi-structured approach allowing for conversations to flow naturally and any interesting points brought up to be explored and elaborated on.

In order to protect the privacy of the participant, each item and account was given a nickname assigned by the participant, in order to communicate sensitive information such as a password or an account name. For example a nickname for the participant's password that is used to access their email could be *'EmailPassword'* or *'password1'*. Participants were given the opportunity to revisit answers they had previously provided in order to review the nickname and the access methods.

Procedure: This study was reviewed and approved by the University of Dundee's Ethics Committee (*UOD-SSEREC-DoC-UG-2020-004*) before any study sessions were carried out. Before each interview, the participant was sent an information sheet and digital consent form containing information about the project. Interview topics were split into two parts: 1) discussion of account security based on the participant's experiences and views and 2) eliciting the participant's account ecosystem by creating their Account Access Graph.

The interview started by asking questions to gauge demographic information. Participants were then systematically asked what accounts or items they have under specific categories: Devices, Password Managers, Emails, Social Media, Finance, Shopping, Entertainment, Gaming, Other and a summary of all the passwords. Participants did not declare every account they have ever created as it would be impractical due to the number of *'one off'* accounts a person creates but were urged to mention accounts that were important to them in each category, or that store sensitive information such as banking details.

Once all account information was collected, the participant was asked questions relating to how they go about finding information security advice, with this following the study's interview script. Participants were asked questions to elaborate on their day to day online security, specifically regarding their views, practices and strategies that were formulated from their lifestyles and experience with online security.

Analysis Technique: Every attempt was made to keep the interviews impartial. However, a potential avenue where bias may be present is that the author was present when each interview session was conducted. A structured interview guide was used to reduce the risk of bias. Following guidance from [11], interviews were transcribed and anonymised before analysis. Individual sections of the interviews were then analysed independently using open coding [45] where the following process was used:

1. **Generating Initial Codes:** The lead author transcribed all interviews and subsequently took notes of initial codes. These were then collated and developed into a codebook.
2. **Evaluation of Codes:** The lead and secondary author discussed all codes and developed initial descriptions of each.
3. **Coding of Full Data Set:** The lead author then coded the complete dataset using the updated set of descriptors made in Step (2).
4. **Defining Themes:** The lead and secondary authors reviewed the final coding and identified similarities to create thematic groups. This was carried out as a collaborative session where all codes were examined.

The final outcome of our analysis is a broad understanding of older adults' security practices and not of the codes themselves. As such, inter-rater reliability is not relevant [28].

3.2 Results

The number of accounts that our participants reported to have in active use ranged from 6 to 21 with a median and average of 12. This is lower than the average of 16–26 accounts a person was found to have in previous studies [12, 34,35,48]. All participants had one or more email accounts, financial accounts and social media accounts, and two or more shopping accounts. All participants used several devices to access their online accounts. Multi-factor authentication was only used when it was mandatory.

Whilst the primary purpose of this first interview was to collect information regarding older adults account ecosystem to analyse and use within the second interview in this study, we also gathered information related to their general mindset regarding online security. A brief summary of this is given below.

Security Practices Used by Older Adults. Older adults use a number of security practices to keep their accounts secure online. Participants discussed their usage of passwords, password management systems, and wariness when using online services.

Passwords: From the participants that were interviewed all of them indicated that they follow what they feel is basic account security hygiene. They stated they did not reuse passwords: *"every password for every account is unique"* (P1) as, *"the domino effects to all your other accounts when one password gets compromised is clear"* (P7). P2 described their password creation strategy as *"taking a password and changing it around, so that every password is a little different and not the same as another one that I have"*.

Password Management: Memory was a critical factor to all of the participants, using memory alone to remember passwords was not a fit for purpose solution. Their password management strategies were paramount in the participants independence to use their online accounts. Only one participant (P3) stated they use a paid digital password manager the rest of the participants stated they used unencrypted password management methods such as *"writing passwords down in an address book"* (P4), or *"store my passwords in a word document"* (P2).

> P7: *"Using a password to unlock my phone is not something I can do, when you are my age you tend to find yourself forgetting things quite often ... however I can't write the password down for the same reason, if I ever forget to take my book with me, then I wouldn't be able to use my phone"*

Online Wariness: All the participants also stated they are very careful when it comes to being online, as they are *"very suspicious"* (P1) when it comes to clicking on any links online when browsing or *"links within emails in case it's spam"* (P3). Out of the 7 participants, P2 and P6 stated they go out of their way to maintain their online security *"by using Apple products as they have more protections out of the box"* (P2) and *"clearing the browser cache to remove any cookies"* (P6) in order to add another layer of security.

Every participant mentioned their reason for their efforts stems from an urge to feel a sense of security, *"If an attacker found one issue they would feel motivated to find more"* (P7). Being highly aware that adults of their age are regularly victims of fraud and cyber attacks, a fear 75% of the participants share was *"becoming another target"* (P3).

Mindset of the Older Adults Regarding Online Security. The mindset of being secure online is something all the older adults share. Participants discussed the different mindsets they have established through their experiences of trying to be safe online.

Attitudes Towards Security: Each of the participants hold the belief that it is *"very important"* (P4) to be secure online, especially when it comes to *"accounts that handle financial transactions"* (P5) such as banks and *"online shopping websites"* (P5). All the participants stated that their motivations and mindset stemmed from fear of "becoming a victim" (P1) of cyber crime and undertaking *"a financial loss"* (P5). P3 even brought up the view that *"hackers are a lot smarter than me ... they will find new ways to scam people"*, thus P3 finds *"it's our own responsibility"* to stay secure and up to date with the current best practices.

Perceptions of Security: All the participants feel that *"they are reasonably secure"* (P1) when it comes to their account security and being online. Each participant stated they are *"doing the best I possibly can within my ability"* (P7). All the participants stated they have *"never previously been a victim"* (P4) of an attack which leads to creating a sense of validation that *"I must be doing something right"* (P1) as their efforts are effective and *"don't need to worry just yet"* (P5) about their online security at the moment. An interesting view that was brought up by two participants (P2 and P3) was that third parties also play a role in insuring their online safety. In P3's case it came down to *"doing research to see if you can trust a company to keep their systems secure for example my bank"* and P2 stated that *"my children will pull me up if I am doing anything I shouldn't be"* and act as a safety net to mitigate actions that may lead to being a victim of fraud or an attack.

4 Engaging Older Adults in Account Security

In order for us to develop a better understanding of the older adults' account security practices while also enabling them to develop an understanding of their security vulnerabilities, we created a web application that provides a personalised account security report. The web application served as a basis for the second interview and highlighted the security vulnerabilities in a participant's account ecosystem which we found in the annotated account access graphs that we created from the first interview.

4.1 Security Goal and Threat Model

The security goal that our analysis focuses on is to prevent unauthorised access to our participants' online accounts. The account graphs that we elicited in the first interview modeled all possibilities to access the participant's online accounts under the assumption that they contain all relevant information. This assumption may not be true, as participants could have withheld some information or our systematic elicitation could have missed an access path.

In view of the security goal and our participants' demographic, the main threat actors to our participants' account security are online (remote) adversaries and (local) thieves, but not burglars who we assume to be interested in other valuables than accounts.

We consider threats arising from online password compromise and device theft or inadvertent loss. We do not consider threats arising from online scams, such as phishing emails, direct account compromise from attacks on the service provider, compromise due to application vulnerabilities, such as insecure password managers, and we do not consider threats that would arise from eavesdropping, such as shoulder-surfing attacks.

Specifically for password secrecy, the main relevant threats are offline password guessing attacks and credential stuffing attacks.

4.2 Assessment of Vulnerabilities

To assess the participants' online account security, we studied all access paths to their accounts in the elicited account graph under the threat model in Sect. 4.1. That is, we considered:

- whether access to an account was possible starting from a single credential (password or device) which implies single factor authentication,
- the security of each password with respect to offline password guessing attacks and credential stuffing attacks, and
- the security of each device in case the device is stolen, i.e., whether the device is protected by a PIN or biometric for example.

To assess whether our participants were vulnerable to credential stuffing attacks we looked for reused passwords in the account graph. This relied on the participants correctly reporting that two or more accounts used the same password.

To assess whether our participants were vulnerable to offline password guessing attacks, we used a simple scheme to classify the participants' individual passwords strengths. Our top priority was to prevent the participant from inadvertently revealing any information about their actual passwords other than an estimate of their passwords' strengths. We therefore provided the participants with a very simple decision procedure: (1) A password created by a password manager is strong. (2) A password that the participant generated themselves and considered to be strong is of average strength. (3) If neither (1) nor (2) apply, then the password is weak.

Our simple classification of the participant's password strength is based on the following reasoning.

1. A password generated by a password manager is very likely to provide much stronger protection against guessing attacks than a human generated password of the same length.
   To differentiate between these two cases, we consider a password generated by a password manager to be strong and a human generated password to be at most of average strength.
2. A password that a participant thinks is weak, is very likely weak.
   Thus passwords classified by the participant as weak are considered to be weak and otherwise considered to be of average strength.

We discuss the limitations of this approach in Sect. 7.1.

4.3   Reporting on the Analysis of the Account Ecosystem

We sorted our findings of each older adult's account ecosystem into three categories: *Critical Issues*, *Achieving Best Practices* and *Current Successes*. These categories were chosen to motivate the participants to take on the given security recommendations. The first two categories are used to prioritize the recommendations. The positive examples in the third category are intended to both confirm good practices and to provide the participant with confidence that they are capable of being secure. The three categories contained the following tests.

Fig. 1. Two web app pages. Initial page showing security grade (left) and a page highlighting a reused password issue (right).

Critical Issues. This category concerns vulnerabilities that compromise the older adult's account security and should be fixed as soon as possible. We looked for and classified three types of issues as critical: reused passwords, weak passwords (as self-reported by the user) and devices that give access to an account but are themselves not protected by a password, PIN code, or biometric authentication method.

Achieving Best Practices. This category deals with vulnerabilities that should be addressed only after any critical issues are removed. Our best practice tests covered the following criteria: The use of password managers, use of multi-factor authentication, and password strength as reported by the user. Passwords are reported on in this category instead of the critical issues category when the participant considers them to be long and strong, but the password was generated by the participant instead of a random password generator.

Current Successes. This category highlights good practices the user is already following but may not be aware of. These results are used to motivate the user by validating their efforts in being secure. The tests for this category are the union of all the tests of the previous two categories. We report in this category the favourable test outcomes. For example, the older adult's use of a password manager or strong passwords would be acknowledged here.

4.4 Displaying Security Information

Security information is presented to participants using several techniques. First, a participant is presented with a holistic letter grade in order to contextualise the effectiveness of their current security practices as shown in Fig. 1. The letter grade is computed as a sum of scores. Scores were given for

- The percentage of reused passwords
- The number of accounts not employing multi-factor authentication

- Use of a "password manager" (can be a paper notebook)
- The percentage of passwords classified as average strength as discussed in Sect. 4.2
- The percentage of passwords classified as weak strength
- The percentage of devices that are protected by a PIN, password, or biometric

Second, on separate pages specific issues and information are brought to the participant's attention. An explanation is given what each issue is, which accounts are affected and a usable solution of how to fix the vulnerability is provided as seen in Fig. 1 on the right.

The detailed security information was split into the three categories described in Sect. 4.3. Within each of the categories, and in line with best practice advice [9], the order of displaying the information was based on priority, the most important issues were displayed to the user first. As shown in Fig. 1 on the example of reused passwords, we ensured that a clear heading was created for each issue and that the supporting summary explaining the issue used simple non-technical words [21, 39]. Users were presented with a list of what accounts were specifically at risk due to individual vulnerabilities and the display of information concluded with a short concise section for recommendations.

5   Older Adults' Awareness of Security Risks

The purpose of our second user study was to improve our understanding of the reasons behind older adults' account management practices. We used semi-structured interviews, combined with a guided walk-through of our security analysis, described in Sect. 4, as a method to allow participants to discuss their own account security setups. This allowed participants to first demonstrate their own awareness of security risks in their setups and then to reflect on our analysis of their security ecosystems and the impacts that it may have.

5.1   Study Setup

Demographic Information: All 7 of the original participants were contacted again. Due to the sensitive nature of the account ecosystem information, each account ecosystem could only be discussed with the participant that it belongs to. Everyone other than P3 and P6 from the previous user study decided to take part in the evaluation thus all the participants will be referred to with the same identifiers.

Interview Script: An interview script (see Appendix B) was developed and used to maintain consistency and coherence between the interviews. The script was designed for a semi-structured interview to allow for conversations to flow naturally allowing any points or views that were brought up to be explored and elaborated on. Interviews took place using video conferencing software.

Account Security Analysis: The previously described web application reporting on the results of the security analysis was shared with participants during the study. The interviewer shared their screen with participants in order to provide a soft onboarding experience and to guide participants through the different options that were available in the application. Participants were given an opportunity to reflect on individual points that were brought up and were encouraged to discuss any issues as part of the semi-structured interview process.

Procedure: This study was reviewed and approved by the University of Dundee's Ethics Committee (*UOD-SSEREC-DoC-UG-2020-004*) before any study sessions were carried out. The study took 20 min of the participants' time. At the start of the study each participant was asked questions to record awareness of their own security before seeing their results of the account security analysis. Once these questions were answered the web application was shown to the participants. After the participants had time to view and understand the results of the analysis, the second half of the interview questions were asked in order to capture the participants' reflections of their current security with regards to the results of the analysis.

Analysis Technique: We used a similar analysis technique to that used in the first study of this paper. All sessions were transcribed, anonymised, and annotated before analysis.

5.2 Results

Our analysis technique applied a deductive approach where we intended to focus on highlighting data that would specifically assist in answering our research question. We report on the perceptions that older adults have regarding their online accounts, their awareness of current security vulnerabilities, and their awareness of how their security practice can be improved.

Perceptions of the Most Important and Secure Accounts Within Account Ecosystems. When classifying which accounts are the most important our participants discussed two factors that they consider. Firstly, which account contains the most valuable data and information and secondly which accounts are the most connected within their personal account ecosystems.

P1 and P7 stated their most important accounts purely due to the connectivity within their account ecosystems was their main email account as *"it links to almost all of my accounts"* (P7). However P7 went on to add *"my email account isn't as important as my financial accounts but none the less still very important"* which was a view that was shared by P2 and P5, who stated their most important account were their financial accounts.

All participants indicated that *"any accounts that handle financial transactions"* (P5) such as a *"bank"* (P4) were the accounts within their ecosystem that required more attention than the other accounts to secure, due to the risk of financial loss.

By our own assessment of participants' account access graphs, each of the participants' primary email account should be considered to be among the most important accounts. For a majority of the participants their email account recovers access to at least one financial account. For all participants it recovers access to most of the accounts they mentioned during the first interview and in particular to several shopping accounts.

Awarenesses of Current Security Vulnerabilities. P2, P4 and P7 expected their potential vulnerabilities to be passwords related. P4 discussed that they were *"sure the analysis will say something about my devices not being password protected"* and P7 acknowledged that their *"email password may not be as strong as it ought to be"*, P4 ended their answer by stating they were *"not sure what to expect really I went in with an open mind"*. However P1 and P5 stated they were not aware of any security vulnerabilities that were present.

Once the analysis results were shown to the participants, P2 was surprised that before they would *"never considered the possibility of my devices being stolen and what they means for my other accounts"* as physical access to their devices meant that any of their accounts could also be accessed because there was a digital unencrypted file containing their passwords. P7 went on to state *"I wasn't too sure how secure it was to write down my passwords"* referring to their non digital password management strategy of writing passwords down in a notebook thus avoiding password reuse and being able to choose stronger passwords as they were not relying on memory to use them. For P1 seeing their results (no critical issues, some best practice issues) validated the efforts and strategies they had in place: *"I'm just surprised I did so well ... it's nice to see I'm on the right track"*.

Awareness of What Can Be Done to Increase Account Security. Prior to seeing their results, P2 and P7 indicated that if they were to do anything it would *"probably be changing my passwords to stronger ones"* (P2), which are "up to date with current standards" (P7). P2 went on to add they *"knew it might be an issue at some point but never got around to changing them"*, but once seeing the analysis P2 concluded that *"I knew my passwords needed some work but not to this extent, this has been really eye opening ... I will definitely changing all my passwords, right after this actually!"*. P7's reaction after seeing their analysis was that *"I will definitely have to look into what counts as a strong password in today's standard."*

Prior to the results of the analysis, P1 and P5 stated they were *"doing the best I can"* (P1). P5 and P4 said they have *"no idea"* (P4) for the same reason that P1 brought up *"I can't think of anything I could do better"* in order to be more secure. After the results of the analysis brought up the critical issue that P5 reused a financial account password for several shopping accounts, the reply was that *"I'll be changing my [financial account] passwords as ... it was a bit silly to use the same password for some of my other accounts too"*.

6   Discussion

Our findings contextualise the account management strategies used by older adults and the reasoning behind their adoption. This gives an insight into older adults' security habits, their mental model of account ecosystem security, and the practices they choose to implement. We discuss the specifics of the strategies that tend to be used by older adults and the goals and reasons behind managing their accounts with such strategies.

The older adults have shown their mindsets and awareness to their own account security throughout the study in this project. It was found that some of the currently advised security practices, such as not to reuse passwords or use long password [15], may not take into account the needs and context of the older adult. The older adults must make their own risk assessments to gauge if the protection they will acquire from a new security practice is worth the effort to implement and alter their mental security model. As found in our study, the usability of the practice, understanding of what the practice is and how it affects their mental model of security and finally the trust that the practice is sound and secure are the fundamental barriers that must be accounted for when the older adult is deciding whether to implement a practice. We discuss our results grouped into these three areas below.

6.1   Usability and Risk Assessment

Each of the older adults in their own way was a victim of expectation to use unusable security practices or practices that are not fit for purpose when considering the needs and situations of the older adult.

Each of the strategies and alterations mentioned in the results were products of the participants' own risk assessments. In the case of P4 and P7, the risk of not remembering the correct authentication information for a device and thus losing access was deemed more realistic and relevant than the risk of the device being stolen. The creation of P2's digital unencrypted file containing passwords was due to similar concerns. Their file is shared with children as a form of digital inheritance [29] to act as a method to access online accounts, posthumously, should this be required.

6.2   Trust and Reliance on Third Parties

The older adults' views on trusting third parties to protect them are split. There are some who state that the third parties you trust with your sensitive information have a duty to maintain the confidentiality of the information. Others, however, state that the full responsibility and control must remain with themselves. A commonality between the two mindsets is that they only give away information if they trust the third party.

6.3 Understanding of Account and Password Security

It was found that all the interviewed older adults implemented a digital or a physical password management strategy. This is a good start, as the older adults were aware of the risks attached to reusing passwords, and some went out of their way to ensure that each password is unique. However not all of the strategies are secure. We found that more than 70% of the passwords were generated by the older adults themselves, rather than a password manager and are thus potentially not very strong. For example, it was found that one participant's technique to create unique passwords was to create transformations of a base password. This strategy creates a false sense of security, because modification of basic passwords is a common strategy [8]. Once an individual password leaks, an attacker aware of the strategy has a significant advantage in correctly guessing the password for another account. Since the older adults are already not relying on memory to access a password, it would be worthwhile to support them to improve their understanding of how to automatically and securely generate random passwords with tools that their operating systems provide out of the box, such as the Safari web browser in macOS and the Edge web browser in Windows.

Basing security practices on weak memory alone creates other avenues where the older adults could be at risk. It was discovered when analysing the older adults personal ecosystems, that a considerable risk to their online security could originate from physical risks. If an unprotected device were to be stolen from an older adult it could give access to all the accounts within their ecosystem. Indeed we found that some participants did not have protections such as PINs or biometrics enabled on their devices, as mentioned above for P4 and P7. For others, their protection relied solely on their device's password. Thus the information required to unlock a device would also give the attacker access to the older adult's password manager. This was present in the account ecosystem of P3, where the password required to unlock a device is the same password required to access their password manager application. Similarly in the case of P2 where once the attacker bypasses the password for a device (which was referred to as weak in strength by the participant) the attacker would have access to an unprotected file used to manage their passwords.

It was also found that a number of the older adults initial perceptions of which accounts were the most important to secure came down to what valuable data and information that account held such as financial accounts. When reflecting this view with the analysis results it was found that the older adults' banking accounts were the most secure within the whole account ecosystem. However, another very important account that was identified was the older adults' primary email. Most of the accounts the older adults have are linked to their email account in that it could be used as a recovery method to access these accounts by means of a password reset. Thus it was recommended that the email account should be the account that is the most inconvenient and difficult for an attacker to compromise, by using a very strong password and enabling multi-factor authentication.

6.4 Password Generation and Password Management Advice

We advised our participants to let a random password generator produce passwords for them and to write passwords down in a notebook or store them in a password manager. This advice differs from NCSC [30] guidance in that we do not recommend that users generate their own passwords for the reasons stated in Sect. 4.2. NIST 800-63-3 [14] defines a "password" as a memorized secret. We do not advocate memorizing passwords. The NCSC [30] also recommends storing passwords in the web browser.

There are three reasons for our advice. First, given the threat of credential stuffing attacks (Sect. 4.1), different passwords must be used for different accounts. Thus our advice must consider the fact that our participants will need to generate several different passwords. Everyone, not only our participants' demographic, has difficulties memorizing multiple passwords [37].

Second, based on previous password studies (e.g., [4, 24, 41]), we expect people to generate weak passwords. We expect that this is exacerbated by the pressure to generate different passwords for different accounts and the need to generate memorable passwords. Using a random password generator and writing the passwords down or storing them in a password manager solves this problem and is safe under our threat model.

Third, while the NCSC [31] and NIST [15, Section 5] recommend sensible password policies, not every website or password protected system today adheres to these policies. A password manager can generate passwords adhering to various policies, while studies (e.g. [4, 24, 41]) have shown a human would likely generate a weak password.

7 Conclusion

The motivation for this paper's study is to support and empower older adults to protect and defend themselves from cyber attacks that could compromise their account security. As a first step towards this goal we have investigated what the account management strategies used by older adults are and why these strategies are adopted.

We conducted two semi-structured interviews with older adults. In the first interview with 7 older adults we captured their account ecosystem and gained insight into their approach to account security. We analyzed their account ecosystems to assess the effectiveness of their security practices. We then created a web application to present the vulnerabilities that were found and to provide guidance to the older adults on how to improve their online security. The web application was presented to 5 of the 7 older adults in the second interview where we gained a better understanding of what our participants perceive as their current risks compared to what their actual risks are.

Our study tackles the narrative that older adults behave insecurely online. We have found that the older adults in our user study tend to be more wary when online, and will research topics extensively before implementing a security practice. They are wary and careful when it comes to being online and trusting websites or clicking on links. We have also found that their perceptions of security were not far from the reality of the situation.

We conclude that a security practice must conform to three key factors for an older adult to successfully deploy it: Usability, Trust, and Understanding. A deficiency in one or more of these can lead to older adults altering the security practice to work for them. These alterations can be safe such as employing non digital password management by using a notebook to store their passwords in order to avoid password reuse. They can also be risky such as choosing to not password-protect their mobile devices for fear of forgetting the password.

7.1   Limitations

In this work, we collected detailed online account security information and discussed this in depth with participants. We acknowledge that our sample size (n = 7, n = 5) is small and lower than local standards for HCI work (Remote Interviews; mean = 16, SD = 6 [5]). However, it is recognised that studies involving representative users (in our case technology literate older adults) will not have a similar number of participants when compared to traditional HCI experiments [40].

All the participants were recruited from the 'Bytes and Blether' group part of the User Centre located at University of Dundee [7]. This is an initiative by the university to teach technological literacy to older adults. Thus all the participants have access to resources and information on using current technology, have an awareness of security and privacy issues, and may have a greater interest in information technology than the general older adults demographic.

As detailed in Sect. 4.2, we had to rely on the participants' own assessment of their passwords' strengths and provided them with a simple self-assessment procedure. We rated the participants' passwords as weak if the participants themselves considered their password to be weak. We rated a password to be of average strength if the participant considered it to be strong, but the password was not generated by a random password generator and we rated it to be strong only if it was generated by a random password generator. While password leak studies (e.g. [4]) and password composition studies [24, 41] have shown that people tend to generate weak passwords, it is nevertheless plausible that our simple self-assessment procedure misclassified some participants' passwords. For example, it has been previously observed (e.g. [41]) that people misjudge password strength. Two other potential sources of error are the possibility that the self-assessment procedure was misunderstood or that a random password generation tool was used in a manner that produces weaker than expected passwords.

7.2   Future Work

There is much work left to do to help older adults to protect themselves when online. Consideration whether an older adult can effectively implement a security practice must be carried out by reflecting and investigating if the tool or practice complements the mindset and strategies used by older adults in regards to usability, trust and understanding. Our web application is a prototype to both help older adults understand the security of their account ecosystem better and enable a conversation with us to understand their needs better. In future work we plan to extend the scope of the web application to include more automated analysis techniques, consider different threat models and provide advice on a wider range of topics and authentication methods such as single sign-on.

It is worth repeating the account ecosystem interview and personalised security analysis for demographics other than just older adults. This would allow us to understand the needs and context of the users in the specific demographic and to adapt the web application and provided guidance accordingly.

Acknowledgments. We are grateful to Karen Renaud for her excellent suggestions on how to improve the paper and the anonymous reviewers for the careful reading and helpful comments. We would also like to thank all members of the Bytes and Blether group at the University of Dundee that took part in this work.

A   Interview 1 Script

Demographic

1. What is your age bracket? (a) 60–69 (b) 70–79 (c) 80–89 (d) 90–99 (e) 100+
2. What sex would you classify yourself as? (a) male (b) female (c) transgender (d) non-binary (e) other (f) prefer not to say
3. What is/was your occupation
4. How do you personally rate your technological literacy?

Finding Information Security Advice

1. How important do you think it is to be secure online?
2. How do you decide what your online security practices are?
3. Do you face any challenges implementing online security for your situation?
4. How do you prefer this type of information being presented to you?

Day to Day Security

1. What do you do to keep yourself secure online? – Why?
2. Are you worried about your online security? – Why?
3. What do you wish was easier regarding online security?

Account Ecosystem. I will now ask you questions about your account ecosystems. For each item you introduce you will give it a nickname such as Social1, Password2 or EmailOL. This is so that you can protect your privacy and not disclose any of your passwords. Please *do not* share any sensitive information such as passwords and PINs. We can revisit questions you have answered.

1. What devices do you use to access the internet?

(a) For each device give it a nickname. (Examples: Laptop1, WorkPhone2)
(b) What are the login methods and things you need to access it?
   i. Give a nickname for each entity needed or refer to the nickname that entity was given if already mentioned in the interview.
   ii. Is this method a recovery method for this account?
(c) Can you view messages and notifications on this device when it is locked?
(d) Are there any comments you have on this device you would like to share?
Repeat (a)–(d) for every Device.
2. Do you use password managers to access any of your accounts?
   (a) Give each password manager a nickname. (Examples: PM1, Manager1)
   (b) What are the login methods and things you need to access it?
      i. Give a nickname for each entity needed or refer to the nickname that entity was given if already mentioned in the interview.
      ii. Is this method a recovery method for this password manager?
   (c) Do you have open sessions (logged in permanently) with this password manager?
      i. For each open session assign a nickname for each entity or refer to the nickname that entity was given if already mentioned.
   (d) Are there any comments you have on this password manager you would like to share?
Repeat (a)–(d) for every password manager.

The sub-questions 2(a)–2(d) are also asked for each of the Questions 3–9, replacing "password manager" by "account".

3. What email addresses do you have access too?
4. What social media accounts do you use to stay connected?
5. What accounts do you have to access your online finances? What social media accounts do you use to stay connected?
6. What accounts do you use for online shopping? What social media accounts do you use to stay connected?
7. What accounts do you use for entertainment? What social media accounts do you use to stay connected?
8. What accounts do you use for gaming? What social media accounts do you use to stay connected?
9. Are there any more accounts or items you feel we have missed? What social media accounts do you use to stay connected?
10. Look over the passwords you mentioned.
    (a) How secure do you think your password is?
       i. Strong = A password created by a password manager.
       ii. Average = A password *you* made yourself that *you* consider strong.
       iii. Weak = A password you made yourself that you consider weak *or* one that does not fit in the other two categories.
    (b) What are the login methods and things you need to access this password?
       i. Give a nickname for each entity needed or refer to the nickname that entity was given if already mentioned in the interview.
       ii. Is this method a recovery method to access this password?
    (c) Are there any comments on this password you would like to share?
Repeat (a)–(c) for every password in this category.

B Interview 2 Script

Checking the Participants Awareness of Their Security

1. What did you think was the most important part of your account ecosystem?
2. Are you aware of any account security vulnerabilities you may have?
3. Which of your accounts do you think are the most important to keep secure?
4. Are you aware of anything you can do to improve your account security?

Reflections

1. Were there vulnerabilities found within the analysis based on a security practice that you originally thought secure?
2. Are there any practices you currently do you thought were not secure but disproved by the analysis?

References

1. Age UK: Computer training courses - it training services, August 2020. https://www.ageuk.org.uk/services/in-your-area/it-training/. Accessed 21 Sept 2021
2. Age UK: Uncovering the extent of cybercrime across the UK, June 2020. https://www.ageuk.org.uk/discover/2020/06/cybercrime-uk/. Accessed 21 Sept 2021
3. Alves, L.M., Wilson, S.R.: The effects of loneliness on telemarketing fraud vulnerability among older adults. J. Elder Abuse Negl. 20(1), 63–85 (2008)
4. Bonneau, J.: The science of guessing: analyzing an anonymized corpus of 70 million passwords. In: IEEE Symposium on Security and Privacy, SP 2012, 21–23 May 2012, San Francisco, California, USA, pp. 538–552. IEEE Computer Society (2012)
5. Caine, K.: Local standards for sample size at CHI, pp. 981–992. Association for Computing Machinery, New York (2016)
6. Carpenter, B.D., Buday, S.: Computer use among older adults in a naturally occurring retirement community. Comput. Hum. Behav. 23(6), 3012–3024 (2007)
7. Crabb, M., Menzies, R., Waller, A.: The user centre. In: History of HCI 2020 (2020)
8. Das, A., Bonneau, J., Caesar, M., Borisov, N., Wang, X.: The tangled web of password reuse. In: NDSS, vol. 14, pp. 23–26 (2014)
9. Egelman, S., Cranor, L.F., Hong, J.: You've been warned: an empirical study of the effectiveness of web browser phishing warnings. In: Proceedings SIGCHI Conference on Human Factors in Computing Systems, pp. 1065–1074 (2008)
10. Fagan, M., Albayram, Y., Khan, M.M.H., Buck, R.: An investigation into users' considerations towards using password managers. HCIS 7(1), 1–20 (2017)
11. Flick, U.: The SAGE Handbook of Qualitative Data Analysis. Sage (2013)
12. Florencio, D., Herley, C.: A large-scale study of web password habits. In: Proceedings 16th International Conference on World Wide Web, pp. 657–666 (2007)
13. Frik, A., Nurgalieva, L., Bernd, J., Lee, J., Schaub, F., Egelman, S.: Privacy and security threat models and mitigation strategies of older adults. In: 15th Symposium Usable Privacy and Security (SOUPS 2019), pp. 21–40. USENIX Association (2019)
14. Grassi, P.A., Garcia, M.E., Fenton, J.L.: Digital identity guidelines (2017). NIST Special Publication 800-63-3 (2017)

15. Grassi, P.A., et al.: Digital identity guidelines: authentication and lifecycle management. NIST Special Publication 800-63B (2017)
16. Grimes, G.A., Hough, M.G., Mazur, E., Signorella, M.L.: Older adults' knowledge of internet hazards. Educ. Gerontol. **36**(3), 173–192 (2010)
17. Grimes, G.A., Hough, M.G., Signorella, M.L.: Email end users and spam: relations of gender and age group to attitudes and actions. Comput. Hum. Behav. **23**(1), 318–332 (2007)
18. Hammann, S., Crabb, M., Radomirovic, S., Sasse, R., Basin, D.: I'm surprised so much is connected. In: Proceedings 2022 CHI Conference on Human Factors in Computing Systems, pp. 620:1–620:13 (2022)
19. Hammann, S., Radomirović, S., Sasse, R., Basin, D.: User account access graphs. In: Proceedings 2019 ACM SIGSAC Conference on Computer and Communications Security, pp. 1405–1422 (2019)
20. Haque, S.T., Wright, M., Scielzo, S.: A study of user password strategy for multiple accounts. In: Proceedings Third ACM Conference on Data and Application Security and Privacy, pp. 173–176 (2013)
21. Harbach, M., Fahl, S., Yakovleva, P., Smith, M.: Sorry, I don't get it: an analysis of warning message texts. In: Adams, A.A., Brenner, M., Smith, M. (eds.) FC 2013. LNCS, vol. 7862, pp. 94–111. Springer, Heidelberg (2013). https://doi.org/10.1007/978-3-642-41320-9_7
22. Hornung, D., Müller, C., Shklovski, I., Jakobi, T., Wulf, V.: Navigating relationships and boundaries: concerns around ICT-uptake for elderly people. In: Proceedings 2017 CHI Conference on Human Factors in Computing Systems, pp. 7057–7069 (2017)
23. Ives, B., Walsh, K.R., Schneider, H.: The domino effect of password reuse. Commun. ACM **47**(4), 75–78 (2004)
24. Kelley, P.G., et al.: Guess again (and again and again): measuring password strength by simulating password-cracking algorithms. In: IEEE Symposium Security and Privacy, SP 2012, pp. 523–537. IEEE Computer Society (2012)
25. Knowles, B., Hanson, V.L.: The wisdom of older technology (non)users. Commun. ACM **61**(3), 72–77 (2018)
26. Lee, N.M.: Fake news, phishing, and fraud: a call for research on digital media literacy education beyond the classroom. Comm. Educ. **67**(4), 460–466 (2018)
27. Martin, N., Rice, J.: Spearing high net wealth individuals: the case of online fraud and mature age internet users. Int. J. Inf. Secur. Priv. (IJISP) **7**(1), 1–15 (2013)
28. McDonald, N., Schoenebeck, S., Forte, A.: Reliability and inter-rater reliability in qualitative research: norms and guidelines for CSCW and HCI practice. Proc. ACM Hum. Comput. Interact. **3**(CSCW), 1–23 (2019)
29. Moncur, W., Waller, A.: Digital inheritance. In: Proceedings RCUK Digital Futures Conference. ACM, Nottingham (2010)
30. National Cyber Security Centre: Improve your online security today. https://www.ncsc.gov.uk/cyberaware/home. Accessed 21 Sept 2021
31. National Cyber Security Centre: Password administration for system owners. https://www.ncsc.gov.uk/collection/passwords/updating-your-approach. Accessed 21 Sept 2021
32. Nicholson, J., Coventry, L., Briggs, P.: "If It's important it will be a headline": cybersecurity information seeking in older adults, pp. 1–11. Association for Computing Machinery, New York (2019)
33. OFCOM: Adults' Media Use & Attitudes report 2020/21. https://www.ofcom.org.uk/research-and-data/media-literacy-research/adults/adults-media-use-and-attitudes. Accessed 21 Sept 2021

34. Pearman, S., et al.: Let's go in for a closer look: observing passwords in their natural habitat. In: Proceedings 2017 ACM SIGSAC Conference on Computer and Communications Security, pp. 295–310 (2017)

35. Pearman, S., Zhang, S.A., Bauer, L., Christin, N., Cranor, L.F.: Why people (don't) use password managers effectively. In: 15th Symposium on Usable Privacy and Security (SOUPS 2019), pp. 319–338. USENIX Association, Santa Clara (2019)

36. Peek, S.T., et al.: Older adults' reasons for using technology while aging in place. Gerontology **62**(2), 226–237 (2016)

37. Pilar, D.R., Jaeger, A., Gomes, C.F.A., Stein, L.M.: Passwords usage and human memory limitations: a survey across age and educational background. PLOS ONE **7**(12), 1–7 (2012). https://doi.org/10.1371/journal.pone.0051067

38. Ray, H., Wolf, F., Kuber, R., Aviv, A.J.: Why older adults (don't) use password managers. In: 30th USENIX Security Symposium, USENIX Security 2021, pp. 73–90. USENIX Association (2021)

39. Redmiles, E.M., Liu, E., Mazurek, M.L.: You want me to do what? A design study of two-factor authentication messages. In: 13th Symposium on Usable Privacy and Security, SOUPS 2017. USENIX Association (2017)

40. Sears, A., Hanson, V.L.: Representing users in accessibility research. ACM Trans. Access. Comput. **4**(2) (2012)

41. Shay, R., et al.: Designing password policies for strength and usability. ACM Trans. Inf. Syst. Secur. **18**(4), 13:1–13:34 (2016)

42. Simons, J.J., Phillips, N.J., Chopra, R., Slaughter, R.K., Wilson, C.S.: Protecting older consumers 2019–2020: a report of the federal trade commission to congress (2020). https://www.ftc.gov/reports/protecting-older-consumers-2019-2020-report-federal-trade-commission. Accessed 21 Sept 2021

43. Stobert, E., Biddle, R.: A password manager that doesn't remember passwords. In: Proceedings 2014 New Security Paradigms Workshop, pp. 39–52 (2014)

44. Tennant, B., et al.: eHealth literacy and web 2.0 health information seeking behaviors among baby boomers and older adults. J. Med. Internet Res. **17**(3), e70 (2015)

45. Tracy, S.J.: Qualitative Research Methods: Collecting Evidence, Crafting Analysis, Communicating Impact. Wiley, Oxford (2019)

46. Vroman, K.G., Arthanat, S., Lysack, C.: "Who over 65 is online?" Older adults' dispositions toward information communication technology. Comput. Hum. Behav. **43**, 156–166 (2015)

47. Wang, C., Jan, S.T., Hu, H., Bossart, D., Wang, G.: The next domino to fall: empirical analysis of user passwords across online services. In: Proceedings Eighth ACM Conference on Data and Application Security and Privacy, pp. 196–203 (2018)

48. Wash, R., Rader, E., Berman, R., Wellmer, Z.: Understanding password choices: how frequently entered passwords are re-used across websites. In: Twelfth Symposium on Usable Privacy and Security (SOUPS 2016), pp. 175–188 (2016)

Found in Translation: Co-design for Security Modelling

Albesë Demjaha[1]([✉]), David Pym[2,3], and Tristan Caulfield[3]

[1] University College London and The Alan Turing Institute, London, UK
[2] Institute of Philosophy, University of London, London, UK
[3] University College London, London, UK
{albese.demjaha.16,d.pym,t.caulfield}@ucl.ac.uk

Abstract. *Background.* In increasingly complex and dynamic environments, it is difficult to predict potential outcomes of security policies. Therefore, security managers (or other stakeholders) are often challenged with designing and implementing security policies without knowing the consequences for the organization. *Aim.* Modelling, as *a tool for thinking*, can help identify those consequences in advance as a way of managing decision-making risks and uncertainties. Our co-design approach aims to tackle the challenges of problem definition, data availability, and data collection associated with modelling behavioural and cultural aspects of security. *Method.* Our process of modelling co-design is a proposed solution to these challenges, in particular for models aiming to incorporate organizational security culture. We present a case study of a long-term study at Company A, where using the methods of participatory action research, humble inquiry, and thematic analysis, largely shaped our understanding of co-design. We reflect on the methodological advantages of co-design, as well as shortcomings. *Result.* Our methodology engages modellers and system stakeholders through a four-stage co-design process consisting of (1) observation and candidate data availability, (2) candidate model design, (3) interpretation of model consequences, and (4) interpretation of domain consequences. *Conclusion.* We have proposed a new methodology by integrating the concept of co-design into the classical modelling cycle and providing a rigorous methodology for the construction of models that captures the system and its behaviours accurately. We have also demonstrated what an attempt at co-design looks like in the real-world, and reflected upon necessary improvements.

Keywords: Security Co-design · Security modelling · Security culture

1 Introduction

Security managers are responsible for meeting the organization's security objectives. Most commonly, managers set a security policy as a way of clearly outlining these objectives and providing further guidance on how to follow them. While the security manager's primary concern is to keep the organization secure and ensure policy compliance, challenges arise from complex factors that may impede the

© Springer Nature Switzerland AG 2022
S. Parkin and L. Viganò (Eds.): STAST 2021, LNCS 13176, pp. 108–128, 2022.
https://doi.org/10.1007/978-3-031-10183-0_6

effectiveness of the security policy. Factors obstructing compliance with security policy may include how the policy itself is written, the level of difficulty associated with compliance, the organization's security culture (or lack thereof), or irrelevant threats represented in the policy. Unfortunately, these factors are often unknown at the time of policy design and security managers face the challenge of setting and championing a security policy that may have undesirable consequences for the organization. The inability to predict such consequences may create uncertainty and risk for the security manager. Modelling provides the opportunity to explore the consequences of a particular decision. Models can help system owners (in this case security managers) manage the complexity of their system by creating appropriate simplifications of the system and its components. In increasingly complex and dynamic environments, it is important to identify ways of exploring potential consequences of decisions before making decisions. Modelling, a 'tool for thinking', is a way of managing uncertainty and risk associated with decisions. By using a range of concepts from security (behavioural) economics as well as mathematical systems modelling, models can be built to make predictions about policy choices and aid security managers in future security decisions.

However, rigorous and useful modelling presents many challenges. Typically, on the one hand, the system's managers wish for it to be modelled in order to answer questions about its design or behaviour. They may be experts in the system's design, its behaviour, or its domain of application, but may have little or no knowledge of the languages, methodologies, or data-capture requirements of modelling. On the other hand, modellers, experts in the languages and methodologies of modelling, may have little understanding of many aspects of the behaviour of the system, the context within which the domain experts' questions are asked, and little knowledge of what data may be available to be collected.

It is, therefore, necessary that in order to construct models that capture the system and its behaviours accurately, capture the system's managers' questions adequately, and do so in such way that the required supporting data can be collected, it is necessary that the system's managers and the modellers cooperate in the construction of the model.

Our thesis is that this requirement can be addressed rigorously by introducing the concept of co-design into the classical modelling methodology, as depicted in Fig. 1. We summarize here the necessary modifications, which are explored in detail in Sect. 4.

- We introduce—see Fig. 2 in Sect. 4—a translation zone in place of the simple 'induction' of models step;
- This translation zone is the space in which the stakeholders—system owners and users and modellers—interact in order to co-design an adequate model;
- The translation zone supports the development of shared understanding of the system, the questions about the system, the modelling methodology and its limitations, and the availability of relevant data.

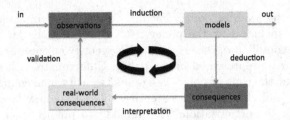

Fig. 1. The classical mathematical modelling cycle. (see, e.g., [21])

Security provides a systems perspective that is both quite generic and for which co-design is particularly important. Although there is evidence to suggest that security culture drives policy compliance [8], cultural and behavioural aspects of security are not commonly considered when modelling security policy. The importance of culture in security has been highlighted long ago [20]; however, its representation is often oversimplified [24], or too complex to model usefully.

Modelling security culture through a co-design approach can help facilitate the required system and context knowledge to represent culture more accurately. Opportunities to capture observations of the cultural and behavioural aspects influencing security policy can be identified by engaging stakeholders from an early stage. Constructs from traditional and behavioural economics can then be used to characterize those observations in ways that are better suited for modelling by considering theories such as bounded rationality and herd behaviour [6].

1.1 Contributions and Structure

Contributions:

- We identify challenges with modelling in general, and those of modelling behavioural and cultural aspects of security in particular;
- We introduce co-design into the classical modelling cycle and develop a methodology for security modelling that addresses the identified challenges. Our process of co-design facilitates collaboration and mutual learning between modellers and stakeholders towards achieving a mutually beneficial goal;
- We demonstrate how components of co-design translate into the real world by unpicking a case-study at Company A and reflecting on the advantages and disadvantages of the used methods as well as identifying opportunities for improvement.

Structure:

- In Sect. 2, we introduce the rôle of modelling in understanding and supporting policy-formulation and decision-making in security. We consider the challenges that can be observed in coordinating the identification and collection of relevant data and the design and construction of models;

- We explain the impact of culture and behaviour on security policy compliance in Sect. 3, and summarize why behavioural and cultural aspects should be captured when modelling security. We then observe the challenges that may arise when attempting to characterize culture less vaguely and model it in a way that is useful in practice;
- Before introducing our new methodology in Sect. 4, we first provide an overview of co-design and discuss existing co-design work in modelling and security. We introduce our approach in the form of a co-design methodology that is a modification of the classical modelling cycle;
- In Sect. 5, we present a case-study which largely shaped our understanding of co-design [10]. Through reflections, we discuss the methods and approaches that worked, as well as shortcomings. Finally, we summarize the contents of this paper in Sect. 6.

2   Modelling for Security

Models play an important role in the way we understand, analyze, and make decisions about security. We can identify many types of models that arise in this setting. Here are a few key examples.

- Access control models: these are typically formulated using algebraic or logical methods. For example, Bell-LaPadula, Biba, and the many models they have inspired, use algebraic methods. An alternative approach is to use logical methods to specify access control rules. This too has been developed quite substantially in a large literature;
- Models of attack–defence strategies: these are typically game-theoretic, in which the game's players represent attackers and defenders with varying assumptions about the knowledge of the players and their levels of investment;
- Policy models: these illustrate the consequences of policy choices on, for example, trade-offs between performance and security attributes. Often these are simulation models, such as impulse–response models, which explore the response of a systems to attacks under varying policy régimes;
- Behavioural economics models: these illustrate behavioural choices within organizations. For example, the Compliance Budget [4], which can also be analysed logically [1], examines the trade-off between the commitment of individuals' (limited) resources to organizational operational objectives and those committed to compliance with organizational security policies;
- Penetration models: these may use, for example, stochastic processes to capture an attackers expected degree of penetration a system with a given defensive posture.

In all these examples, albeit to differing extents, constructing the models adequately requires their co-design by the system's owners, users, and modellers.

2.1   Challenges of Modelling

There are many problems that can arise when constructing models, and many of them have been described and explained in the work of Michael Pidd—see, for example, [22] and the many articles in [23]. For a more mathematical perspective, see [7] and for a 'systems thinking' perspective on engineering, see [18].

Challenges can arise during the initial phases of modelling, when the purpose and specification of the model is decided, during the construction of the model, and also during the eventual use of the model.

Before a model can be built, it is necessary to understand what its purpose is and what it should do. Beginning model construction or data collection before the purpose of a model has been identified can lead to a number of problems:

- Collecting data before determining the modelling approach to be used. The required data can vary significantly depending on the chosen modelling approach. By collecting the data in a silo, the data that has been collected may not be adequate for the modelling method in mind;
- Conducting large-scale data collection prior to determining the purpose of the model. When this occurs, the problem identification is driven and restricted by the data that has been already collected. Important contextual knowledge may be missing in the data-set because of the data collection happening prior to any careful objective identification;
- Neglecting communication with stakeholders (e.g., the system owner) at an early stage can lead to an incomplete identification of the problem to be modelled. The system owner is likely to hold critical information about the system and its issues, and can help with identifying modelling objectives.

Prior to model construction, it is essential to identify the data that are required and the limitations to what can be collected. Failure to do so can lead to the following problems:

- Deciding to model a system without considering the expert knowledge of the system stakeholders. Stakeholders might hold critical knowledge about whether constructing such a model is even a possibility given the limitations of data availability;
- Some models may require the understanding of processes for which data cannot be collected. The system stakeholders may have the required understanding of the processes even if data collection about those processes is not possible. This further emphasizes the importance of stakeholder involvement;
- The necessary data collection may be too expensive to conduct or require a long time to set up. This may mean that the data becomes unusable or irrelevant by the time it has been collected.

There are problems that can impact the eventual use of the model:

- Lack of stakeholder involvement may lead to a disconnect between the identified model objectives and the real world issues present in the system. If the model objectives are not aligned with the real world problems, the model might end up being useless for the system stakeholders;

– When doing modelling as part of interdisciplinary work, there is a risk that domain experts will work in a disjoint manner. If the objectives of the expert collecting the data and the modeller are not aligned, the end result of the model might not be useful for either.

Finally, a few generic issues are always present: 'the map is not the territory' [16]; the level of detail/complexity of the model must be appropriate to address the problem—Einstein's principle; the model should be available when needed—a less good model that is available when needed may be more useful than a better model that is not; and cost-effectiveness—cost of creating the model should be justified by the benefits of having the model.

Looking carefully at these problems it is possible to see that they are in some sense circular: the data that needs to be collected depends on the purpose of the model and the modelling approach selected, but these choices are in turn constrained by the availability of data and affected by the modeller's understanding of the system. The challenge is to develop an approach to modelling that resolves this circular dependency; we propose to do this by involving modellers and stakeholders in an iterative process of co-design that creates a shared understanding of the system to be modelled, identifies the purpose of the model, and ensures that the specified model is aligned with the needs of the stakeholders and fits within the limitations created by data availability.

3   Modelling Behavioural and Cultural Aspects of Security

Compliance with security policy is largely affected by employee behaviour and the elements that influence these behaviours [4]. The behaviour and decision-making of people are already complex and can be further complicated by social, cultural, or other influencing factors in the organization.

Insights from behavioural economics can aid the understanding of people's decision-making and interaction with the system, which subsequently help better modelling of such behaviour [6]. Simplified abstractions of complex phenomena such as security culture may particularly benefit security managers and other system owners tasked with the management of security behaviours in ever-changing ecosystems. Modelling certain dimensions of security culture, or groups interacting within that culture, may help characterize security culture in a more meaningful and practical way for system stakeholders.

3.1   Challenges of Modelling Behavioural and Cultural Aspects

The complexity of security culture creates certain challenges when trying to model it. The following are some examples of such challenges:

– The concept of culture is complex and difficult to articulate in a tangible manner [11]. Although culture has been studied for a very long time and is a widely used concept, its meaning is often portrayed in an intangible way. When modelling culture, there is a need to focus on tangible components of culture, which can be used to establish cultural and behavioural parameters [11];

- There is no accepted and practical definition of security culture [19]. Originating from organizational culture, the concept of security culture has received a lot of attention in security research and the literature has been expanding rapidly. However, work on security culture rarely provides a more in-depth explanation about how the adapted model of organizational culture translates to the context of security [24]. This further complicates modelling cultural aspects of security;
- Culture is a dynamic phenomenon, often impacted by unexpected change or turbulence [25]. Culture may have stable components, but it is dynamic in nature and continuously changing. While it may be a more difficult and lengthier process, the stable components of culture may change as well under unexpected and extreme circumstances [25]. When modelling culture, it may be difficult to anticipate such extreme circumstances, which could significantly impact the cultural parameters in the model;
- Representing culture in a model could introduce a two-fold risk. The first would be ending up with a reductionist view—taking an approach that is too simplistic in representing the influence of culture on behaviour. This would produce yet another insufficiently detailed representation of security culture. The second would be that of over-elaboration—creating an overly complex representation of culture, perhaps rendering the model unusable in a real-world context [11].

The complex nature of culture in general—and that of security culture in particular—is what makes the opportunity to model culture appealing. The ability to represent culture more practically—in a model—has the potential of becoming a useful tool for system owners challenged with the task of managing security behaviours in a complex and dynamic ecosystem. A possible representation of culture could be in the form of cultural and behavioural parameters derived from moving components of culture, or by categorizing system stakeholders into distinct behaviour groups.

While the benefits to modelling culture in a practical manner may be obvious, there are inhibitors—similar to the modelling challenges above—that may limit the ability to do so. In order to represent cultural components or behaviour groups adequately and accurately, there is a necessity for real-life observations of that very culture. In addition to the observations of culture, there is a requirement for an in-depth understanding of the ecosystem. The availability of such knowledge is often limited, whereas the collectability of such data is sometimes not a possibility for various reasons.

System owners and other stakeholders hold critical knowledge about the ecosystem and the moving components of that system. The experience, knowledge, and information of the stakeholders about the system as well as culture to be modelled complement the expertise of the modeller. By involving stakeholders from the stage of problem identification, and receiving their willingness to participate, much more accurate representations of culture and system components can be created for the model. The complexity of a system—and culture—can be captured more correctly through a process of mutual learning between the system stakeholders and the modeller.

4 Co-design for Security Modelling

4.1 What is Co-design?

Co-design is normally associated with user-centred design and participatory design [9]. As it is largely influenced by the latter, co-design is often considered to be an updated term for participatory design [9]. The core principle of co-design is that it encourages *collaboration* between all stakeholders in the design process. A useful definition that thoroughly captures the process of co-design is that by Kleinsmann and Valkenburg [15, p. 2–3]:

> 'Co-design is the process in which actors from different disciplines share their knowledge about both the design process and the design content. They do that in order to create shared understanding on both aspects, to be able to integrate and explore their knowledge and to achieve the larger common objective: the new product to be designed.'

Benefits such as improved creativity and idea generation as well as better knowledge and cooperation between stakeholders have been associated with co-design [28]. Steen [27], argues that co-design can be viewed as a process of *abduction*. Dorst [12] provides a similar perspective by arguing that abduction is fundamental to design thinking. When using abduction as a technique in co-design, problems and potential solutions are explored in an iterative process whereby *problem and solution co-evolve* [27, p. 18].

4.2 Co-design and Modelling

The closest representation of co-design in modelling work can be found in *participatory modelling* (PM) which can be defined as 'a purposeful learning process for action that engages the implicit and explicit knowledge of stakeholders to create formalized and shared representations of reality' [30, p. 1]. PM emerged as a result of the realization that stakeholders can contribute useful knowledge, experience, and skills—and that stakeholders are more likely to comply with policies if they are engaged in the process of developing those policies [31].

Participatory modelling is sometimes referred to as collaborative modelling or co-modelling, terms which are often used interchangeably as there are no clear distinctions between them [2]. Basco-Carrera et al. [2] attempt such a distinction and associate collaborative modelling more strongly with co-design as it is better suited for contexts with high cooperation. PM, on the other hand, involves a lower level of cooperation.

Methods such as participatory and collaborative modelling have come into use because of an increased emphasis on stakeholder involvement in fields such as water resources management. In fact, the majority of PM work has been done in areas such as environment and planning, water resources management, and resource and environmental modelling [2,17,30,31].

An ideal approach to PM would be to involve stakeholders in most (if not all) stages of modelling [31]. However, this is not always the case, and there are different 'ladders' of stakeholder participation which distinguish between different levels of involvement [2]. In contrast to PM, co-design focusses more strongly on high participation, which suits our methodological approach.

4.3 Co-design and Security

To the best of our knowledge, there is a scarcity of works in security research that focus on participatory modelling or co-design. Ionita et al. [14] implement participatory modelling principles to evaluate whether such a collaborative approach would improve the quality of the final models. They tested their approach in the context of risk assessment and got favourable results from the participatory modelling. Beautement et al. [3] demonstrate the importance of capturing data that represents a real-world environment. To achieve this, they propose a methodology consisting of passive and active data collection cycles—meant to collect accurate data about security behaviours and attitudes in organizations [3]. Heath, Hall, and Coles-Kemp [13] focus on the security design of a home banking system by intersecting aspects of co-design and participatory physical modelling. More specifically, participants interact with different security scenarios by using LEGO kits and achieve positive insights by doing so.

While the above examples demonstrate co-design thinking [3]—and attempts to create an interaction between co-design and modelling [13]—no comprehensive methodology has been proposed for co-designing security modelling, at least not one that reflects *our* understanding of co-design. Our approach focusses on a deeper involvement of stakeholders, by ensuring mutual objectives from early on, and continued participation—but also co-creation—throughout the entire co-design process.

4.4 Our New Methodology

In order to build a model, the modeller has three requirements: an understanding of the modelling objectives, an understanding of the system to be modelled, and the knowledge or data about the system required to construct the model. In order for a model to be useful for a system manager (the model user or 'customer'), the modelling objective must be aligned with the manager's desired analysis. The modeller and the manager must have a shared understanding of the model objectives. The model must also fit within the limitations of what information the modeller can learn and collect about the system. A well-specified model with a shared understanding between modeller and manager is useless if the modeller has no access to the information required to build it.

These limitations on data collection come in two forms. First, there is information that is impossible to collect; this is a hard limit—perhaps because of time, monetary, or physical limitations that cannot be overcome. Second, there are limitations imposed by the willingness of system stakeholders to participate in the modelling process. In large socio-technical ecosystems, as frequently found in the security domain, there are many sources of data and many stakeholders, without whose cooperation it can be challenging to gain access to their knowledge of the systems of which they are a part.

We propose a process of model co-design that aims to facilitate the construction of models that meet these criteria. We start by giving a definition:

Model co-design is a process that engages modellers and system stakeholders cooperatively in the acts of objective identification and model specification, design, and construction with the aims of aligning model objectives with the needs of the stakeholders, and designing a model that is feasible given the limits of data availability, which are discovered as part of the process.

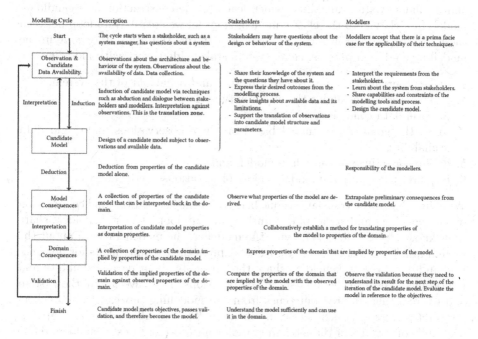

Fig. 2. Modelling cycle, translation zone, and co-design.

We can express this process as a modification of the classic modelling cycle, which is shown in Fig. 1. The classic modelling cycle starts at the point of observation—it assumes the objectives of the model are already specified—and moves in a cycle. Observations of the system are made and a candidate model is constructed; the consequences of the model are interpreted as real-world (or domain) consequences and then validated against observations of the real system. If the model does not match the real system, the candidate model is refined and the process repeats. When the modeller is satisfied that the model performs appropriately the cycle is finished. The perspective of this classic cycle is very modelling- and modeller-centric.

In our conception of co-design, modellers and stakeholders work together to determine the objectives of the model, which are refined based on observations of the system, the data required to produce a model, and the limits of data availability. Figure 2 presents our *co-design cycle*.

The co-design cycle starts when a stakeholder, such as a system manager, wants to understand something about the system. This may, for example, be due to a desire to understand an aspect of observed system behaviour, or a question about policy choices or system management. The stakeholder then begins to work with a modeller, if the modeller believes their techniques are applicable. The modeller can be a person or team, and possibly be unfamiliar with the system of interest.

Next come the main elements of the co-design cycle: observation of the system and candidate data availability, which leads to the construction of a candidate model. In a change to the classic modelling cycle, we create a sub-loop between these two stages, and it is this sub-loop that forms the *translation zone* in the modelling co-design process. Here, system stakeholders work with modellers to

1. make observations about the architecture and behaviour of the system,
2. make observations about the availability of data,
3. perform data collection,
4. refine the goals of the model based on these observations, data, and data availability,
5. design (or induce) a candidate model, and
6. interpret the candidate model against observations—returning to (1).

We define this as the translation zone because of the interactions and cooperation of the modellers and stakeholders during this sub-loop. The stakeholders share their knowledge of the system with the modeller; the modellers learn about the system from the stakeholders. Modellers express their requirements for information and data; the stakeholders share their insights about data availability and limitations. The stakeholders share the questions they have about the system and express their desired outcomes from the modelling process; the modellers interpret these requirements as a specification. The modellers share the capabilities and constraints of the modelling tools and process; the stakeholders refine their requirements based on this understanding of what can be modelled. The modellers design the candidate model; the stakeholders support the translation of observations into model structure and parameters.

The candidate model is then interpreted by stakeholders and modellers against observations, and the cycle repeats. This is an iterative dialogue between stakeholders and modellers that seeks to converge on a shared understanding of the system, of the data available, and of the objectives and capabilities of the model.

The rest of the co-design cycle closely follows the classic modelling cycle, but we define the rôles that stakeholders and modellers play during these parts of the process, as shown in Fig. 2. The modellers deduce the model-consequences from the candidate model, while the stakeholders observe this step to learn more about the operation of the model. These are consequences *in terms of the model*, not in terms of the system itself, so they must be interpreted. The modellers and the stakeholders collaboratively establish a method for translating properties of the model to properties of the domain; the result are the domain properties that are implied by the properties of the model.

Next comes validation. Here, the stakeholders must compare these model-implied domain properties to the observed properties of the model. The modellers observe this because understanding validation failures—where model-implied properties and observed properties do not match—is important for the construction of a new candidate model in the next iteration. If validation is successful, the candidate model is accepted and the cycle is complete.

What the Co-design Cycle Achieves. We described above a number of challenges that often arise during modelling. This co-design approach has the potential to help modellers and stakeholders to overcome some of these challenges. Many of the challenges arise because of uncertainty on the part of the modeller: about which data should be collected, what data is available, and even what problem should be modelled. Other challenges arise because of the stakeholders' lack of involvement: stakeholders may ask an initial question, but it might not be the right question to arrive at answers that will be useful to them, or they may have necessary insights into the system that get ignored because they are never asked. For security problems, organizational culture is often a very important factor (for example, in the way policy decisions will play out); without the engagement of stakeholders, it may be impossible to capture the culture sufficiently well enough to make a good model.

A co-design modelling process will bring both modellers and stakeholders together in a cooperative process to produce a model that deepens the understanding of all stakeholders involved; it helps understand the system and helps make better decisions about it. Part of the value of building models of things is that it enforces a careful consideration of the thing itself—it actually forces one to think about what it is, in ways that are perhaps more rigorously characterized than they would be otherwise. This careful consideration also applies to the formulation of questions about the system of interest: it will encourage a more rigorous, more precise, more reflected formulation of questions. Co-creating the questions (or problem) is just as important as co-creating the model. Better questions allow for a better understanding of what a model needs to do, and what data is needed for it.

Co-design also makes it more likely that more data will be available to the modellers: stakeholders may have a great deal of knowledge about the system, and in the case of modelling culture, the stakeholders' behaviour *is* the data that is needed. A process that creates an understanding of why data is needed, through a shared understanding of the model and its purpose, can help gain access to the stakeholders who have this information, as we show below.

5   Case Study: Reflections

To demonstrate how an attempt to co-design looks like in a real-world context, as well as reflect on potential improvements, we present an in-depth case-study of a single company, previously published in [10].

5.1   The Organization

Here we provide a brief profile of Company A, focussing on the historical security context of the organization as well as their current security structure, policies, and processes. A more detailed description of the company can be found in [10]. *Profile:* The company—hereafter referred to as *Company A*—is a medium-large sized company operating within the finance and technology sector. Company A is based in the United Kingdom and specializes in financial forecasting. The company has grown significantly over the last few years—the start-up mentality it had in the beginning has slowly shifted to a more corporate one. Starting at around two hundred employees about two decades ago, it now has close to a thousand employees.

So far, Company A has been incredibly successful in the work that it does. In order to protect the work that it produces, the company also places great value on its information assets by investing heavily on security measures. They have developed their security expertise throughout the years—so much so that—it is mistaken for a security company rather than a finance and technology one.
Security Context: Company A's security measures were almost non-existent in the beginning. The company had a much more informal attitude towards security and only basic controls. Then, Company A suffered an information security breach in the form of an insider attack [10]. This breach seriously threatened the company's financial and reputational stability and could have potentially ended the business. Fortunately they were able to predominantly contain the breach and the damage. However, this particular experience emphasized the necessity for a better security strategy and more mature processes.

Fast forwarding some years after the incident—Company A resembles almost a completely different organization. It has a post-shock organizational security structure. This means that the security structure was created as a result of a *shock*, that being the breach in this particular case. To ensure that a similar breach does not occur again, Company A invested significantly in security technology and staff. The security increase is also noticeable when entering the premises of the organization as there are multiple CCTV cameras and physical barriers to control movement in different areas.
Structure, Policies, and Processes: The security division comprises around ten percent of Company A. The increase in size changes the security communication

and impacts the processes and policies. After the incident, several security policies were created—some of them are redundant, some are jargon-heavy, some contradict others, and most are located inconsistently. Security rules are also outlined in the Staff Handbook, to which all newcomers and existing employees are contractually bound.

According to the policies, non-compliance with security leads to disciplinary action, but Company A has no formal and systematized way of tracking non-compliance—some incidents may go unnoticed, while others receive unexpected disciplinary action. An inconsistent approach to disciplining non-compliance may negatively impact the legitimacy of the policies and, in turn, lead to increased workarounds. In addition, having a set of scattered policies rather than a single central policy can further complicate employees' ability to comply with security. Given these observations, there has been an initiative at Company A to centralize the security policy in order to achieve consistency.

5.2   Methodology

The engagement with the organization started when the Chief Information Security Officer (CISO) of Company A had made certain observations about the security division and had questions about the impact of security on the company's business processes. The CISO and one of the authors had been discussing the questions about Company A's security function. As a result of mutual interest in the topic—as well as the author's capabilities to capture the factors they had discussed—they decided to research the questions by constructing a conceptual model of Company A's security processes, policies, and behaviours, focussing on the following objectives: (1) to explore and evaluate the daily security processes in the company, (2) to identify potential friction, (3) to explore the meaning and role of security culture in general and within the organization, and (4) to identify potential improvements.

The research for this case-study was led by one of our researchers, embedded in Company A for a period of 6 months. By working at the security division, the researcher was able to immerse in the role of a security employee and simultaneously conduct research. The methods used were guided by our engagement with Company A and the context of the organization [10]. While the case-study was conducted during the early stages of our understanding and development of co-design, we recognized the importance of focussing on the engagement and participation of stakeholders and adopted existing methods to achieve this.

The Study: The case-study at Company A consists of long-term diary entries and semi-structured interviews with security staff. We used the following methods during the research: *participatory action research* (PAR) [29], *humble inquiry* [26], and *thematic analysis* (TA) [5]. The diary entries served primarily as a process of familiarization with Company A and its processes, and as a way to contextualize the findings. Semi-structured interviews with fifteen security managers at Company A were conducted focussing on the objectives that were agreed on with the CISO. The interview questions were guided by regular discussions with the CISO as well as the researcher's independent observations.

Participatory Action Research, Humble Inquiry, Thematic Analysis: Participatory action research is an approach to action research that focusses predominantly on the action and participation of stakeholders impacted by the research [29]. In exploring issues and questions that are significant to stakeholders, PAR emphasizes their role as co-researchers in the process of inquiry and research. PAR encourages the understanding of factors such as: what people do, how they interact with the world and others, what they value, and the discourses through which people understand and interpret their world [29]. These factors are much akin to those required to understand the culture of an organization.

At Company A, the researcher had the opportunity to observe the employees on a daily basis—absorbing a detailed account of their actions, values, and interaction with the world. The PAR factors above—in line with the model objectives—were additionally explored during the interviews with the security managers. Other principles of participatory action research further guided the case-study at Company A—PAR is a process that is *social, participatory, practical and collaborative, emancipatory, critical, reflexive,* and *transformative.* An account of applying these principles in practice can be found in [10].

As we developed our understanding of co-design, the researcher used Schein's method of *humble inquiry* [26], which encourages effective communication and positive relationships with participants, to conduct interviews. It treats participants as *co-researchers* rather than as interviewees. Interviews conducted in this way are meant to benefit both parties by having a conversation based on curiosity and honesty.

We used *thematic analysis*—a widely used method for analysing qualitative data—to analyse the interviews with the security managers. The purpose of TA is to identify patterns in the data by creating codes that are later on grouped into relevant themes. The method consists of several steps such as data familiarization, the generation of the initial codes, the search and revision of themes, up to the naming of the final themes [5]. The field researcher had detailed knowledge of the data and thus conducted the primary coding, which was then reviewed by one of the other researchers [10]. We agreed on the final themes jointly.

5.3   Main Findings

We produced eight themes from the thematic analysis of the interviews. The themes relate to Company A's overall approach to security and the employees' perceptions and attitudes towards security. The main findings from [10] are briefly summarized in Table 1.

5.4   Reflections

We designed and conducted the Company A case-study while we were at the beginning of developing a co-design methodology for security modelling. The study was preliminary, aimed at developing a conceptual model, and meant to be

Table 1. Themes from thematic analysis.

Theme and Description
Post-shock security
The impact of the information security breach is reflected in the security structure and practices of Company A.
Security theatre undermines policy
The heavy implementation of visible security controls for the sake of *appearing* secure undermines the legitimacy of the security policies at the company.
Security is like detention
Non-security staff are treated as *enemies* when not complying with security, which leads to a blame culture in the company.
Security is a blocker
The productivity of non-security staff often suffers because of restrictions imposed by security controls.
Lack of effective communication
The justification behind implementing such strict security controls is not adequately communicated across the organization.
Zero-risk appetite
The tolerance for taking security risks is almost non-existent in Company A, which often compromises productivity.
Sensible security is likely to work
The security division believes that less strict but better suited security controls are likely to increase compliance with security policies.
Behaviour change is required
Unlearning of old behaviours and behaviour change is required in order to create better security habits over time.

followed up by larger-scale research, which might have involved more mathematical types of modelling. Unfortunately, because of organizational restructuring, the co-design with Company A ended earlier than expected.

Important lessons, which significantly shaped our understanding of co-design, emerged from conducting this case-study. The individual methods that we implemented, such as participatory action research and humble inquiry, helped us learn which aspects of co-design would work and which should be improved. The work we did with Company A provided an interesting perspective and valuable reflections, which significantly influenced the co-design work presented here.

We summarize our reflections below.

Co-creating Objectives: The research objectives for the Company A case-study were jointly created between us and the CISO. We wanted to ensure that the questions the CISO wanted to explore were aligned with our research goals and vice-versa. These aligned objectives were stated early on in the field researcher's job description and the methods were then adapted based on the context and other organizational factors. For example, one factor that impacted the method of the research was the availability of the security managers. Compromises were made jointly to ensure that the objectives were followed and that the research was beneficial for all actively involved stakeholders. We encountered a limitation in our attempt to co-create the objectives. Although there was initial buy-in for the research from the senior executives, we did not agree on the long-term objectives with them as we did with the CISO. This led to misalignment of goals later on and influenced the continuation of the co-design.

Involvement in Research: The collaboration with the CISO and other relevant stakeholders was present throughout the research. Continuous discussions with the CISO helped shape the design of the interviews and encouraged the managers' willingness to participate. The interview study was approved as well as championed by the CISO of Company A. This simplified the arrangement of the interviews with the participants and set a positive tone for the conversations during the interviews. Furthermore, the involvement of the security managers in the research carried on as they were keen to contribute to the research and be informed of the outcomes.

Building Relationships: In addition to the CISO's involvement and support, something else that positively impacted the experience was the researcher's opportunity to build relationships with the employees of Company A, including the security managers. The ability to work alongside the participants for months before interviewing them meant that the researcher could build a relationship based on trust and mutual goals. Building such relationships also influenced the authenticity of the researcher's cultural and behavioural observations and the possibility to make such observations in the first place.

Mutual Learning: When embedded in the company, the researcher worked on several projects and tasks that were not directly related to the research. This was an opportunity to work together with many employees from the security division as well as other departments. During these collaborations, there were many instances of mutual learning. The security division were able to learn about the behavioural and cultural aspects of security from the researcher, while the researcher learned a lot about how the security systems and processes worked in practice. This process of mutual learning created a space for symmetric relationships functioning through translation zones between both technical and human-centred security—as well as between security research and application. A shortcoming of the mutual learning process was the lack of formalization during the initial phases of learning while the researcher was getting familiar with the systems and processes. More structuring and documentation of the knowledge exchange between the system owners and the researcher would have benefited the construction of the conceptual model.

Mapping Case-Study Reflections to Our Co-design Process: Our co-design methodology was directly informed by the methodological principles and reflections at Company A. Below we map the components from the case-study to the corresponding components in our methodology (as shown in Fig. 3).

1. The process of *co-creating the objectives* with the CISO of Company A, as well as the inability to co-create the objectives with the rest of the senior executives, emphasizes the importance of clarifying the mutual objectives from the very beginning. This maps to the first stage in the modelling cycle— *Observation and Candidate Data Availability*. Here the observations or questions about the system originating from stakeholders, are communicated to modellers to explore collaboration opportunities. If there is alignment between the questions the stakeholder wants to ask and the modelling techniques the modeller aims to apply, they co-create the objectives towards a mutually beneficial aim.
2. In between the first and second stage of the modelling cycle, lies the *translation zone* between the stakeholders and the modellers. This space of the co-design methodology corresponds to the multiple levels of *mutual learning* at Company A. In the translation zone, stakeholders and modellers exchange knowledge and experiences.
3. The reflections on *involvement in research* and *building relationships* highlight the significance of involving stakeholders in the research end-to-end. An extended interaction creates opportunities to build relationships and trust, as was the case with the researcher and the employees of Company A. Strong relationships create better collaboration opportunities while the involvement of stakeholders throughout the entire process improves the feasibility and quality of the research. As such, these two components correspond to *all the stages in the co-design process.*

Summary: Even though some of our reflections suggest that there is space for improvement, the experience at Company A has been largely positive. It gave us the opportunity to trial a set of methods, the principles of which closely relate to our understanding of co-design, that further emphasize the necessity for stakeholder involvement. The engagement of stakeholders at Company A was worthwhile as it enabled observations and data collection from a wide range of people and significantly aided our understanding of the system. As a result of this early co-design process, we were successfully able to draw mutual conclusions— from the observations and conceptual modelling—summarized in Sect. 5.3.

The biggest shortcoming was the inability to continue the co-design process, which stopped at the stage of designing a conceptual *candidate model*. The later stages of the co-design process, such as developing a more accurate model as well as validating it are missing from the current case-study. Another study must be repeated in the future in order to apply all the stages of our co-design process.

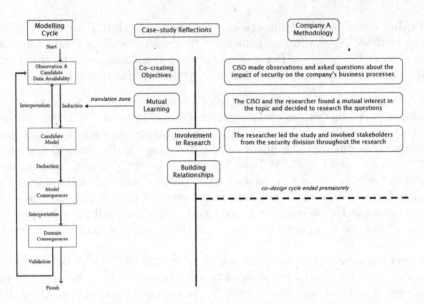

Fig. 3. The mapping of the case-study components to the co-design modelling cycle.

6   Conclusion

In this paper, we have proposed a new methodology by integrating the concept of co-design into the classical modelling cycle and providing a rigorous methodology for the construction of models that capture the system and its behaviours accurately. Our definition of co-design focusses on the ongoing *engagement between modellers and stakeholders* in the process of *objective identification and model specification, design, and construction* with the goal of achieving *alignment* between the model objectives and the needs of the stakeholders, and designing *a feasible model* given the constraints of data availability, which are explored as part of the co-design process.

We have presented an in-depth case-study of Company A, marking the beginning of our understanding and development of co-design. We reflect on the methods used in the case-study that shaped our co-design methodology by extracting positive experiences and shortcomings from approaches such as *co-creating objectives, involvement in research, building relationships*, and *mutual learning*.

Our co-design approach aims to tackle the challenges of problem definition, data availability, and data collection associated with modelling behavioural and cultural aspects of security. It does so by capturing the system's managers' questions adequately, in such a way that the required supporting data can be collected, and the managers and modellers can cooperate in the construction of the model. Co-designing a security model in such a way focusses on more accurate and practical representation of behavioural and cultural aspects of security, which can help security managers with their policy decisions.

In future work, we intend to further validate our co-design methodology by going through all the stages of the cycle with system stakeholders in an organization.

References

1. Anderson, G., McCusker, G., Pym, D.: A logic for the compliance budget. In: Zhu, Q., Alpcan, T., Panaousis, E., Tambe, M., Casey, W. (eds.) GameSec 2016. LNCS, vol. 9996, pp. 370–381. Springer, Cham (2016). https://doi.org/10.1007/978-3-319-47413-7_21
2. Basco-Carrera, L., Warren, A., van Beek, E., Jonoski, A., Giardino, A.: Collaborative modelling or participatory modelling? a framework for water resources management. Environ. Model. Softw. **91**, 95–110 (2017)
3. Beautement, A., Becker, I., Parkin, S., Krol, K., Sasse, A.: Productive security: a scalable methodology for analysing employee security behaviours. In: Twelfth Symposium on Usable Privacy and Security (SOUPS 2016), pp. 253–270. USENIX Association, Denver, CO, June 2016. https://www.usenix.org/conference/soups2016/technical-sessions/presentation/beautement
4. Beautement, A., Sasse, M.A., Wonham, M.: The compliance budget: managing security behaviour in organisations. In: Proceedings of the 2008 New Security Paradigms Workshop, pp. 47–58 (2008)
5. Braun, V., Clarke, V.: Using thematic analysis in psychology. Qual. Res. Psychol. **3**(2), 77–101 (2006)
6. Caulfield, T., Baddeley, M., Pym, D.: Social learning in systems security modelling. Constructions **14**(15), 3 (2016)
7. Collinson, M., Monahan, B., Pym, D.: A Discipline of Mathematical Systems Modelling. College Publications, London (2012)
8. D'Arcy, J., Greene, G.: Security culture and the employment relationship as drivers of employees' security compliance. Inf. Manage. Comput. Secur. (2014)
9. David, S., Sabiescu, A.G., Cantoni, L.: Co-design with communities. a reflection on the literature. In: Proceedings of the 7th International Development Informatics Association Conference, pp. 152–166. IDIA Pretoria, South Africa (2013)
10. Demjaha, A., Caulfield, T., Sasse, M.A., Pym, D.: 2 fast 2 secure: a case study of post-breach security changes. In: 2019 IEEE European Symposium on Security and Privacy Workshops (EuroS&PW), pp. 192–201. IEEE (2019)
11. Dignum, V., Dignum, F.: Perspectives on Culture and Agent-based Simulations, vol. 3. Springer, New York (2014). https://doi.org/10.1007/978-3-319-01952-9
12. Dorst, K.: The core of 'design thinking' and its application. Des. Stud. **32**(6), 521–532 (2011)
13. Heath, C., Hall, P., Coles-Kemp, L.: Holding on to dissensus: participatory interactions in security design. Strateg. Des. Res. J. **11**(2), 65–78 (2018). https://doi.org/10.4013/sdrj.2018.112.03
14. Ionita, D., Wieringa, R., Bullee, J.W., Vasenev, A.: Investigating the usability and utility of tangible modelling of socio-technical architectures. No. TR-CTIT-15-03 in CTIT Technical Report Series, Centre for Telematics and Information Technology (CTIT), Netherlands, May 2015
15. Kleinsmann, M., Valkenburg, R.: Barriers and enablers for creating shared understanding in co-design projects. Des. Stud. **29**(4), 369–386 (2008)

16. Korzybski, A.: Science and Sanity: An Introduction to Non-Aristotelian Systems and General Semantics. Institute of GS, Brooklyn (1958)
17. Landström, C., Whatmore, S.J., Lane, S.N., Odoni, N.A., Ward, N., Bradley, S.: Coproducing flood risk knowledge: redistributing expertise in critical 'participatory modelling'. Environ. Plann. A **43**(7), 1617–1633 (2011)
18. Lawson, H.B.: A Journey Through the Systems Landscape. College Publications, London (2010)
19. Malcolmson, J.: What is security culture? does it differ in content from general organisational culture? In: 43rd Annual 2009 international Carnahan Conference on Security Technology, pp. 361–366. IEEE (2009)
20. Martins, A., Elofe, J.: Information security culture. In: Ghonaimy, M.A., El-Hadidi, M.T., Aslan, H.K. (eds.) Security in the Information Society. IAICT, vol. 86, pp. 203–214. Springer, Boston (2002). https://doi.org/10.1007/978-0-387-35586-3_16
21. McColl, J.: Probability. Butterworth-Heinemann, Elsevier (1995)
22. Pidd, M.: Tools for thinking-modelling in management science. J. Oper. Res. Soc. **48**(11), 1150–1150 (1997)
23. Pidd, M.: Systems modelling: theory and practice. Syst. Model. Theor. Pract. **1**, 20 (2004)
24. Reid, R., Van Niekerk, J., Renaud, K.: Information security culture: a general living systems theory perspective. In: 2014 Information Security for South Africa, pp. 1–8. IEEE (2014)
25. Schein, E.H.: Organizational Culture and Leadership, vol. 2. Wiley, Hoboken (2010)
26. Schein, E.H., Schein, P.A.: Humble Inquiry: The Gentle Art of Asking Instead of Telling. Berrett-Koehler Publishers, San Francisco (2021)
27. Steen, M.: Co-design as a process of joint inquiry and imagination. Des. Issues **29**(2), 16–28 (2013)
28. Steen, M., Manschot, M., De Koning, N.: Benefits of co-design in service design projects. Int. J. Des. **5**(2), 46–53 (2011)
29. Stephen, K., Robin, M., Denzin, N., Lincoln, Y.: Participatory action research: communicative action and the public sphere. Denzin, N.K., Lincoln, Y.S. (eds.), The Sage Handbook of Qualitative Research, United Kingdom: Sage Publications, pp. 559–604 (2000)
30. Voinov, A., et al.: Tools and methods in participatory modeling: selecting the right tool for the job. Environ. Model. Softw. **109**, 232–255 (2018)
31. Voinov, A., et al.: Modelling with stakeholders-next generation. Environ. Model. Softw. **77**, 196–220 (2016)

From the Present to the Future

Positioning Diplomacy Within a Strategic Response to the Cyber Conflict Threat

Karen Renaud[1,2,3,4](✉) ⓘ, Amel Attatfa[2] ⓘ, and Tony Craig[1] ⓘ

[1] University of Strathclyde, Glasgow, UK
{karen.renaud,anthony.craig}@strath.ac.uk
[2] Abertay University, Dundee, UK
a.attatfa1900@abertay.ac.uk
[3] Rhodes University, Grahamstown, RSA
[4] University of South Africa, Gauteng, RSA

Abstract. *Background.* Nation states unleash cyber attacks targeting other nation states (e.g. WannaCry, SolarWinds), termed "offensive cyber operations". When such aggressions are deemed, according to the UN Charter, to constitute *a threat to the peace, breach of the peace, or act of aggression towards a nation state*, governments might choose to respond. Responses can range from silence all the way to retaliation, at the other end of the scale. The emergence of cyber diplomacy suggests a less militant and potentially powerful response option. Barrinha and Renard [5] explain that the rise of cyber diplomacy has coincided with "a growing contestation of the values, institutions and power dynamics of the liberal-created cyberspace". (p. 3). The question is: how could cyber diplomacy fit into a strategic threat management plan?

Aim. To position cyber diplomacy within a strategic response to nation state offensive cyber operations.

Method. To help us to position cyber diplomacy's role in this domain, we first examine historical cyber conflicts, and governments' responses to these, as well as testing the factors that might explain response choice. We then review a number of proposed options for managing cyber conflicts.

Results. We propose a comprehensive "Five D's" strategic framework to manage the threat of offensive cyber operations. Cyber diplomacy is included, acknowledging its emerging and potentially powerful role in managing cyber conflicts in the future.

Conclusions. Cyber diplomacy has recently emerged and it has not yet been widely deployed. We show how it can be positioned within a strategic framework for managing the threat of offensive cyber operations from other nation states.

Keywords: Offensive cyber operations · Cyber diplomacy · Strategic management of threats

ⓒ Springer Nature Switzerland AG 2022
S. Parkin and L. Viganò (Eds.): STAST 2021, LNCS 13176, pp. 131–152, 2022.
https://doi.org/10.1007/978-3-031-10183-0_7

1   Introduction

Cyber attacks can be perpetrated by a range of agents, including script kiddies, cyber criminal gangs and nation states [25]. The targets, too, range from individual citizens [50], to companies [47] all the way to nation states. It is increasingly clear that this is a present and serious threat [11,29], which Barker says has increased 100% over the last 3 years [4]. In this paper, we are interested in nation states targeting other nation states in the cyber realm, to "*disrupt their peace*"[1]. Sigholm and Larsson [61] argue that these kinds of attacks are a natural extension of traditional military and intelligence operations to the cyber arena.

In 1996, USA President Clinton established the Commission of Critical Infrastructure Protection[2]. He wanted to ensure that electricity communications and computer networks would be protected from attack[3]. At the time, no one could have anticipated the likes of the wide-ranging SolarWinds cyber attack of 2020 [68], which did indeed impact electricity utilities [74]. Using Lin's terminology of an "*offensive cyber operation*" [39] to describe 'nation state on nation state' cyber aggressions, we will refer to these events as **OCOs** in this paper.

The cyber conflict database published by Valeriano and Maness [73] lists 266 OCOs that occurred from 2000 to 2016, confirming the reality of the threat. The actual incidence is likely to be even higher, given significant under-reporting [31].

Article 51 of the UN Charter gives countries the right of self-defense, permitting forceful responses to "armed attacks"[4], which includes cyber aggressions [58]. Even so, most of these cyber-related incidents do not trigger any significant response from the target country [41].

Governments have a number of options in responding to OCOs [3,42]. Our focus, in this paper, is on the deployment of cyber diplomacy, which can be defined as "*the use of diplomatic tools and the diplomatic mindset to resolve issues arising from cyberspace*" [1, p. 60]. We commenced by exploring the nature of governments' responses to OCOs, the factors that trigger these, and the occurrence of diplomatic responses. We then considered various proposed strategies for managing the OCO threat, including diplomacy. Finally, we produced a proposed framework for managing OCO threats, which includes cyber diplomacy. Our research questions are thus:

RQ1: *Which factors influence responses to OCOs, and how often was diplomacy the response?*

RQ2: *What proposals have been advanced for managing OCO threats on a global scale?*

RQ3: *How could cyber diplomacy fit into a strategic response to the OCO threat?*

---

[1] https://www.cyberarmscontrol.org/post/article-39-of-the-un-charter-cyber-as-a-threat-to-international-peace-and-security.

[2] http://www.ieee-security.org/Cipher/Newsbriefs/1996/960723.EOonCIP.html.

[3] https://fas.org/irp/offdocs/eo13010.htm.

[4] https://legal.un.org/repertory/art51.shtml.

Section 2 reviews the related literature and identifies factors that are likely to influence responses to OCOs. Sections 3, 4 and 5 address RQ1, RQ2 and RQ3 respectively, cultimating in the "Five D's" strategic framework for managing OCO threats. Section 6 discusses the paper's findings and concludes, with Sect. 7 acknowledging the limitations of our empirical investigation.

2   Background: Nation State Cyber Aggressions

We commence by defining OCOs, to ensure that this discussion is well grounded. Lin [39] defines an OCOs as: *"military operations and activities in cyberspace for cyber attack against and (or) cyber-exploitation of adversary information systems and networks"*. This umbrella term including cyber attacks and exploitations, which can be destructive or non-destructive (e.g. espionage).

What distinguishes OCOs from cyber attacks that target individual computer users or companies? Murray [43] argues that cyber aggressions targeting "citizenry", as opposed to "individual citizens", are characterised by the intention to harm the target *nation* by denying it the use of its resources. OCOs may disrupt essential services (e.g., WannaCry[5] which disrupted the UK's National Health Service), destroy resources (e.g., the Stuxnet[6] OCO on Iran's nuclear centrifuges), manipulate information or information systems (e.g. the SolarWinds[7] supply chain OCO), or steal intelligence [52]. Sometimes, the impact cascades into the physical domain, as occurred in the Not-Petya cyber aggression [22], affecting the lives of significant numbers of Ukrainian citizens.

Pomerlau [52] explains that cyber attacks from non-state actors generally aim to coerce targets or gain financially. Attacks by nation states targeting other nation states, on the other hand, are motivated by geopolitics. Rosenzweig [57] presents a typology of cyber aggressions, in terms of the mass harm caused. He commences with cyber mischief at the lowest level advancing to cyber crime, cyber espionage, cyber terrorism and cyber war harming the most citizens of the target country. As such, the closer one gets to the top of Rosenzweig's typology, the more likely it is that the nation state is the target, and governments might feel compelled to respond in some way.

2.1   Choosing a Response

Baram and Sommer [3] suggest a range of responses to OCOs, based on whether governments: (1) admit the OCO occurred (e.g., [9]), (2) attribute the OCO to a country, (3) both[8] or (4) neither[9]. It is worth emphasising that attribution

---

[5] https://www.kaspersky.co.uk/resource-center/threats/ransomware-wannacry.

[6] https://www.csoonline.com/article/3218104/what-is-stuxnet-who-created-it-and-how-does-it-work.html.

[7] https://www.cisecurity.org/solarwinds/.

[8] https://microsites-live-backend.cfr.org/cyber-operations/search?keys=not+petya.

[9] https://www.dailymail.co.uk/sciencetech/article-2637899/eBay-refused-admit-massive-cyber-attack-thought-customer-data-safe.html.

is challenging [18,59]. Countries might engage, directly or indirectly, via a third party, or camouflage their OCO [35,56,70]. If governments *do* decide to attribute an OCO to the aggressive actions of another state, Moret and Pawlak [42] provide a long list of potential responses, which *does* include diplomacy, but also includes a military response at the upper end of the scale.

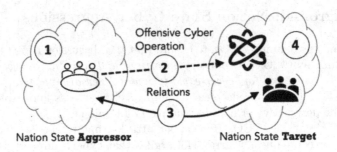

Fig. 1. Four dimensions influencing the choice of response to an OCO: (1) Aggressor, (2) OCO severity, (3) Aggressor vs. Target, (4) Target

Response Choice Architecture: We currently have little understanding of the factors that might influence the choice of response. As a first foray, we identify four dimensions of the choice architecture that could be influential. These are: (1) the attributes of the state-sponsored aggressor, (2) the severity of the cyber operation, (3) the relations between the two countries, and (4) the attributes of the target state. There are undoubtedly many others, which could be the focus of future research. Yet, these offer a broad framework for exploring the nature of responses to OCOs.

First, the aggressor (#1 in Fig. 1). **(1)** The power of the state sponsor of an OCO could shape the response from the target state [2]. Some approaches in the International Relations literature suggest that a country's power allows it to influence the behaviour of others [77]. With no international arbiter of conflict, the balance of power between states is what determines who can do what to others. A powerful state could therefore be better able to deter harsher responses from the target of a cyber operation.

Second, the OCO (#2 in Fig. 1). **(2)** the severity of the OCO is likely to be influential in terms of triggering a response. Analysts have drawn a distinction between cyber operations that are exploitative and those that are destructive [34,39]. Exploitative operations, such as acts of cyber espionage, aim to observe or exfiltrate data from the target's computer systems. Destructive attacks aim to change or destroy computer systems, or the information stored within them. Another distinction made by scholars is between "low-cost, low-payoff" disruptions and "high-cost, high-payoff" attacks against critical infrastructure targets [72]. We might expect more severe OCOs to trigger proportionally robust responses from target states as they try to deter further harm via punishment mechanisms [46, p. 55].

Third, (3) (#3 in Fig. 1) pre-existing diplomatic relations between the aggressor and target nations. Pairs of countries that have closer diplomatic relations may have more communication channels available to resolve incidents peacefully. A lack of diplomatic relations might trigger a more robust response.

Fourth, the target country's characteristics (#4 in Fig. 1).

(4a) The general level of Internet dependence in a country could feed into perceived vulnerability, threat, and thus the kind of response to an OCO The more devices connected to the Internet, the more extensive the attack surface and thus greater potential harm from OCOs [37]. For example, North Korea has an advantage over the United States in the event of a cyber war, given the differences in Internet dependence [63, p. 151]. With more potential for cyber security breaches, a state may be increasingly motivated to punish OCOs and deter them in the future.

(4b) The power of the target country, approximated by its Gross Domestic Product (GDP). States with more economic power are likely to have the capacity to adopt robust responses. Powerful states also have more motivation to retaliate to protect their prestige.

(4c) Power in international relations is related to the alliance partnerships that states can draw on to project influence or deter OCOs. Without the resources or alliances, weaker states in international politics will be limited in how they can respond to an OCO.

3   RQ1: Historical Responses

In this section, we seek to scope the influence of the aforementioned factors on governments' responses to OCOs. This analysis is inductive rather than theory directed, due to the absence of existing theories to build on. The proposed model is depicted in Fig. 2, with variables detailed in Table 1.

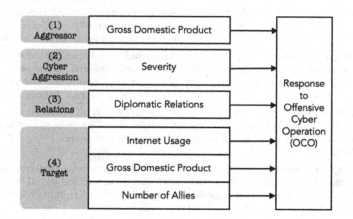

Fig. 2. Proposed model of factors influencing responses to OCOs

Table 1. Measurement of variables

Variable	Measurement
(1) Aggressor Power: The wealth of the OCO aggressor will influence the robustness of the response to an OCO.	We used the GDP of the aggressor state (constant 2010 USA dollars) as a measure of its wealth and power.
(2) OCO Severity: The more destructive an OCO, the stronger the response from the target government	We relied on the variable provided by the Cyber Operations Tracker, which classifies attack mechanisms as defacement, distributed denial of service (DDoS), doxing, espionage, financial theft, data destruction, sabotage, and multiple (Definitions provided on the Cyber Operations Tracker (CFR) website[12]. To simplify severity analysis, we re-coded this information as either *destructive* or *non-destructive*, which maps onto the distinction made by Lin [39]. Destructive OCOs either cause damage to physical infrastructure or to data, and include data destruction and sabotage. Non-destructive attacks include defacement, DDoS, doxing, espionage, and financial theft. There was one instance where the type of OCO was coded as "several", which we re-coded as "missing".
(3) Diplomatic Relations: The weaker the diplomatic relations between the target and aggressor, the more robust the response from the target to an OCO	We used data on diplomatic exchanges from the Correlates of War [6] that indicates if a country has any diplomatic presence in another, including *charges d'affairs*, ministers, or ambassadors, or else has zero diplomatic representation in another country. The data ends in the year 2005 it may reflect an historical rather than present state of relations.
(4a) Target's Internet Use: The more citizens using the internet, the larger the vulnerable attack surface.	As a proxy for Internet dependence, we used World Bank data on the percentage of the country's population that has used the internet in the past 12 months.
(4b) Target Power: The wealth of the OCO target will influence the robustness of the response to an OCO.	We used the GDP of the target state (constant 2010 USA dollars) as a measure of its wealth and power.
(4c) Target's Allies: Target countries with more international allies should adopt more robust responses to OCOs	We counted the number of defence pacts each target country had signed using the formal alliances (v4.1) dataset from the Correlates of War [6]. A defence pact is determined if a signed treaty between states includes providing defence to one or more state involved

3.1   Methods

We draw on data from the Council on Foreign Relation's Cyber Operations Tracker. At the time the data was downloaded in 2020, the Cyber Operations Tracker data included 481 OCOs from 2005 to 2020. These are limited to publicly known, state-sponsored OCOs (OCOs). Of these 482 OCOs, the response chosen by the target state was recorded for 86 instances.

Given the limitations of this data, we do not claim generalisation possibilities. Until more data comes to light, however, the Cyber Operations Tracker provides the only source of information on cyber operations *and* governments' responses to them. We therefore use this data source to discover if there are any correlations between our selected factors and the nature of the response chosen in response to an OCO.

We analyse this incident-level data set where each row gives information about one of these 86 OCOs as well as the target state and the state aggressor. In some cases, multiple countries are listed as targets. In these cases, there were also responses from multiple targets, so the number of observations in the data set was expanded so there is a unique row of data for each involved government. The data set thus expanded to 91 observations.

3.2   Dependent Variable: State Response to OCO

Our dependent variable is a binary measure of the type of response a state has taken in responding. For this we recode the information provided by the Cyber Operations Tracker, which categorises target government responses into seven types as described in Table 2. Denouncement is the most common response and is evident in 53.5% of OCOs.

Table 2. Frequency of target government response variable

Type of response	Freq	%
Denial	1	1.1
Confirmation	14	15.4
Denouncement	49	53.9
Criminal charges	17	18.7
Sanctions	6	6.6
Hack-back	2	2.2
Unknown	2	2.2
Total	91	100.0

Table 3. Frequency of re-coded target government response variable

Type of response	Freq	%
Active (criminal charges, sanctions, hack-backs)	25	28.1
Passive (denial, confirmation, denouncement)	64	71.9
Total	89	100.0

To create a simpler indication of the strength of response that is more amenable to logistic regression analysis, we recoded the range of responses into two categories: (1) active, and (2) passive. Responses where the state takes action against the state sponsor of the OCO are coded as 'active', and include criminal charges, sanctions, hack-backs and diplomacy. Responses where the state did not take action against the state sponsor are coded as 'passive', and include denial, confirmation, and denouncement. The scale of response is therefore a binary variable taking one of two values: 0 or 1, where 1 indicates a stronger response from the target state. There are two instances where there was a suspected response, yet the precise actions were unspecified. These are coded as 'missing', leaving the final number of cases assessed at 89. Table 3 shows that more robust, active responses occur 28.1% of the time. In the next section, we describe the results of a logistic regression model where we measure the effect that each factor has on the likelihood of a state adopting a more active response to a cyber attack.

3.3   Empirical Findings

Table 4 provides the results of the logistic regression analysis, examining the effect of each of our factors on the scale of response taken by the target of an OCO. The coefficient shows the change in the odds of the target state carrying out an active response if there is a one unit increase in the value of each independent variable, while controlling for the effects of the other independent variables. An odds ratio above 1 indicates a positive relationship between the independent variable and the robustness of response, while a ratio below 1 indicates a negative association. For each independent variable, the coefficient is displayed along with the robust standard error, the p value indicating statistical significance at the 95% confidence level, and the lower and upper confidence interval limits. P values under 0.05 are considered statistically significant ($p < 0.05$). The model uses listwise deletion of missing values which limits the analysis to 64 observations when all variables are included in the same model. The first factor we test is the economic power of the suspected state sponsor of the OCO, measured by its GDP. Despite a slight positive relationship, the result is not statistically significant. The power of the aggressor therefore does not seem to have a deterrent effect on the kind of response chosen by the target. The severity of the OCO is not a good predictor of diplomatic response type either.

Table 4. Logistic regression of cyber response type (active or passive)

Independent variable	Coefficient (Odds ratio)	Robust standard error	P value	Lower 95% Confidence level	Upper 95% Confidence level
Aggressor's GDP (Log)	1.13	0.36	0.696	0.61	2.10
Severity of OCO	1.12	1.49	0.931	0.08	15.07
Diplomatic relations	0.63	0.70	0.677	0.07	5.67
Internet usage of target (%)	1.05	0.04	0.217	0.97	1.15
Target's GDP (Log)	1.56	0.60	0.251	0.73	3.31
Number of allies of target	1.29	0.16	0.042	1.01	1.65
Constant	0.00	0.00	0.065	0.00	4.20

Note: 64 observations. Constant estimates baseline odds. GDP of aggressor and target is log transformed to reduce skew.

For each independent variable, the coefficient is displayed along with the robust standard error, the p-value indicating statistical significance at the 95% confidence level, and the lower and upper confidence interval limits. P-values under 0.05 are considered statistically significant (p¡0.05). The model uses list-wise deletion of missing values which limits the analysis to 64 observations when all variables are included in the same model.

The first factor we test is the economic power of the suspected state sponsor of the OCO, measured by its GDP. Despite a slight positive relationship, the result is not statistically significant. The power of the aggressor therefore does not seem to have a deterrent effect on the kind of response chosen by the target. The severity of the OCO is not a good predictor of diplomatic response type either.

This suggests that destructive OCOs which damage digital or physical infrastructure do not invoke a more active response than non-destructive OCOs, such as website defacement, DDoS, or espionage. It is possible that states view certain non-destructive OCOs as equally threatening to their national security. Cyber espionage, for instance, can cause serious economic and reputational harm, which might lead to similar responses to those in response to destructive OCOs. Indeed, there is ongoing debate on whether cyber espionage should be seen as part of norm inter-state interactions or whether it warrants a military response [66].

There is a negative correlation between mutual diplomatic representation between the target and state-sponsor of an OCO and the chosen response, shown by a coefficient below 1, but it is very small and statistically insignificant. The nature of cyber responses therefore does not seem to be influenced by pre-existing diplomatic relations, at least under this metric. It is likely that most nation states engaged in cyber conflict already have poor relations or are engaged in strategic rivalry, in which case diplomatic relations may be less relevant.

The fourth factor is the level of internet usage in the target state. Again, there is a very low association between the percentage of the population using the internet and the robustness of the OCO response, which lacks statistical significance. Responses to OCOs do not increase in severity with increases in internet usage.

The target state's power, approximated by its GDP (constant US dollars) is our next factor. Here we see a larger coefficient, suggesting a positive association between the victim's GDP and robustness of response taken. The finding is not too surprising given the skew in the data towards the United States as a target country. However, the effect is not statistically significant when controlling for the effects of other variables in the model, with large errors and wide confidence intervals. It remains an open question whether the United States' diplomatic responses are a result of its economic resources.

The strongest correlation in this analysis is between the number of allies that the target country has, and the robustness of its response to an OCO (0.507). As a country gains more allies, it tends to carry out harsher responses, including criminal charges, hack-backs, or sanctions, and this association is statistically significant (0.000). The United States has both a large number of allies globally and has often taken strong action against OCOs, according to the CFR data, so we cannot rule out a spurious relationship here. Nevertheless, it raises the possibility that a country like the United States is able to implement strong responses *because* of its international power and influence, as gauged here through alliances.

3.4   Findings and Limitations

Chosen cyber responses appear to be driven mostly by the international status of the target country. Alliances reflect and reinforce a country's global influence and power in the international system. Countries with more power are able to attract others into their sphere of influence.

That said, it is important to acknowledge the prominence of the United States in the data supporting this analysis. This is to be expected, given that it is the largest economy in the world, the most studied with respect to cyber security "as a great power" [12], and with a large numbers of international alliances, which makes it an attractive target. It is also in the top five countries most at risk of OCOs[13], and ranked in the top 5 of countries in terms of cyber security maturity [13]. Twenty-two of 25 responses coded as 'active' involved the United States. This analysis suggests that America's global influence might also play a role in explaining their willingness to punish cyber aggressions, and there is evidence that they are also helping other countries to repel OCOs [67, 75].

The analysis was carried out using the available data from the Cyber Operations Tracker, but we should be cautious about the conclusions we draw. As the authors of the data repository openly admit, the data is based on publicly known OCOs with a potential bias towards English speaking countries given the greater openness to reporting these events in the West. Further research is needed to understand how non-Western countries respond to OCOs.

Another limitation in the data is that it only captures responses to cyber-attacks that have been openly declared by the victim and misses responses that occur in secret. At this stage, we have little way of knowing the responses that have occurred unless these make their way into the public domain. This could help us interpret our finding that a high-status country such as the United States, is likely to engage in robust responses, given that powerful states are likely to be less deterred from openly confronting cyber aggressions. The data set probably under reports the way low status countries choose to respond to OCOs.

At a minimum, this analysis has helped describe the existing data on how states have responded in the past, and started a discussion of possible explanations. Having done so, we proceed to RQ2, to consider proposals for managing OCO threats.

4   RQ2: Proposed OCO Threat Management Possibilities

With a limited understanding of factors that trigger OCOs, we now consider advanced options for managing OCO threats. To judge these options, we will use

---

[13] https://nordvpn.com/cri/.

Brantly's [8] deterrence dimensions, given that we are looking at this issue from a response perspective. Brantly claims that deterrence efforts have to have three core components: (1) having formulated the intention to protect the nation's cyberspace (credibility), (2) having the capabilities to implement that intention (capability), and (3) the communication of the intention and capability to a potential aggressor (communication).

4.1   A Cyber Geneva Convention

In 1949, the Geneva Conventions were ratified by 196 countries. These are international treaties that contain the most important rules limiting the barbarity of war. They protect people who do not take part in the fighting (civilians, medics, aid workers) and those who can no longer fight (wounded, sick and shipwrecked troops, and prisoners of war)[14].

Would a "Cyber" Geneva Convention be feasible? Brad Smith from Microsoft proposed exactly this in 2017 [64], with the idea of protecting citizens during peace times. In particular, signatories would have to agree not to target critical civilian electrical, economic and political infrastructures. This sounds sensible until you realise that there is no widely accepted definition of 'critical infrastructure' [44]. Jacobson [30] argues against Microsoft's proposal from a Danish perspective. He argues that such a digital convention would risk re-opening already concluded international agreements. Such an agreement might also serve to hamper existing cyber activities engaged in by smaller countries to protect themselves. Jacobson believes that involvement in the EU, NATO, the United Nations, as well as enhancing cooperation with the private sector, would enhance security in cyberspace better than a Cyber Geneva convention. Hollis [27] points to the fact that even those advocating for an international law for information operations are sceptical of a cyber 'Geneva Convention' given the volatility of technological innovation and development. This approach thus appears to fail on Brantly's *credibility* dimension.

4.2   Cyberspace as Ostrom's "Commons"

Elinor Ostrom was a political scientist at Indiana University who won a Nobel Prize for her research into how communities ought to co-operate to share resources. She referred to such shared resources as a "commons". Ostrom proposed eight principles for managing a commons [76]. Principle number six is: *"Use graduated sanctions for rule violators."* Ostrom's 7th principle specifies that resolution of disagreements between users of commons should be accessible and low-cost. This ensures that problems are solved rather than ignored and engenders inclusivity.

If Ostrom's 6th and 7th principles are not being respected by all Internet users, a cyber "tragedy of the commons" could exist, with some nations committing aggressions with impunity, essentially being bullies on the commons

---

[14] https://www.icrc.org/en/doc/war-and-law/treaties-customary-law/geneva-conventions/overview-geneva-conventions.htm.

playground. Rankin *et al.* [54] explains this could end up destroying the very resource the world increasingly depends on.

At first glance, treating the Internet as a commons appears to be a viable approach to managing inter-country cyber aggressions, especially if these principles are enforced by an international body, such as the UN. However, we first have to consider whether cyberspace qualifies as a commons.

Kanuck [33] points out that other "commons" have been discovered by humans, not created by them. Kanuck argues that designating the Internet as a commons would require decisions to be made about how much, and which specific portions, of cyberspace would be governed according to these principles. It is likely that countries would consider their own essential infrastructures not to be part of the commons, but rather subject to individual property rights.

Fitzpatrick [23] argues that a sustainable sharing of "a commons" is only possible if reliable mechanisms are established to enforce compliance with agreed rules of usage. However, Kanuck [33] argues that the lack of transnational judicial cooperation makes any such enforced compliance infeasible. The other difficulty is that the reliable identification of legitimate users remains elusive. If it is not possible to identify people reliably, as passports do in the physical realm, it is hard to make people accountable for bad behaviours to sanction or exclude them. Applying such remediation to nation states is probably infeasible, and these are the infractions we are discussing here. This approach appears to fail on Brantly's *capability* dimension, making the idea of treating cyberspace as a commons infeasible.

4.3   Establishing Alliances

Based on our empirical investigation, even given the limitations, it seems that the way to be more powerful in cyberspace is to establish alliances with other countries, and sign treaties to formalise these. Accumulating allies to protect yourself is an age-old tactic. Cleopatra is said to have courted Mark Antony specifically because she saw his value as an ally[15]. The impact of the USA in swinging the outcome of both World Wars emphasised their value as an ally. Even today, many countries consider the USA a valuable ally [62], especially when a treaty is in place. On 19 July 2021, a senior USA administration stated: *"No one action can change China's behavior in cyberspace and neither can just one country acting on its own"* [65], confirming the power of international cooperation and collaboration.

Yet, the mere fact of having allies is not an absolute deterrent, when it comes to being targeted. Who the allies are, and their standing in the political sphere, also makes a difference. Clare [15, p. 545] argues that *"allies only effectively deter challenges against those partners that are of a greater strategic importance"*. Was this why the USA condemned the WannaCry ransomware OCO and joined the UK in attributing it to North Korea [7], even though the kill switch activated by the UK's Marcus Hutchins neutralised the threat before it compromised the

---

[15] https://www.scholaradvisor.com/essay-examples/cleopatra-relationships/.

USA's systems [45]? Perhaps it was because of the USA and UK's long standing Five Eyes Intelligence Alliance, or their history of being allies during recent conflicts.

This approach ensures that states benefit from the *capabilities* of their allies, and establishes their enhanced *credibility* in responding to OCOs. Our investigations suggest that this makes them able to respond to cyber aggressions, making the deterrence actions credible. The idea of forming alliances, if treaties exist, ensures that such alliances are salient, and *communicated* to others.

We need to reiterate, at this point, that our data was dominated by OCOs targeting the USA. The USA has many strong alliances. It might not be possible for other states to implement this strategy, nor is it guaranteed to give them the power to respond, perhaps in kind, to OCOs. Hence, this option is unlikely to be a globally feasible option.

4.4 The United Nations Approach

In 1945, after two of the biggest conflicts in the 20th century, the United Nations (UN) was created to maintain international peace and security, give humanitarian assistance to those in need, protect human rights, and uphold international law[16][26]. At the time, no one could have anticipated cyber aggressions. The United Nations (UN) formulated eleven 'Cyber Norms' in response to the realisation that nation state cyber aggressions were occurring with increasing regularity [24].

Usually the action or response of the UN tends to be strategic, via treaties, conventions, written recommendations and consensus regarding specific issues [40]. The UN does actively engage "in the field". UN peacekeepers are a military peace-keeping group intervening in parts of the world where interventions are required. In the cyber context, the UN has been working actively e.g., by means of non-proliferation of mass weapons. This is because, should these weapons fall into the hands of malicious groups or private parties, the consequences could be dire and dangerous on a global level.

Considering Brantly's [8] mitigations in this respect, we can see the UN's *capability* as residing in its standing as an international body and recognition by the International Community. The UN's *credibility* [21] has been questioned a number of times, notably due to events and episodes that have occurred throughout its history that raised a number of critiques from different parties with reference to its functioning and management of crisis. Lastly, the UN has been quite active when it comes to its *communication*, putting in place a special department of communication [71]. Since its creation in 1946, a year after the UN's establishment, it has tackled disinformation and misinformation, specifically online [20].

---

[16] https://www.un.org/en/about-us/history-of-the-un.

4.5 Cyber Diplomacy

Torres and Riordan [69] explain that one of the UN's major roles is to establish norms of behaviour, which they have done. The second is to promote cyber diplomacy. Cyber diplomacy is defined as *"a set of diplomatic practices concerned with the broadly defined governance of cyberspace."* [53, p. 2].

It seems sensible for governments to engage in diplomacy efforts, both cyber and traditional, to ensure that tense situations, perhaps post-OCO activity, do not escalate into open war. Conflicts have been prevented in the past when the leaders of the involved countries have met and resolved their differences to prevent escalation and eventual outright war. The Cuban missile crisis of 1962 is a case in point [32]. Kennedy and Khrushchev met and found a way to stand down their forces and a potentially devastating nuclear conflict was avoided. Diplomacy also seems indicated when an aggression has already been committed, such as SolarWinds, so that responses are measured and effective.

Levinson [38] argues that a law enforcement approach is unlikely to be an effective strategy in addressing nation state cyber aggressions, and this argument is echoed by O'Connell [51]. There are examples where the USA has preferred diplomacy to other approaches. Maness and Valeriano [41] determined that when China has engaged in attacking the United States, the United States has responded with diplomatic efforts. They have attempted to improve relations instead of responding by hacking back, for example.

With respect to Brantly's three dimensions [8], cyber diplomacy fulfills all of them. In 2016, the European Union wrote about the role of cyber diplomacy in building *capabilities* across the European Union. *Communication* is built into the definition of cyber diplomacy. *Credibility*, which encompasses governments' intention to act against the threat, and their formulation of strategies, is also built into the descriptions of cyber diplomacy and could be seen as the *raison d'être* for its existence. We now proceed to position cyber diplomacy within a strategic response to OCOs.

5 RQ3: Positioning Cyber Diplomacy

We now consider how a strategic approach could be formulated for managing the OCO threat. Instead of including only deterrence aspects, Carlin [10] suggests a 'Whole-of-Government Approach to National Security Cyber Threats'. Carlin recommends including the three D's: *deterrence, detection* and *disruption.* Cohen *et al.* [17] extend this with *defeat.* Based on the previous discussion, we extend this with a fifth dimension: *cyber diplomacy.*

Deterrence: Nye proposes a four-pronged deterrence approach: punishment, defence, entanglement and norms. Nye argues that this can *"reduce the likelihood of adverse acts causing harm in the cyber realm. They can complement one another in affecting actors' perception of the costs and benefits of particular actions"* [46, p. 62]. Punishment is challenging in the cyber domain, due to the aforementioned attribution difficulty, compromising the **credibility** of the deterrence. Defence is related to implementing good cyber hygiene, signalling *capability* of deterrence efforts. Entanglement suggests creating dependencies between two states such that an attack would hurt the aggressor as well as the target. Finally, formulating and communicating norms imposes a reputational cost on aggressors, This fulfils the *communication* deterrence dimension.

Detection: Detection happened months, if not years, after the fact for the SolarWinds OCO [36] and for the Yahoo breach, which has also been attributed to unnamed "state sponsored actors" [19]. It might be that detection is being neglected in favour of deterrence. CISCO [14] recommends a number of ways to detect infiltration, including (1) identifying mysterious emails, (2) noting unusual password activity, (3) identifying suspicious pop-ups, and a (4) slower than usual network. These can be categorised either as anomaly detection (1–3) or performance monitoring (4).

Disruption: The third of Carlin's recommendations is disruption. This could include economic sanctions, coordination with other intelligence bodies such as the Five Eyes to share information and coordination with the private sector [10].

Defeat: Cohen *et al.* [17] explain that defeat refers to the efforts taken to reduce the number and severity of OCOs and to ensure that society can recover quickly from adverse cyber events. They advocate building resilience, which includes: implementing technical measures, human resource development, training exercises and, crucially, plans for recovering from the impact of OCOs that *do* succeed. Hence defeat includes the concept of *prevention*, as well as recovery.

Diplomacy: Cyber diplomacy has recently emerged as a viable mechanism to be used in this domain [1]. There is evidence that the USA has already started using diplomacy when engaging with particular countries [41].

5.1   The Five D's Framework:

In formulating the framework, we have to be cognisant of the cyber attack life cycle stages proposed by the USA's Cyber Threat Framework [48]: (1) preparation, (2) engagement, (3) presence, and (4) effect/consequence. The framework needs to include strategic responses for each of these phases.

Figure 3 brings everything together in a comprehensive framework describing how states can build a strategic response to the nation state cyber threat. The five D's (three from Carlin [10], one from Cohen *et al.*'s defeat and the fifth being cyber diplomacy) are mapped to Brantly's capability, credibility and communication dimensions [8].

This framework combines the preventive and reformative approaches to harm prevention [60]. We demonstrate how establishing alliances and the UN Norms would fit into these conceptualisations, as well as the formulation of plans for responses *pre-OCO*. Each of the "Five D" activities is expanded upon within their demarcated space in the diagram.

5.2   Countries' Cyber Security Strategies

Governments across the globe have formulated cyber security strategy documents[17] reflecting a growing understanding that the best way to manage cyber threats is to mount a strategic response, not a reactive tactical one. The existence of these policies demonstrates these countries' *credibility* in managing cyber threats. What is their strategy for dealing with OCOs?

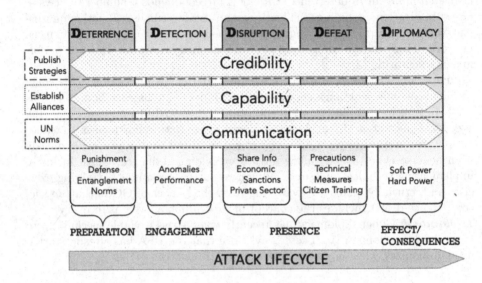

Fig. 3. The "Five D's" nation state cyber threat management framework

Renaud *et al.* [55] analysed the cyber security strategy policies of the Five Eyes countries and China. Their analysis produced a list of government responsibilities mentioned by these countries' cyber strategy policies. All refer to the need to *"manage and mitigate cyber threats"*, but do not provide a framework for specifically managing the OCO threat.

All also mention the responsibility to engage internationally and share information, which confirms the need to *communicate* with others and thereby to enhance their own *capabilities*. Interestingly, the USA alone mentions their responsibility to extradite cyber criminals, arguably a strong *deterrence* aspect. Detection is likely to be included in *"Coordinate reporting of vulnerabilities"* and *"Measure state of cyber security"*. Disruption, defeat and diplomacy are not mentioned in the responsibility list. However, the Five Eyes countries are likely to be engaging in disruption and defeat activities, preferring not to mention these in their strategy documents, so as not to leak information that could benefit countries who might consider an OCO in the future.

---

[17] https://www.itu.int/en/ITU-D/Cybersecurity/Pages/National-Strategies-repository.aspx.

It is also likely that these countries' governments do indeed have plans for dealing with OCOs that they have chosen not to share with the general public. Indeed, the USA announced that they had plans to prevent such an OCO on their 2020 election [49] and Cluley [16] reports that the USA is offering a reward for help in catching state-sponsored ransomware attackers. Moreover, the Biden administration just appointed their first National Cyber Director [28], with a remit to *"prepare the federal government's response to cyberattacks and cyber campaigns of **significant consequence**"* (emphasis added by authors). This description suggests that a strategic response to OCO threats might well be part of the National Cyber Director's remit too.

6   Discussion and Conclusion

Cohen *et al.* [17] emphasise and highlight the importance of plans in coping with and offsetting the effects of OCOs. The "Five D's" framework's main contribution lies in its bringing all aspects of a strategic response into one framework, and pointing the way towards OCO mitigations. It enables a formulation of plans and implementation of measures *before* any OCOs occur. This paper reported on research carried out to answer the three research questions laid out in the introduction.

To answer **RQ1**, we identified and tested the influence of a number of factors that could play a role in triggering a robust response to an OCO. We discovered that diplomacy did not appear in reported responses to OCOs.

We then proceeded to advance a number of suggestions for managing the OCO threats. In addressing **RQ2**, only cyber diplomacy appears to satisfy all of Brantly's [8] dimensions.

Finally, to address **RQ3**, we propose a "Five D's" framework for a strategic response to managing the OCO threat. The framework is grounded in the research literature, and highlights the emerging and crucial role of cyber diplomacy in this space.

The factors we tested to answer RQ1 need to be augmented to provide a more comprehensive view of response influences. We hope that other researchers will help us to refine and improve the framework presented in Fig. 3 so that it can bécome a useful resource for governments wanting to manage OCO threats to their own citizenry.

As future work, it would be worth investigating the impact of geopolitical factors on the cyber aggression realm, and especially the interplay of physical geography, pre-existing alliances and/or disputes due to physical proximity and emerging cyber capabilities. This investigation would seek to reveal the influence of physical proximity on cyber activities and aggressions. However, it must be acknowledged that the interconnectiveness of the world currently, might make geographical location less of an influential factor than it might have been two decades ago.

7   Limitations

As acknowledged in Sect. 3.4, our empirical investigation is USA centric, which means that we cannot easily generalise our findings. It is challenging to obtain better data sets but when these are published, we plan to run our analysis again on the more comprehensive data set to determine which factors significantly influence responses to OCOs.

References

1. Attatfa, A., Renaud, K., De Paoli, S.: Cyber diplomacy: a systematic literature review. Procedia Comput. Sci. **176**, 60–69 (2020)
2. Baldwin, D.A.: Power and International Relations: A Conceptual Approach. In: Walter Carlsnaes, T.R., Simmons, B.A. (eds.) Handbook of International Relations. Princeton University Press, Princeton (2016)
3. Baram, G., Sommer, U.: Covert or not covert: national strategies during cyber conflict. In: 11th International Conference on Cyber Conflict (CyCon), vol. 900, pp. 1–16. IEEE (2019)
4. Barker, I.: Nation state attacks increase 100 percent in three years (2021). https://betanews.com/2021/04/08/nation-state-attacks-increase/
5. Barrinha, A., Renard, T.: Power and diplomacy in the post-liberal cyberspace. Int. Aff. **96**(3), 749–766 (2020)
6. Bayer, R.: Diplomatic Exchange Data set, v2006.1. (2006). https://correlatesofwar.org/data-sets/diplomatic-exchange
7. BBC: Cyber-attack: US and UK blame North Korea for WannaCry (2017). Accessed 1 May 2021. https://www.bbc.co.uk/news/world-us-canada-42407488
8. Brantly, A.F.: The cyber deterrence problem. In: 10th International Conference on Cyber Conflict (CyCon), pp. 31–54. IEEE (2018)
9. Brown, G.D.: Why Iran won't admit Stuxnet was an attack. Joint Force Quart. **63**(4), 70–73 (2011)
10. Carlin, J.P.: Detect, disrupt, deter: a whole-of-government approach to national security cyber threats. Harv. Nat'l Sec. J. **7**, 391 (2015)
11. Carpenter, P.: Cybersecurity and nation-state threats: what businesses need to know (2021). https://www.forbes.com/sites/forbesbusinesscouncil/2021/04/16/cybersecurity-and-nation-state-threats-what-businesses-need-to-know/?sh=18d005817c21
12. Cavelty, M.D., Egloff, F.J.: Hyper-securitization, everyday security practice and technification: cyber-security logics in Switzerland. Swiss Polit. Sci. Rev. **27**(1), 139–149 (2021)
13. cipher: Which Country is #1 in Cybersecurity? (2021). Accessed 10 July 2021. https://cipher.com/blog/which-country-is-1-in-cybersecurity/
14. CISCO: cyber diplomacy in the European union (2017). Accessed 2 May 2021. https://www.cisco.com/c/dam/m/en_ca/business-transformation/pdf/5-ways-to-detect-a-cyber-attack.pdf
15. Clare, J.: The deterrent value of democratic allies. Int. Stud. Quart. **57**(3), 545–555 (2013)
16. Cluley, G.: Us offers $10 million reward in hunt for state-sponsored ransomware attackers (2021). Accessed 17 Jul 2021. https://www.tripwire.com/state-of-security/security-data-protection/us-offers-10-million-reward-in-hunt-for-state-sponsored-ransomware-attackers/

17. Cohen, M., Freilich, C., Siboni, G.: Four Big "Ds" and a Little "r": a new model for cyber defense. Cyber Intell. Secur. **1**(2), 21–36 (2017)

18. Coppinger, D.S.: Aggression in Cyberspace: Framing an Operational Response. Technical Report, Naval War Coll Newport RI Joint Military Operations Department (2010)

19. Cuthbertson, A.: Yahoo data breach is 'Most Audacious Hack of All Time' (2016). Accessed 30 Apr 2021. https://uk.news.yahoo.com/yahoo-data-breach-most-audacious-163029811.html

20. Department of Global Communications: 5 ways the UN is fighting 'infodemic' of misinformation (2020). Accessed 2 May 2021. https://www.un.org/en/department-global-communications/

21. Earle, P.C.: Lockdowns have killed what's left of the united nations' credibility (2020). Accessed 30 Apr 2021. https://www.aier.org/article/lockdowns-have-killed-whats-left-of-the-united-nations-credibility/

22. Fayi, S.Y.A.: What Petya/NotPetya ransomware is and what its remidiations are. In: Latifi, S. (ed.) Information Technology - New Generations. AISC, vol. 738, pp. 93–100. Springer, Cham (2018). https://doi.org/10.1007/978-3-319-77028-4_15

23. Fitzpatrick, D.: Evolution and chaos in property right systems: the third world tragedy of contested access. Yale LJ **115**, 996–1048 (2005)

24. GOV.UK: Implementing norms in cyberspace (2020). Accessed 30 Apr 2021. https://www.gov.uk/government/publications/implementing-norms-in-cyberspace

25. Hald, S.L., Pedersen, J.M.: An updated taxonomy for characterizing hackers according to their threat properties. In: 2012 14th International Conference on Advanced Communication Technology (ICACT), pp. 81–86. IEEE (2012)

26. Hanhimäki, J.M.: The United Nations: A very Short Introduction. Oxford University Press, Great Britain (2015)

27. Hollis, D.B.: Why states need an international law for information operations. Lewis Clark L. Rev. **11**, 1023–1061 (2007)

28. Hunton privacy blog: white house to nominate first national cyber director (2021). Accessed 18 Jul 2021. https://www.huntonprivacyblog.com/2021/04/14/white-house-to-nominate-first-national-cyber-director/

29. ID agent: 10 facts about nation-state cyberattacks that will keep you up at night (2020). https://www.idagent.com/blog/10-facts-about-nation-state-cyberattacks-that-will-keep-you-up-at-night/

30. Jacobsen, J.T.: En "digital Genèvekonvention" er ikke i Danmarks interesse. Internasjonal Politikk **76**(2), 73–88 (2018)

31. Jensen, L.: Maritime cyber security: it's all about the money (2021). Accessed 1 May 2021. https://improsec.com/cyber-blog/maritime-cyber-security-its-all-about-the-money

32. Jervis, R.: The cuban missile crisis: what we know, how did it start, and how did it end. In: Scott, L., Hughes, R.G. (eds.) The Cuban Missile Crisis: A Critical Reappraisal (Cold War History). Taylor & Francis, Oxon (2018)

33. Kanuck, S.: Sovereign discourse on cyber conflict under international law. TEx. L. REv. **88**, 1571–1597 (2009)

34. Kello, L.: The meaning of the cyber revolution: perils to theory and statecraft. Int. Secur. **38**(2), 7–40 (2013)

35. Kostadinov, D.: The attribution problem in cyber attacks (2013). Accessed 30 Apr 2021. https://resources.infosecinstitute.com/topic/attribution-problem-in-cyber-attacks/

36. Lakshmanan, R.: Here's how solarwinds hackers stayed undetected for long enough (2021). Accessed 30 Apr 2021. https://thehackernews.com/2021/01/heres-how-solarwinds-hackers-stayed.html
37. Lee, E.: More dependence on internet leads to more cyberattacks worldwide (2017), vOA News. Accessed 8 May 2021. https://www.voanews.com/silicon-valley-technology/more-dependence-internet-leads-more-cyberattacks-worldwide
38. Levinson, M.: Why law enforcement can't stop hackers (2011). Accessed 1 May 2021. https://www.cio.com/article/2402264/why-law-enforcement-can-t-stop-hackers.html
39. Lin, H.S.: Offensive cyber operations and the use of force. J. Nat'l Sec. L. Pol'y **4**, 63–86 (2010)
40. Lustik, L.: Can the UN prevent cyber-attacks? (2018). Accessed 1 May 2021. https://thenewcontext.org/can-the-un-prevent-cyber-attacks/
41. Maness, R.C., Valeriano, B.: The impact of cyber conflict on international interactions. Armed Forces Soc. **42**(2), 301–323 (2016)
42. Moret, E., Pawlak, P.: The EU cyber diplomacy toolbox: towards a cyber sanctions regime? (2017). European Union Institute for Security Studies (EUISS). Accessed 8 May 2021. https://www.iss.europa.eu/sites/default/files/EUISSFiles/Brief24Cybersanctions.pdf
43. Murray, G.R., et al.: Toward creating a new research tool: Operationally defining cyberterrorism (2019), oSF Preprints
44. Newbill, C.M.: Defining critical infrastructure for a global application. Ind. J. Global Legal Stud. **26**, 761–780 (2019)
45. Newman, L.H.: How an accidental 'Kill Switch' Slowed Friday's massive ransomware attack (2017). Accessed 1 May 2021. https://www.wired.com/2017/05/accidental-kill-switch-slowed-fridays-massive-ransomware-attack/
46. Nye, J.S., Jr.: Deterrence and dissuasion in cyberspace. Int. Secur. **41**(3), 44–71 (2016)
47. Office of the director of national intelligence: NCSC director warns of nation-state cyber threats to law firms in June 4 remarks at ILTA LegalSEC summit 2019 (2019). https://www.dni.gov/index.php/ncsc-newsroom/item/2002-ncsc-director-warns-of-nation-state-cyber-threats-to-law-firms-in-june-4-remarks-at-ilta-legalsec-summit-2019
48. Office of the director of national intelligence: cyber threat framework (undated). https://www.odni.gov/index.php/cyber-threat-framework
49. O'Flaherty, K.: U.S. government confirms plan to defend 2020 election against cyberattacks (2019). https://www.forbes.com/sites/kateoflahertyuk/2019/08/28/us-government-plan-to-halt-election-cyberattacks-misses-one-major-issue/?sh=7c1017de2041
50. Oved, M.C.: Journalist's phone hacked by new 'invisible' technique: all he had to do was visit one website. Any website. (2021). https://www.thestar.com/news/canada/2020/06/21/journalists-phone-hacked-by-new-invisible-technique-all-he-had-to-do-was-visit-one-website-any-website.html
51. O'Connell, M.E.: Cyber security without cyber war. J. Confl. Secur. Law **17**(2), 187–209 (2012)
52. Pomerleau, M.: State vs. non-state hackers: different tactics, equal threat? (2015). https://defensesystems.com/articles/2015/08/17/cyber-state-vs-non-state-haclers-tactics.aspx
53. Presidency: European union: cyber diplomacy in the European union (2019). Accessed 2 May 2021. https://eucyberdirect.eu/wp-content/uploads/2019/12/cd_booklet-final.pdf

54. Rankin, D.J., Bargum, K., Kokko, H.: The tragedy of the commons in evolutionary biology. Trends Ecol. Evol. **22**(12), 643–651 (2007)

55. Renaud, K., Orgeron, C., Warkentin, M., French, P.E.: Cyber security responsibilization: an evaluation of the intervention approaches adopted by the five eyes countries and China. Public Adm. Rev. **80**(4), 577–589 (2020)

56. Rid, T., Buchanan, B.: Attributing cyber attacks. J. Strat. Stud. **38**(1–2), 4–37 (2015)

57. Rosenzweig, P.: Cyber warfare: how conflicts in cyberspace are challenging America and changing the world. ABC-CLIO (2013)

58. Schmitt, M.N. (ed.): Tallinn Manual 2.0 on the International Law Applicable to Cyber Operations. Cambridge University Press, Cambridge (2017)

59. Shackelford, S.J., Andres, R.B.: State responsibility for cyber attacks: competing standards for a growing problem. Geo. J. Int'l L. **42**, 971 (2010)

60. Sharma, U., Sharma, S.K.: Principles And Theory In Political Science Vol# 1. Atlantic Publishers & Dist, New Delhi (2000)

61. Sigholm, J., Larsson, E.: Determining the utility of cyber vulnerability implantation: The heartbleed bug as a cyber operation. In: 2014 IEEE Military Communications Conference, pp. 110–116. IEEE (2014)

62. Silver, L.: U.S. is seen as a top ally in many countries - but others view it as a threat (2019). Accessed 30 April 2021. https://www.pewresearch.org/fact-tank/2019/12/05/u-s-is-seen-as-a-top-ally-in-many-countries-but-others-view-it-as-a-threat/

63. Singer, E.O.: From reproductive rights to responsibilization: fashioning liberal subjects in Mexico City's new public sector abortion program. Med. Anthropol. Quart. **31**(4), 445–463 (2017)

64. Smith, B.: Keynote address at the RSA conference: the need for a digital Geneva convention (2017), president and Chief Legal Officer, Microsoft

65. Starks, T.: US blames China for Microsoft hacking, ransomware attacks as part of global condemnation (2021). Accessed 19 Jul 2021. https://www.cyberscoop.com/china-microsoft-exchange-server-indictments-us-allies/

66. Terry, P.C.: Don't do as I do-The US response to Russian and Chinese cyber espionage and public international law. German Law J. **19**(3), 613–626 (2018)

67. The associated press: US, Estonia partnered to search out cyber threat from Russia (2020). Accessed 2 May 2021. https://www.usnews.com/news/politics/articles/2020-12-03/us-estonia-partnered-to-search-out-cyber-threat-from-russia

68. Tidy, J.: Solarwinds: Why the sunburst hack is so serious (2020). Accessed 31 Dec 2020. https://www.bbc.com/news/technology-55321643

69. Torres, M., Riordan, S.: Policy brief: the cyber diplomacy of constructing norms in cyberspace (2020). Accessed 30 Apr 2021. https://www.ieeiweb.eu/wp-content/uploads/2020/10/T20_TF5_PB4_ok.pdf

70. Tsagourias, N.: Cyber attacks, self-defence and the problem of attribution. J. Conflict Secur. Law **17**(2), 229–244 (2012)

71. United nations: telling the UN story in many languages, powered across platforms. (undated). Accessed 30 April 2021. https://www.un.org/en/department-global-communications/

72. Valeriano, B., Jensen, B.M., Maness, R.C.: Cyber strategy: The Evolving Character of Power and Coercion. Oxford University Press, New York (2018)

73. Valeriano, B., Maness, R.C.: The dynamics of cyber conflict between rival antagonists, 2001–11. J. Peace Res. **51**(3), 347–360 (2014)

74. Vavra, S.: NSA warns defense contractors to double check connections in light of Russian hacking (2021). Accessed 30 April 2021. https://www.cyberscoop.

com/nsa-warns-defense-contractors-operational-technology-connections-russia-solarwinds/

75. Vercellone, C.: Ukraine is getting more help to build cyber capabilities (2020). Accessed 3 May 2021. https://www.fifthdomain.com/international/2020/03/04/ukraine-is-getting-more-help-to-build-cyber-capabilities/

76. Walljasper, J.: Elinor Ostrom's 8 principles for managing a commons (2011). Accessed 22 Apr 2021. http://www.onthecommons.org/magazine/elinor-ostroms-8-principles-managing-commmons

77. Waltz, K.N.: Theory of International Politics. Reading, Mass.: Addison-Wesley Pub. Co., Boston (1979)

SOK: Evaluating Privacy and Security Vulnerabilities of Patients' Data in Healthcare

Faiza Tazi[1] , Josiah Dykstra[2] , Prashanth Rajivan[3] ,
and Sanchari Das[1(✉)]

[1] University of Denver, Denver, CO 80208, USA
{Faiza.Tazi,sandas}@du.edu
[2] Designer Security, LLC., Severn, MD 21144, USA
josiah@designersecurity.com
[3] University of Washington, Seattle, WA, USA
prajivan@uw.edu

Abstract. Interactions in healthcare systems, by necessity, involve sharing sensitive information that must be protected. Thus, to understand the existing privacy and security research conducted in the context of healthcare organizations, we conducted a systematic literature review of $N = 205$ papers that examine the security and privacy of patient data . . We found that current research focuses heavily on the technological solutions, which are presented to benefit large-scale medical facilities such as hospitals, but generally ignore the unique security challenges of smaller private practices which might not have the resources to protect patient data. Additionally, only 18 ($<9\%$) papers have conducted user studies to understand the patient and staff's risk perception of healthcare data. We conclude by identifying research gaps and provide potential solutions to enable robust data security for sensitive patient data.

Keywords: Literature review · Healthcare Data Privacy and Security

1 Introduction

With increased digitization in the healthcare sector, privacy risks and security concerns about data storage, access, and transfer among healthcare providers and patients have subsequently increased as well [55,174]. Thus, information security has become an ongoing challenge in the healthcare sector with critical data breaches exposing sensitive records of millions of patients [10]. One such major data breach occurred in 2015 when a phishing scam exploited the credentials of five employees at *Anthem*, a health insurance organization, compromising the Personally Identifiable Information (PII) of 80 million individuals [194]. Data breaches in healthcare could occur for a variety of reasons, including a lack of employee awareness about data security, technological shortcomings, and the dearth of technological implementations [53]. Despite the proliferation of data security focused research in the community, the field lacks a comprehensive

© Springer Nature Switzerland AG 2022
S. Parkin and L. Viganò (Eds.): STAST 2021, LNCS 13176, pp. 153–181, 2022.
https://doi.org/10.1007/978-3-031-10183-0_8

synthesis and analysis of the body of healthcare privacy and security research especially from the user[1] perspective [14].

Towards this, we conducted a systematic literature review to provide a holistic overview and a basis for the research undertaken in this area which has been proven to be helpful in other domains [125]. We collected 2,903 research articles on data security and privacy preservation in healthcare organizations. Thereafter, we did a thematic analysis on a selected set of $N = 205$ papers. From the $N = 205$ papers, we further discuss insights from $n1 = 97$ papers that focused on the technological implementation. Finally, we present an in-depth analysis of $n2 = 18$ papers that are focused on the human (user) factors. We found that the majority of the security research done in healthcare focused on the technologies with a severe lack of focus on understanding and improving the human factor aspect. Furthermore, even among the work focused on technologies, we observed a gap in the research with applications to private practice healthcare organizations. The disparity is noteworthy.

Our contributions through this work are as follows:

- While other Systematizations of Knowledge (SoKs) have been published on specific technologies related to healthcare, ours is among the first to perform a systematic approach for structuring existing knowledge on security and privacy in healthcare organizations.
- In this SoK we make a holistic observation on security and privacy in healthcare and point out gaps that remain to protect patients' health data.
- To the best of our knowledge, our SoK is the first paper to focus on an overview of privacy and security research of patient data from a human perspective.

Our study concludes that the technological solutions are outpacing the foundational analysis of the ways the healthcare workforce is using and defending patient data today. Moreover, the existing research focuses on a narrow scope of medical settings which neglects the large population of patients and healthcare workers engaged in private healthcare practices.

2   Method

Our systematic literature review includes a corpus of 205 papers published till February 14, 2021, collected from different digital libraries. The literature review comprised of six steps: (i) database search, (ii) title screening, (iii) abstract screening, (iv) full-text screening, (v) data extraction, and (vi) thematic analysis. *Inclusion Criteria*: Papers were included if they were: (1) Published in a peer-reviewed publication including journals and conferences; (2) Written and available in English; and (3) Focused on the security and privacy of data in healthcare organizations. We contacted publication venues and authors to obtain papers that were not available for public access, and obtained all the papers in our list.

---

[1] Throughout this work, we will refer to all individuals with access and responsibility for protecting healthcare data, including patients and healthcare workers, as *users*.

Exclusion Criteria: Papers were excluded if: (1) Papers were presented as a work-in-progress (posters, extended abstracts, etc.); (2) The content analysis showed that the research was not directly related to patient/consumer health-related data security and/or privacy in healthcare organizations; and (3) The collected articles were part of patents or book chapters.

Figure 1 details all the steps carried out throughout this analysis.

Search	N= 2903	Database Search: ACM DL, Google Scholar, SSRN, ScienceDirect, IEEE Xplore, PubMed
Screening	N=352	Title Screening (Google Scholar)
	N=280	Duplicate Removal
	N=231	Quality Screening (Removal of work in progress)
Analysis	N = 205	Abstract and Full-text Screening
	n1 = 97	Technical Solutions
	n2= 18	User Studies

Fig. 1. A snapshot of the data collection, screening, and analysis methodology along with the number of papers screened in each stage of the literature review.

2.1   Database and Keyword-Based Search

We conducted our search by exploring seven digital technology and medical databases: ACM DL, Google Scholar, SSRN, ScienceDirect, IEEE Xplore, PubMed, and MEDLINE. We specifically searched healthcare-focused journals in MEDLINE but were not able to find any relevant papers based on our topic of research, so we removed it from our database list. Our selection process was based on an iterative evaluation. We started by defining appropriate keywords for our subject matter. This was followed by filtering the results to meet our requirements. Subsequently, a systematic analysis was conducted on the final collection of research articles. This procedure was adapted from prior literature reviews by Stowell et al. [185], Das et al. [51,52], and other related works [123,127,139].

After the initial search to obtain the keywords we collected the papers through a keyword-based search as mentioned above, using the Publish or Perish[2] software for retrieving articles from Google Scholar. Thereafter, we

---

[2] https://harzing.com/resources/publish-or-perish.

explored individual digital libraries to collect papers relevant to this research. Boolean search strings were developed for searching databases including up to 88 AND/OR operators and 17 NOT operators across the following keyword terms: *Healthcare Data Security, Healthcare Data Breach, Healthcare Data Theft, Medical Data Theft, Medical Data Security, Medical Data Breach, Patient Data Security, Patient Data Theft, and Patient Data Breach.* Our initial database and keyword-based search resulted in a total of 2903 papers.

2.2 Title Screening: Google Scholar

We noticed that every other digital library except Google Scholar has a limited number of papers. Thus, we avoided title-based screening for these digital libraries. We conducted a title-based search with the above-mentioned keywords in Google Scholar. We also removed any patents or citation options from Google Scholar. In the title-based search we looked for the keywords in the title itself to emphasize on the relevance, resulting in a total of 352 papers.

2.3 Duplicate and Work-in-Progress Removal

In the next phase, we conducted the step of duplicate removal. We removed 72 duplicate articles, which left us with 280 papers. We also removed any papers which were a work in progress such as posters, extended abstracts, etc. We screened out self-identified work-in-progress papers or reviewed the paper to see if the papers were works-in-progress. Due to the varying nature of publication of these works we could not demarcate the papers based on their page numbers with an assumption that work-in-progress papers are short. However, we removed any papers which were shorter than four pages. After this procedure, we were left with a data set of 231 papers.

2.4 Abstract and Full-Text Screening

Each individual research paper was assessed to determine its relevance to the topic of our research by reviewing the abstract and full-text. To do this, two researchers trained in qualitative coding determined the relevance of the individual papers to the research by analyzing the abstract and full-text. If there were any discrepancies with determining the relevance to the research then a third researcher was introduced to resolve the issue. Thus, 26 papers were excluded in this phase. After this screening, there remained a total of $N = 205$ papers on which we conducted our detailed thematic analysis [51].

2.5 Analysis

Our final set of data included a total of $N = 205$ papers on which we conducted detailed analysis in two parts. First, a thematic analysis was conducted to evaluate specific aspects of the papers including technical applications and policies. Thereafter, a detailed analysis of the user studies was conducted to understand more about the user issues as per the goal of this work.

Table 1. Distribution of the number of papers based on the thematic analysis

Themes	No. of papers
Technological solutions	97 (47.32%)
Healthcare frameworks	34 (16.58%)
User studies	18 (8.78%)
Data storage & Management	18 (8.78%)
Overviews	16 (7.80%)
Ethical and legal implications	10 (4.89%)
Case studies - Data breaches	6 (2.93%)
Systematic literature reviews	6 (2.93%)

Thematic Analysis: To perform a thematic analysis, we reviewed the abstract, methods, results, discussion, and conclusion of the 205 collected papers obtained from full-text screening. Two researchers evaluated this collection of papers by first reviewing 20 randomly selected papers to generate the codebook. The codebook consisted of 119 open codes which were themed into eight overarching themes including: technological solutions proposed, evaluation of current model with privacy frameworks, systematic literature reviews, evaluation of patient data focusing on the big data storage and management, ethical and legal implications of research, author notes and overview of the current healthcare practices to protect user data, case studies on particular incidents occurred as in data breaches, and finally the user studies.

Table 1 shows the distribution of the papers as per the categorization of all of the 205 papers. This can be further examined in Fig. 2. Any paper that included any form of user study, even if that was not the paper's primary theme, was marked in the user study category. This was specified given the user-focused aspect of the paper. After conducting the first set of analysis, we performed another set of thematic analysis to categorize the papers which studied technological solutions to address healthcare privacy and security challenges. Given the large number of technical solution-focused papers, we have detailed them in Table 2 to explore more on what type of technical solutions were proposed by the prior works.

User Study Analysis: After the two phases of thematic analysis, we conducted a detailed user study analysis where we focused on the $n2 = 18$ user studies. We extracted the quantitative and qualitative findings to assess what user and technical perspectives of the healthcare-focused research was conducted by the prior studies. We have provided details of both the technical solutions analyzed in this work and the user studies in the following section.

Out of the 18 user-focused studies, four were qualitative [1,24,48,99], 12 were quantitative [23,36,43,49,69,71,80,140,143,162,170,177], and two were mixed-methods studies [28,133]. The quantitative studies included works which imple-

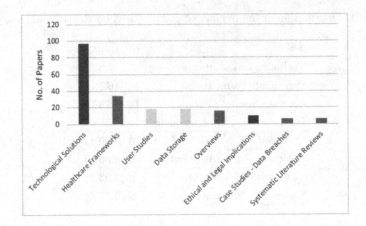

Fig. 2. A snapshot of the themes discussed throughout the analysis

mented nine survey-based studies [23, 49, 69, 71, 80, 143, 162, 170, 177], one cross-sectional studies [36], one in-lab simulation-based study [43], and one randomized control experiment [140]. For qualitative studies, they included three interview-based studies [1, 24, 48] and one field-based research [99]. In the qualitative study, Baker et al. also performed observation evaluations on their studied participants for the interview [24]. For mixed methods, there were two studies, where one study which had a combination of online survey and did content analysis [133], the second study did a semi-structured interview with 16 care managers at 12 health centers in three states participated [28].

3   Findings and Discussions

As described earlier, we first started with the thematic analysis of the collected papers where we found eight overarching themes. Thereafter, we detailed the technical solutions provided by the papers, and finally performed a detailed literature analysis on the small subset of user studies identified. In this section, we will first provide details of the thematic analysis and thereafter, we will provide details and evaluation of the user studies.

3.1   Thematic Analysis

For each of the 205 papers, we collected details about the methods, results, analysis, discussion, and implications. Thereafter, we analyzed the data collected, and categorized them into eight themes as shown in Table 1. For this we particularly looked into the methods, results, and discussions of the mentioned papers. We then performed a detailed analysis on the technical solutions and the user studies, which will be discussed in the later subsections.

Technical Solutions Discussed: Nearly half of the collection, $n1 = 97$ (47.32%) out of $N = 205$ papers, focused on proposing a technology-based solution for the privacy and security issues of the healthcare sector. To understand further, we classified the technical solutions proposed by the authors. Table 2 as well as Fig. 3 show the distribution of the papers based on the several types of technological solutions proposed by the authors to enhance the privacy and security of the data transferred and accessed in the healthcare sector. Many of the papers use a combination of the technical solutions, for example using cryptography for authentication or using encryption to do image processing. However, here we used mutually exclusive codes to focus on the primary solution proposed by the paper after going through the full-text.

Table 2. Distribution of the papers providing technical solutions out of the $n1 = 97$ papers which proposed privacy and security solutions of the healthcare organization

Themes	No. of papers
Data encryption	32 (32.99%)
Blockchain	12 (12.37%)
Image protection	12 (12.37%)
Watermarking	8 (8.25%)
Access control and Authentication	7 (7.22%)
Mathematical modelling	5 (5.15%)
Network-based solutions	5 (5.15%)
Artificial intelligence and Machine learning	4 (4.12%)
Web-based solution	4 (4.12%)
Cloud-based technologies	4 (4.12%)
Edge computing	3 (3.1%)
Treatment continuity	1 (1.03%)

Data Encryption: Out of the $n1 = 97$ technology-focused papers, nearly half of the papers discussed the encryption techniques to protect the data. A total of 32.99% of the papers discussed how patient data can be encrypted and anonymized for robust security of health-related data [6,16,17,25,29–31,42,57, 86,92,96,103,120,147,153,159,161,166,167,188,189,195,197,201,209–211]. For example, Sudha and Ganesan while discussing the lack of security of Electronic Medical Records (EMR) propose a Pervasive Mobile Healthcare where multimedia medical record are protected using an Elliptical Curve Cryptography algorithm [186]. Gupta and Metha discuss the importance of transmission of medical data over unsecured networks, and propose a chaos-based encryption scheme to secure medical images [76].

Blockchain: Another important focus on the technological solution found in our collected sample was on blockchain technology [8,13,33,38,50,72,75,112,

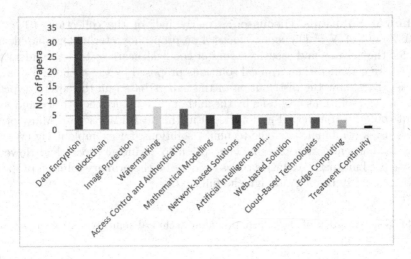

Fig. 3. A snapshot of different technology based solutions for healthcare data privacy and security

149, 154, 155, 181]. These papers explore the peer-to-peer network topology of the blockchain, which implements a distributed ledger technology focusing on the transparency of the network [141]. For example, Brunese et al. propose a blockchain-based technology aimed to protect information exchanges in hospital networks, with particular regard to magnetic resonance images by implementing formal equivalence checking to validate the network of the transiting data [38].

Image Protection: As discussed previously, there are papers which discussed how encryption and blockchain can be used to protect medical data in the form of images. However, we found 12 papers which explored the different technical implementations to specifically protect medical images [18, 21, 27, 40, 42, 62, 97, 102, 114, 171, 173, 182]. For example, Kumar et al. propose embedding patient information into a medical image through data hiding to improve security and confidentiality for diffusion of medical information system [114]. Their proposal was interesting and effective as they not only discussed embedding the text into images, but also the importance of protecting these images.

Watermarking: A particular aspect of image protection was digital watermarking. There were eight papers which focused on the watermarking aspect of medical image protection [22, 65, 66, 98, 137, 165, 182, 200]. Vidya and Padmaja focused on enhancing the security of Electronic Patient Record (EPR) data which enable tele-diagnosis. They propose watermarking by embedding EPR into the facial photograph of the patient and discussed implementing a Photoplethysmography signal from the forefinger tip of the patient for authentication which had a success rate of 98% against security breaches [200].

Access Control and Authentication: Seven papers focused on making the security protocols of the healthcare system robust by addressing the access control and authentication particularly [20, 73, 73, 85, 105, 157, 172]. Izza et al. focused on

Internet of Things-based E-healthcare and radio frequency identification (RFID) authentication scheme for Wireless Body Area Network (WBANs). In their protocol, which they mention to be effective against digital threats implements elliptic curve digital signature with message recovery [85].

Mathematical Modeling: We found that five of the collected papers utilized statistical and other mathematical models to provide solutions to the security threats of the healthcare organization [44, 121, 122, 124, 192]. Chaudhury et al. discusses the Supervisory Control And Data Acquisition (SCADA) systems used for medical data transfer and how Impulsive Statistical Fingerprinting (ISF) can be implemented to substantiate the conversion of sensitive health data through the ISF into a secure Health Level 7 (HL7) format [44].

Network-based Solutions: Five (5.15%) of the papers discussed network-based solutions to resolve the privacy and security complexities of healthcare systems [26, 88, 106, 206, 213]. For example, Wang et al. details the WBAN and introduces the key technologies and characteristics of wireless sensor networks emphasizing node localization. They emphasize the importance of network localization algorithms and performance evaluation indicators on wearable 3D node localization algorithms to protect healthcare data of the patients [206].

AI and ML-based Solutions: Out of $n1 = 97$ papers we found that four (4.12%) papers discussed artificial intelligence and machine learning-based solution to address the privacy and security issues of the healthcare sector [45, 95, 156, 183]. PraveenKumar proposes health and temperature sensors to monitor the patient health data that gets transmitted to a microcontroller. The real time data is then monitored and analyzed using k-means clustering and can guide both patient and doctor knowledge [156].

Web-based Solutions: Web-based solutions were proposed in four papers in our collection, where any form of web-based technical solutions to improve privacy and security of the sensitive data of the patients was discussed [19, 117, 191, 207]. Tian et al. looked into clinical prognosis prediction models based on electronic health record data and developed a web service based on multi-center clinical data called POPCORN. The PrognOsis Prediction based on multi-center clinical data CollabORatioN (POPCORN) focused on the standardization of clinical data expression, the preservation of patient privacy during model training using a multivariable meta-analysis, and a Bayesian framework [191].

Cloud-based Solutions: Four out of 205 papers discussed cloud-based solutions to address the privacy and security issues of patient data protection [12, 58, 101, 134]. Khan et al. presents a secure cloud-based mobile healthcare framework using WBANs where the framework tries to secure the inter-sensor communication by multi-biometric-based key generation scheme [101].

Edge Computing-based Solutions: Several prior papers have discussed edge computing, but we found three papers which focused on edge-computing-based solutions [7, 9, 119]. Edge computing is a distributed, open IT architecture that features decentralised processing by the device itself or by a local computer or server, rather than being transmitted to a data center [175].

Treatment Continuity: An interesting paper by Zhang et al. [214] pointed out a scary aftermath of cybersecurity breaches, which is pausing or preventing continuous treatment of patients suffering from critical ailments. Their proposed solution to address this focuses on automatic retrieval of essential information from the clinical radiation oncology information systems for each under-treatment patient periodically and providing backup through secondary data servers in the event of an attack to one of the servers [214].

Healthcare Frameworks: Of the 205 papers collected, 34 (16.58%) papers studied or introduced new healthcare data management frameworks. A paper was considered under the theme of healthcare frameworks if the main subject of its study is a security, privacy, or design frameworks [5, 11, 15, 35, 37, 39, 60, 67, 70, 83, 84, 90, 110, 113, 115, 116, 118, 126, 128, 132, 135, 145, 150, 152, 160, 164, 178, 180, 198, 208]. These papers particularly describe methods to design a secure and private technology for healthcare data usage. One such paper "A Security Framework for Mobile Health Applications" introduced a security framework for healthcare mobile applications, taking usability and security into consideration [190]. Ibrahim et al. introduced a framework for securely sharing electronic health records over the cloud between different healthcare providers. This framework ensures the confidentiality, integrity, authenticity, availability, and auditability of the electronic health records [82].

Data Storage and Management: Papers were classified as data storage and management if the research done was related to healthcare data access, manipulation, or the different technologies allowing for medical data storage. We found 18 (8.78%) such papers in our corpus [32, 54, 68, 74, 77, 81, 94, 107–109, 129, 138, 151, 163, 168, 179, 202, 205]. In particular, Duque et al. introduce a distributed data management architecture with a focus on the healthcare data security and high performance requirements [54]. On the other hand, Petković was concerned about the reliability of data transmitted through remote patient monitoring systems, since the data is collected by patients with no medical supervision [151]. Petrović addresses this issue by proposing several approaches that minimize the risks and ensure high information reliability.

Overviews: Overview papers include works which consolidate the prior work on healthcare privacy and security by adding details of the current state of privacy and security in the organizations and also adding details of the new technologies implemented. Of the 205 papers, 16 papers (7.80%) discuss or review the healthcare privacy and security domain [2–4, 41, 59, 100, 100, 130, 142, 144, 148, 158, 187, 196, 204]. Of these, Paksuniemi et al. gives an overview of the wireless technologies devices and reveal the importance of implementing security measures in these technologies to enable secure patient monitoring [144]. Moreover, Wang provides an overview of the security threats imposed by smart devices which monitor the patients through internet-connected technologies. Wang details two primary security related issues for Internet-based tele-medicine systems that need to be addressed: (1) medical data protection needs; and (2) system design issues [204].

Ethical and Legal Implications: Of the 205 papers, ten (4.89%) papers studied the ethical and legal ramifications of data leaks occurring due to healthcare data breaches [63, 72, 78, 79, 91, 104, 131, 169, 193, 199]. These papers particularly explore violations in U.S. healthcare standards, including the Health Information Technology for Economic and Clinical Health (HITECH) Act [79] which proposes the meaningful use of interoperable electronic health records throughout the U.S. healthcare delivery system as a critical national goal. Hollis also discusses how beyond medical data secursity, healthcare staff are ethically required to anonymize the data so other staff are unable to uniquely identify a patient through their stored data [78].

Case Studies and Data Breaches: Case studies and data breaches both document real-world outcomes including common violations of security and privacy. Both are insightful to illuminate contemporary issues and research should seek to help develop proactive defenses that decrease the prevalence and impact of incidents and data breaches. We found that six (2.93%) of the 205 corpus papers were case studies and data breaches, classified as such when authors studied a particular organization, data protection practices, or particular incidents of data breaches. Some of these case studies chose different countries for their analysis [34, 46, 61, 136, 176, 212]. The organizations which were studied spanned global geography including India [176], United States [46], Saudi Arabia [34], and Morocco [136].

Yesmin and Carter created an evaluation framework for automated privacy auditing and found that 98.09% of 55,000 accesses of protected health information by staff in a hospital were identified as appropriate and the tool was unable to identify the remaining 1.91% of accesses [212]. Choi et al.'s work estimated changes in health information technology investments by tracking spending by U.S. hospitals between 2012 and 2016. Their results found that health information technology spending increased by 26.0% in one year after a breach [46]. These studies have been critical to understanding the real world but do not mention the stakeholders who were responsible or whose data were breached and how that may impact patients' lives.

Systematic Literature Reviews: Of the 205 papers analyzed, six (2.93%) were systematic literature reviews [47, 87, 89, 93, 146, 203]. These studies gave an overview of the current standards and practices followed in the healthcare sectors while mentioning the importance of the focus on the healthcare privacy and security. However, these studies did not focus or explore the user perspective. For example, Walker et al. implemented a mixed-method systematic review by analyzing about 300, 000 papers and found evidence of high heterogeneity across crude data indicating that the effectiveness of security measures varies significantly in healthcare but concluded without a solution for insiders attack [203].

3.2   Analysis of User Studies

In addition to our analysis of the technical solutions proposed in the collection, we performed a detailed analysis of the user studies ($n = 18$). Our goal was to understand and assess the studies which evaluated user perception towards the privacy and security of their healthcare-related data. We performed a thorough analysis of the user studies and analyzed certain aspects of the study such as type of study conducted, study populations, duration, and medical settings.

Table 3. % of and number of studies in settings with various population densities along with details about the user study durations.

	Qual studies (n = 4)	Quant studies (n = 12)	Mixed-Methods (n = 2)
Population			
Urban	25% (1)	41.67% (5)	0% (0)
Suburban	0% (0)	0% (0)	0% (0)
Rural	25% (1)	0% (0)	0% (0)
Mixed	0% (0)	8.33% (1)	50% (1)
Other	0% (0)	0% (0)	0% (0)
Not reported	50% (2)	50% (6)	50% (1)
Study population setting			
Healthcare Providers	75% (3)	33.33% (4)	100% (2)
Healthcare Students	0% (0)	25% (3)	0% (0)
Patients	0% (0)	8.33% (1)	0% (0)
Mixed	25% (1)	16.66% (2)	0% (0)
General Population	0% (0)	16.66% (2)	0% (0)
Study location			
USA	25% (1)	16.66% (2)	50% (1)
Europe	25% (1)	25% (3)	50% (1)
Europe and USA	0% (0)	8.33% (1)	0% (0)
Asia	0% (0)	25% (3)	0% (0)
Middle East	25% (1)	8.33% (1)	0% (0)
Nigeria	25% (1)	8.33% (1)	0% (0)
Turkey	0% (0)	8.33% (1)	0% (0)

Study Method: Of the 18 user studies in our corpus, 66.66% (12) were quantitative studies. From the quantitative perspective, 50% (9) were surveys [23, 49, 69, 71, 80, 143, 162, 170, 177], 5.56% (1) quantitative descriptive study [36], 5.56% (1) simulation-based study for a quantitative sample [43], 5.56% (1) randomized controlled trials [140]. Of other studies, 11.1% (2) were mixed-methods survey [28, 133] with open-ended questions with a smaller population sample, 5.56% (1) field study [99], and 16.66% (3) qualitative interview-based studies [1, 24, 48]. Among the 18 user studies, only one assessed a proposed technological intervention. This evaluation involved the efficiency and convenience of a mobile app for managing diabetes [1]. Participants noted that one advantage of it was compliance with hospital regulations for patient data security.

Study Duration: For the majority of the studies, the time taken for the completion of the study primarily occurred in a single session (Table 3) [23, 49, 69, 71, 133, 143, 170, 177]. However, an evaluation of a diabetes management app occurred over 12 weeks [1], the randomized controlled trial of telehealth occurred over a 12 month period [140]. Also, a survey of public perception mobile phones' effect on healthcare was repeated in 2013 and 2014 [162], and a field study in Nigeria was conducted over four weeks [99]. Such longitudinal studies are particularly important to understand users' privacy and security perspective and how user perspectives can change (or do not change) over time.

Population Distribution: As shown in Table 3, many of the 18 papers did not report population distribution of the participants (44.44%, 8) [23, 28, 49, 69, 99, 143, 177]. Most of the remainder studies were conducted in urban settings (37.5%, 6) [1, 36, 43, 80, 140, 170], except one (5.56%) which was conducted in a rural setting [24]. No papers reported on suburban population settings.

Study Population Setting: Of nine of the 18 user-focused papers which studied healthcare providers [24, 28, 48, 49, 69, 71, 99, 133, 177], only one studied the patients exclusively [170]. Three papers studied a mixed population of patients and healthcare providers [1, 23, 140]. Mixed method studies focused only on healthcare providers; similarly, 75% of qualitative studies were focused on healthcare providers.

Study Geographical Location: Out of the 18 studies, four were conducted in the USA [24, 28, 140, 162] and five in the European Union [48, 69, 71, 133, 177], and one was conducted in both Europe and USA [49]. One paper that conducted their study with participants in Europe included 30 countries [177] and one included 24 European countries [133]. Only one study was conducted in Turkey [36], two in Africa (both in Nigeria) [23, 99], and two in the Middle East [1, 170]. Three quantitative studies were conducted in Asia specifically India, Malaysia, and Hong Kong [43, 80, 143].

Table 4. % and Number of studies conducted in various healthcare facilities along with the number of study participants for different user studies.

	Qual studies (n = 4)	Quant studies (n = 12)	Mixed-Methods (n = 2)
Studied medical facilities			
Home	0% (0)	16.67% (2)	0% (0)
Hospital	25% (1)	25% (3)	0% (0)
Private practice	25% (1)	0% (0)	0% (0)
Mixed	0% (0)	16.67% (2)	0% (0)
Other medical	50% (2)	41.67% (5)	50% (1)
Not reported	0% (0)	0% (0)	50% (1)
Num participants			
>0, ≤100	75% (3)	0% (0)	50% (1)
>100, ≤500	0% (0)	50% (6)	50% (1)
>500, ≤1000	0% (0)	14.67% (5)	0% (0)
>1000, ≤5000	0% (0)	8.33% (1)	0% (0)
>5000	0% (0)	0% (0)	0% (0)
Not reported	25% (1)	0% (0)	0% (0)

Study Context: Two qualitative studies were conducted in medical settings other than hospitals and private practice [1,99]; one was conducted in private practices [24] and one in three different hospitals [48]. (Table 4). Quantitative studies reported settings including hospitals [69,71,177], medical settings not including hospitals and private practice such as medical schools [36,43,49,80, 143], patients' home environments [162,170], and mixed settings [23,140]. No papers focused on private practice settings. This is again interesting, as privacy and security of medical data is critical irrespective of the setting. Thus, studies focusing on more diverse medical settings are critical.

Number of Participants: One of the 4 qualitative studies did not report the sample size. The most participants reported in one study is 50 participants, the other two studies reported the same number of participants, 14. All the quantitative studies and the mixed method studies reported the sample size. A total of 94 participants were in qualitative studies, 5, 856 (Median=429, IQR=581, Range=50–1242) were in quantitative studies, and 117 (Median=58.5, IQR=42.5, Range=16–101) in mixed studies.

4   Implications

We acknowledge the contribution of these previous works towards enhancing the privacy and security of sensitive patient data. However, we note that more research is needed to fully understand the challenges to healthcare security and privacy.

4.1 Holistic Security Approach

When security or privacy are a secondary goal of the users, research is needed to understand the motivations behind the circumvention of controls. From our analysis of the user studies, we have identified three major themes pertaining to the human factors of information security in healthcare, namely: inconsistent access controls, non-compliant and insecure communication modes, and disruptive update and backup policies. The majority of the past security research involving people in healthcare has focused on understanding how providers may circumvent authentication [184], including the discovery that providers often share login credentials with each other due to inconsistencies in access control policies [24,48].

Access controls and privileges in healthcare are often designed without considering the individual provider's needs or the multitude of tasks conducted by them on a day-to-day basis. Rather, it is often designed in a tiered manner where senior doctors have the most privileges and junior doctors and nurses are assigned limited privileges [24,48,69]. Therefore whenever a provider (e.g., nurse or junior doctor) needs immediate access to a certain system or patient record for providing critical care, but don't have the necessary privileges, credentials are shared, usually by the senior doctors in these settings. This type of credential sharing also occurs when someone needs access at a critical time but has not completed the necessary training [47]. In addition to this, past research also discusses other general, known issues associated with password usage such as using insecure passwords, task interruptions, disabling authentication or keeping machines unlocked for a long periods of time. Access control cards are used to counter these password usage issues, but still do not address the security circumvention issues discussed earlier [177].

The other dominant theme involved secure communication between providers and patients, or lack thereof. Few papers noted that providers often used non-HIPAA compliant messaging software to share test results with the patients and also with each other [1,48]. For example, providers have been known to share images of scan reports with patients using WhatsApp, a popular messaging platform from Facebook. Providers may be placing inappropriate trust on these messaging platforms based on the end-to-end encryption claims made by these platforms. More research is necessary to understand the challenges involving the use of recognized, HIPAA compliant message systems (e.g., American Messaging System or AS) for communicating securely between providers and between providers and patients.

The final theme that emerged from our analysis was regarding the issue of applying security updates and automatic backups. Providers report updates and backups appearing at inappropriate times such as while engaging with patients [48]. More research is necessary to determine the timing of updates that are reasonably quick and non-disruptive to the workflow of the providers.

Unsurprisingly, technologies including encryption, blockchain, cloud, and access controls were popular topics in the research literature. While technology represents an important area for future opportunities and threats in healthcare, they remain distant and disconnected from real-world needs today. Their over-representation in the literature, therefore, overshadows the analysis of security and privacy practices today.

The rollout of any new technology in healthcare is slow given strict legal and compliance constraints. Despite these new technologies, other technical solutions were notably missing that may hold promise for healthcare security and privacy. For example, continuous authentication may aid healthcare workers by using biometrics or hardware tokens to lock and unlock computers when an authorized user is in physical proximity. The user studies of security circumvention suggest that automated security features may be helpful, building on the effectiveness of features such as automated software updates. Additionally, despite the popularity of machine learning solutions in various fields, we were surprised that these solutions were not prominent in our healthcare corpus.

4.2   Focus on Private Practice Healthcare

The studies we analyzed focused heavily on hospitals and other large medical settings despite the fact that those represent a narrow view of all healthcare workplace settings. Hospitals are atypical because they are among the most well-resourced settings for controlling, implementing, and enforcing security and privacy controls. Those resources enable higher than average investment in security and privacy solutions, technical support, and organizational security culture. The problems that manifest in hospitals, and solutions for them, should not be assumed to generalize to other medical settings.

The literature appears to emphasize that improving health is the primary objective in healthcare, with security and privacy among secondary goals. A small businesses may have slimmer margins to apply to those non-primary goals. They need help to prioritize spending and implementation of privacy and security controls and the research community should prioritize the most impactful needs first. In a study of private practice audiology clinics, Dykstra et al. found that expertise, time, and money were reported as the primary limitations of better cybersecurity [56]. While these limitations are not unique to healthcare, they must be more explicitly acknowledged when proposing new security and privacy mitigation measures. For example, one might imagine that a doctor in a single-provider clinic may circumvent a compliant telehealth solution and revert to a non-compliant personal device given a hardware failure in the practice. Thus, a focus on studies reviewing such nuances will be critical especially for private practice and other resource-constrained healthcare organizations.

4.3   Studies in Rural Setting and Developing Nations

Along these lines, we observed scarce security and privacy research related to rural settings and developing nations. The resource limitations of the settings

demand a dedicated study of the population and appropriate technological mitigation techniques. The healthcare sector and research communities alike require
the insights of economics. None of the papers in our survey offered a robust
analysis of the probability of various vulnerabilities that would aid resource-
limited organizations in prioritizing solutions. Economic models, such as the
Gordon-Loeb model, may be effective in suggesting investment strategies [64].
Economics research may also wish to explore the costs and benefits of cybersecurity policy decisions in medical settings, insights about attacker motivations, and
oppositional human factors to disrupt attacker cognition and decision making.

4.4   Understanding the Patient's Perspective

Among the user studies we analyzed, the majority have focused on understanding the security behaviors of healthcare workers. However, patients' perspectives appears to be largely overlooked. Security and privacy requirements should
be informed and driven primarily from the desires of patients about their own
data. Patients as voting citizens influence healthcare laws and regulations in
their choice of elected officials. Patients are also the most directly impacted by
security breaches. More research is necessary to understand the gaps in patients'
understanding about the implications of a security breach to their personal data.
Research is also necessary to understand how much (or how little) trust patients
place in their healthcare organizations in protecting their personal data [111].

5   Limitations and Future Work

Healthcare is a broad and diverse sector with many niche journals and publications. Despite our best efforts, we may have missed important contributions
reported in publications for medical sub-specialities published in paid venues or
otherwise excluded by our search criteria. Future work is needed to understand
when, how, and why healthcare workers circumvent compliant workflows and
tools. Prior work has been focused primarily on authentication-related circumvention and usability and a broader examination is warranted. Further, past
research has drawn heavily from surveys so in-situ data would provide further
grounding and accuracy.

6   Conclusion

As the healthcare sector is increasingly digitized, privacy risks and security concerns about data storage, access, and transfer have greatly increased. However,
the question remains about how the research community is addressing these
concerns from the technical and user perspective. To this aid, we conducted a
detailed systematic literature review after collecting 2,903 papers and themat-
ically analyzing $N = 205$ of them. These peer-reviewed research articles were
published and available over seven digital spaces: ACM DL, Google Scholar,

SSRN, ScienceDirect, IEEE Xplore, PubMed, and MEDLINE. We examined the security and privacy of patient data in healthcare organizations as studied by prior literature. We found that current research focuses primarily on data encryption and frameworks while understudying the user risk perceptive of privacy and security. Along the socio-technical component of healthcare privacy and security, it was concerning to note that < 9% of the papers conducted any user studies. Among those, the studies were influenced by survey designs rather than in-depth, longitudinal user-focused studies. Additionally, these studies focused primarily on larger settings by severely ignoring the organizations with limited resources such as the private healthcare sector. We conclude with actionable recommendations from the rich literature we studied that can enhance the privacy and security aspects of the healthcare sector.

Acknowledgments. We would like to thank the Inclusive Security and Privacy-focused Innovative Research in Information Technology (InSPIRIT) Laboratory at the University of Denver. We would also like to thank Salman Hosain for their initial contribution in this research and Alisa Zezulak for helping with the proofreading of this paper. Any opinions, findings, and conclusions or recommendations expressed in this material are solely those of the authors and do not necessarily reflect the views of the University of Denver, the University of Washington, and the Designer Security.

References

1. Abd-alrazaq, A.A., et al.: Patients and healthcare workers experience with a mobile application for self-management of diabetes in Qatar: a qualitative study. Comput. Methods Program. Biomed. Update **1**, 100002 (2021)
2. Abouelmehdi, K., Beni-Hessane, A., Khaloufi, H.: Big healthcare data: preserving security and privacy. J. Big Data **5**(1), 1–18 (2018). https://doi.org/10.1186/s40537-017-0110-7
3. Abouelmehdi, K., Beni-Hssane, A., Khaloufi, H., Saadi, M.: Big data security and privacy in healthcare: a review. Procedia Comput. Sci. **113**, 73–80 (2017)
4. Abraham, C., Chatterjee, D., Sims, R.R.: Muddling through cybersecurity: insights from the us healthcare industry. Bus. Horiz. **62**(4), 539–548 (2019)
5. Acharya, S., Susai, G., Pillai, M.: Patient portals: Anytime, anywhere, pp. 779–781 (2015)
6. Aiswarya, R., Divya, R., Sangeetha, D., Vaidehi, V.: Harnessing healthcare data security in cloud, pp. 482–488 (2013)
7. Al Hamid, H.A., Rahman, S.M.M., Hossain, M.S., Almogren, A., Alamri, A.: A security model for preserving the privacy of medical big data in a healthcare cloud using a fog computing facility with pairing-based cryptography. IEEE Access **5**, 22313–22328 (2017)
8. Al-Karaki, J.N., Gawanmeh, A., Ayache, M., Mashaleh, A.: Dass-care: a decentralized, accessible, scalable, and secure healthcare framework using blockchain, pp. 330–335 (2019). https://doi.org/10.1109/IWCMC.2019.8766714
9. Alam, M.G.R., Munir, M.S., Uddin, M.Z., Alam, M.S., Dang, T.N., Hong, C.S.: Edge-of-things computing framework for cost-effective provisioning of healthcare data. J. Parallel Distrib. Comput. **123**, 54–60 (2019)

10. Albarrak, A.I.: Information security behavior among nurses in an academic hospital. Health Med. **6**(7), 2349–2354 (2012)
11. Alboaie, S., Nita, L., Stefanescu, C.: Executable choreographies for medical systems integration and data leaks prevention, pp. 1–4 (2015). https://doi.org/10.1109/EHB.2015.7391612
12. Almehmadi, T., Alshehri, S., Tahir, S.: A secure fog-cloud based architecture for MIoT, pp. 1–6 (2019). https://doi.org/10.1109/CAIS.2019.8769524
13. Alshalali, T., M'Bale, K., Josyula, D.: Security and privacy of electronic health records sharing using hyperledger fabric, pp. 760–763 (2018). https://doi.org/10.1109/CSCI46756.2018.00152
14. Altuntaş, G., Semerciöz, F., Eregez, H.: Linking strategic and market orientations to organizational performance: the role of innovation in private healthcare organizations. Procedia-Soc. Behav. Sci. **99**, 413–419 (2013)
15. Alyami, H., Feng, J.L., Hilal, A., Basir, O.: On-demand key distribution for body area networks for emergency case (2014). https://doi.org/10.1145/2642668.2642684
16. Anghelescu, P.: Encryption of multimedia medical content using programmable cellular automata, pp. 11–16 (2012)
17. Anghelescu, P., Ionita, S., Sofron, E.: Block encryption using hybrid additive cellular automata, pp. 132–137 (2007)
18. Arumugham, S., Rajagopalan, S., Rayappan, J.B.B., Amirtharajan, R.: Networked medical data sharing on secure medium-a web publishing mode for DICOM viewer with three layer authentication. J. Biomed. Inf. **86**, 90–105 (2018)
19. Asija, R., Nallusamy, R.: Data model to enhance the security and privacy of healthcare data, pp. 237–244 (2014). https://doi.org/10.1109/GHTC-SAS.2014.6967590
20. Aski, V., Dhaka, V.S., Kumar, S., Parashar, A., Ladagi, A.: A multi-factor access control and ownership transfer framework for future generation healthcare systems, pp. 93–98 (2020). https://doi.org/10.1109/PDGC50313.2020.9315840
21. Ayad, H., Khalil, M.: A semi-blind information hiding technique using DWT-SVD and QAM-16 for medical images, pp. 1–7 (2017)
22. Ayad, H., Khalil, M.: A semi-blind information hiding technique using DWT-SVD and QAM-16 for medical images (2017). https://doi.org/10.1145/3090354.3090433
23. Ayanlade, O., Oyebisi, T., Kolawole, B.: Health information technology acceptance framework for diabetes management. Heliyon **5**(5), e01735 (2019)
24. Baker, A., Vega, L., DeHart, T., Harrison, S.: Healthcare and security: understanding and evaluating the risks, pp. 99–108 (2011)
25. Balamurugan, G., Joseph, K.S., Arulalan, V.: An iris based reversible watermarking system for the security of teleradiology, pp. 1–6 (2016)
26. Bao, S.D., Chen, M., Yang, G.Z.: A method of signal scrambling to secure data storage for healthcare applications. IEEE J. Biomed. Health Inf. **21**(6), 1487–1494 (2017). https://doi.org/10.1109/JBHI.2017.2679979
27. Basavegowda, R., Seenappa, S.: Electronic medical report security using visual secret sharing scheme, pp. 78–83 (2013)
28. Bechtel, J.M., Lepoire, E., Bauer, A.M., Bowen, D.J., Fortney, J.C.: Care manager perspectives on integrating an mhealth app system into clinical workflows: a mixed methods study. Gener. Hospital Psychiatry **68**, 38–45 (2021)
29. Besher, K.M., Subah, Z., Ali, M.Z.: IoT sensor initiated healthcare data security. IEEE Sens. J. **21**(10), 11977–11982 (2020)

30. Bharghavi, G., Kumar, P.S., Geetha, K., Sasikala Devi, N.: An implementation of slice algorithm to enforce security for medical images using DNA approach, pp. 0984–0988 (2018). https://doi.org/10.1109/ICCSP.2018.8524413

31. Bharghavi, G., Kumar, P.S., Geetha, K., Devi, N.S.: An implementation of slice algorithm to enforce security for medical images using DNA approach, pp. 0984–0988 (2018)

32. Bhola, J., Soni, S., Cheema, G.K.: Recent trends for security applications in wireless sensor networks-a technical review, pp. 707–712 (2019)

33. Bhuiyan, M.Z.A., Zaman, A., Wang, T., Wang, G., Tao, H., Hassan, M.M.: Blockchain and big data to transform the healthcare, pp. 62–68 (2018)

34. Binobaid, S., Fan, I.S., Almeziny, M.: Investigation interoperability problems in pharmacy automation: a case study in Saudi Arabia. Procedia Comput. Sci. **100**, 329–338 (2016)

35. Boddy, A., Hurst, W., Mackay, M., El Rhalibi, A.: A study into detecting anomalous behaviours within healthcare infrastructures, pp. 111–117 (2016)

36. Bodur, G., Gumus, S., Gursoy, N.G.: Perceptions of Turkish health professional students toward the effects of the internet of things (IOT) technology in the future. Nurse Educ. Today **79**, 98–104 (2019)

37. Branley-Bell, D., et al.: Your hospital needs you: eliciting positive cybersecurity behaviours from healthcare staff using the aide approach. Ann. Disaster Risk Sci. **3**(1), 1–16 (2020)

38. Brunese, L., Mercaldo, F., Reginelli, A., Santone, A.: A blockchain based proposal for protecting healthcare systems through formal methods. Procedia Comput. Sci. **159**, 1787–1794 (2019)

39. Brunese, L., Mercaldo, F., Reginelli, A., Santone, A.: Formal modeling for magnetic resonance images tamper mitigation. Procedia Comput. Sci. **159**, 1803–1810 (2019)

40. Brunese, L., Mercaldo, F., Reginelli, A., Santone, A.: Radiomic features for medical images tamper detection by equivalence checking. Procedia Comput. Sci. **159**, 1795–1802 (2019)

41. Burke, W., Oseni, T., Jolfaei, A., Gondal, I.: Cybersecurity indexes for ehealth, pp. 1–8 (2019)

42. Cao, F., Huang, H.K., Zhou, X.: Medical image security in a HIPAA mandated PACS environment. Computer. Med. Imaging Graph. **27**(2–3), 185–196 (2003)

43. Chan, K.G., Pawi, S., Ong, M.F., Kowitlawakul, Y., Goy, S.C.: Simulated electronic health documentation: a cross-sectional exploration of factors influencing nursing students' intention to use. Nurse Educ. Pract. **48**, 102864 (2020)

44. Chaudhry, J., Qidwai, U., Miraz, M.H.: Securing big data from eavesdropping attacks in scada/ics network data streams through impulsive statistical fingerprinting, pp. 77–89 (2019)

45. Chen, Y., Chen, W.: Finger ECG-based authentication for healthcare data security using artificial neural network, pp. 1–6 (2017)

46. Choi, S.J., Johnson, M.E., Lee, J.: An event study of data breaches and hospital IT spending. Health Policy Technol. **9**(3), 372–378 (2020)

47. Coventry, L., Branley, D.: Cybersecurity in healthcare: a narrative review of trends, threats and ways forward. Maturitas·**113**, 48–52 (2018)

48. Coventry, L., et al.: Cyber-risk in healthcare: Exploring facilitators and barriers to secure behaviour, pp. 105–122 (2020)

49. Currie, W.: Health organizations' adoption and use of mobile technology in France, the USA and UK. Procedia Comput. Sci. **98**, 413–418 (2016)

50. Dagher, G.G., Mohler, J., Milojkovic, M., Marella, P.B.: Ancile: privacy-preserving framework for access control and interoperability of electronic health records using blockchain technology. Sustain. Cities Soc. **39**, 283–297 (2018)

51. Das, S., Kim, A., Tingle, Z., Nippert-Eng, C.: All about phishing: Exploring user research through a systematic literature review. arXiv preprint arXiv:1908.05897 (2019)

52. Das, S., Wang, B., Tingle, Z., Camp, L.J.: Evaluating user perception of multi-factor authentication: a systematic review. In: Proceedings of the Thirteenth International Symposium on Human Aspects of Information Security & Assurance (HAISA 2019) (2019)

53. Demjaha, A., Caulfield, T., Sasse, M.A., Pym, D.: 2 fast 2 secure: a case study of post-breach security changes, pp. 192–201 (2019)

54. Duque, H., Montagnat, J., Pierson, J.M., Brunie, L., Magnin, I.: Dm2: a distributed medical data manager for grids, pp. 138–147 (2003)

55. Dwivedi, A.D., Srivastava, G., Dhar, S., Singh, R.: A decentralized privacy-preserving healthcare blockchain for IoT. Sensors **19**(2), 326 (2019)

56. Dykstra, J., Mathur, R., Spoor, A.: Cybersecurity in medical private practice: results of a survey in audiology, pp. 169–176 (2020). https://doi.org/10.1109/CIC50333.2020.00029

57. El Bouchti, A., Bahsani, S., Nahhal, T.: Encryption as a service for data healthcare cloud security, pp. 48–54 (2016)

58. Elmogazy, H., Bamasak, O.: Towards healthcare data security in cloud computing, pp. 363–368 (2013)

59. Esposito, C., Castiglione, A.: Cloud-based management of healthcare data: security and privacy concerns and a promising solution

60. Essa, Y.M., Hemdan, E.E.D., El-Mahalawy, A., Attiya, G., El-Sayed, A.: IFHDS: intelligent framework for securing healthcare bigdata. J. Med. Syst. **43**(5), 1–13 (2019)

61. Garner, S.A., Kim, J.: The privacy risks of direct-to-consumer genetic testing: a case study of 23 and Me and ancestry. Wash. UL Rev. **96**, 1219 (2018)

62. Geetha, R., Geetha, S.: Efficient high capacity technique to embed EPR information and to detect tampering in medical images. J. Med. Eng. Technol. **44**(2), 55–68 (2020)

63. Georgiou, D., Lambrinoudakis, C.: Compatibility of a security policy for a cloud-based healthcare system with the EU general data protection regulation (GDPR). Information **11**(12), 586 (2020)

64. Gordon, L.A., Loeb, M.P., Zhou, L., et al.: Investing in cybersecurity: insights from the Gordon-Loeb model. J. Inf. Secur. **7**(02), 49 (2016)

65. Goudar, V., Potkonjak, M.: Addressing biosignal data sharing security issues with robust watermarking, pp. 618–626 (2014). https://doi.org/10.1109/SAHCN.2014.6990402

66. Goudar, V., Potkonjak, M.: On admitting sensor fault tolerance while achieving secure biosignal data sharing, pp. 266–275 (2014). https://doi.org/10.1109/ICHI.2014.44

67. Goudar, V., Potkonjak, M.: A robust watermarking technique for secure sharing of basn generated medical data, pp. 162–170 (2014)

68. Gritzalis, D.: A baseline security policy for distributed healthcare information systems. Comput. Secur. **16**(8), 709–719 (1997)

69. Gritzalis, D., Katsikas, S., Keklikoglou, J., Tomaras, A.: Determining access rights for medical information systems. Comput. Secur. **11**(2), 149–161 (1992)

70. Gritzalis, D., Lambrinoudakis, C.: A security architecture for interconnecting health information systems. Int. J. Med. Inf. **73**(3), 305–309 (2004).

71. Gritzalis, D., Tomaras, A., Katsikas, S., Keklikoglou, J.: Data security in medical information systems: the Greek case. Comput. Secur. **10**(2), 141–159 (1991)

72. Gross, M.S., Miller Jr, R.C.: Ethical implementation of the learning healthcare system with blockchain technology. Blockchain in Healthcare Today, Forthcoming (2019)

73. Guennoun, M., El-Khatib, K.: Securing medical data in smart homes, pp. 104–107 (2009). https://doi.org/10.1109/MEMEA.2009.5167964

74. Guizani, K., Guizani, S.: IoT healthcare monitoring systems overview for elderly population, pp. 2005–2009 (2020)

75. Gupta, A., Bansiya, A.: Utilizing cloud computing for stronger healthcare data security. Int. J. Sci. Res. Eng. Trends **6**, 2384 (2020)

76. Gupta, V., Metha, G.: Medical data security using cryptography, pp. 866–869 (2018)

77. Hammouchi, H., Cherqi, O., Mezzour, G., Ghogho, M., El Koutbi, M.: Digging deeper into data breaches: an exploratory data analysis of hacking breaches over time. Procedia Comput. Sci. **151**, 1004–1009 (2019)

78. Hollis, K.F.: To share or not to share: ethical acquisition and use of medical data. AMIA Summits Transl. Sci. Proc. **2016**, 420 (2016)

79. Holmgren, A.J., Adler-Milstein, J.: Health information exchange in us hospitals: the current landscape and a path to improved information sharing. J. Hospital Med. **12**(3), 193–198 (2017)

80. Hsu, W.W.Q., Chan, E.W.Y., Zhang, Z.J., Lin, Z.X., Bian, Z.X., Wong, I.C.K.: Chinese medicine students' views on electronic prescribing: a survey in Hong Kong. Eur. J. Integr. Med. **7**(1), 47–54 (2015)

81. Huang, C.D., Behara, R.S., Goo, J.: Optimal information security investment in a healthcare information exchange: An economic analysis. Decis. Support Syst. **61**, 1–11 (2014)

82. Ibrahim, A., Mahmood, B., Singhal, M.: A secure framework for sharing electronic health records over clouds, pp. 1–8 (2016). https://doi.org/10.1109/SeGAH.2016. 7586273

83. Ibrahim, A., Mahmood, B., Singhal, M.: A secure framework for sharing electronic health records over clouds, pp. 1–8 (2016)

84. Ivaşcu, T., Frîncu, M., Negru, V.: Considerations towards security and privacy in internet of things based ehealth applications, pp. 275–280 (2016). https://doi. org/10.1109/SISY.2016.7601512

85. Izza, S., Benssalah, M., Drouiche, K.: An enhanced scalable and secure RFID authentication protocol for WBAN within an IoT environment. J. Inf. Secur. Appl. **58**, 102705 (2021)

86. Jabeen, T., Ashraf, H., Khatoon, A., Band, S.S., Mosavi, A.: A lightweight genetic based algorithm for data security in wireless body area networks. IEEE Access **8**, 183460–183469 (2020)

87. Jabeen, T., Ashraf, H., Ullah, A.: A survey on healthcare data security in wireless body area networks. J. Ambient Intell. Humanized Comput. 1–14 (2021)

88. Jaigirdar, F.T.: Trust based security solution for internet of things healthcare solution: an end-to-end trustworthy architecture, pp. 1757–1760 (2018)

89. Jalali, M.S., Razak, S., Gordon, W., Perakslis, E., Madnick, S.: Health care and cybersecurity: bibliometric analysis of the literature. J. Med. Internet Res. **21**(2), e12644 (2019)

90. Janjic, V., et al.: The serums tool-chain: Ensuring security and privacy of medical data in smart patient-centric healthcare systems, pp. 2726–2735 (2019)

91. Jayanthilladevi, A., Sangeetha, K., Balamurugan, E.: Healthcare biometrics security and regulations: biometrics data security and regulations governing PHI and HIPAA act for patient privacy, pp. 244–247 (2020)

92. Joshitta, R.S.M., Arockiam, L., Malarchelvi, P.S.K.: Security analysis of sat_jo lightweight block cipher for data security in healthcare IoT, pp. 111–116 (2019)

93. Kamoun, F., Nicho, M.: Human and organizational factors of healthcare data breaches: the swiss cheese model of data breach causation and prevention. Int. J. Healthcare Inf. Syst. Inf. (IJHISI) **9**(1), 42–60 (2014)

94. Karthick, R., Ramkumar, R., Akram, M., Kumar, M.V.: Overcome the challenges in bio-medical instruments using IoT-a review. Materials Today: Proceedings (2020)

95. Kaur, J., et al.: Security risk assessment of healthcare web application through adaptive neuro-fuzzy inference system: a design perspective. Risk Manage. Healthcare Policy **13**, 355 (2020)

96. Kausar, F.: Iris based cancelable biometric cryptosystem for secure healthcare smart card. Egyptian Inf. J. (2021)

97. Kaw, J.A., Loan, N.A., Parah, S.A., Muhammad, K., Sheikh, J.A., Bhat, G.M.: A reversible and secure patient information hiding system for IoT driven e-health. Int. J. Inf. Manage. **45**, 262–275 (2019)

98. Kelkar, V., Tuckley, K.: Reversible watermarking for medical images with added security using chaos theory, pp. 84–87 (2018). https://doi.org/10.1109/CESYS.2018.8724039

99. Kenny, G., O'Connor, Y., Eze, E., Ndibuagu, E., Heavin, C.: A ground-up approach to mHealth in Nigeria: a study of primary healthcare workers' attitude to mHealth adoption. Procedia Comput. Sci. **121**, 809–816 (2017)

100. Khaloufi, H., Abouelmehdi, K., Beni-hssane, A., Saadi, M.: Security model for big healthcare data lifecycle. Procedia Comput. Sci. **141**, 294–301 (2018)

101. Khan, F.A., Ali, A., Abbas, H., Haldar, N.A.H.: A cloud-based healthcare framework for security and patients' data privacy using wireless body area networks. Procedia Comput. Sci. **34**, 511–517 (2014)

102. Khan, J., et al.: Medical image encryption into smart healthcare IoT system, pp. 378–382 (2019). https://doi.org/10.1109/ICCWAMTIP47768.2019.9067592

103. Khan, J., et al.: Medical image encryption into smart healthcare IoT system, pp. 378–382 (2019)

104. Kierkegaard, P.: Medical data breaches: notification delayed is notification denied. Comput. Law Secur. Rev. **28**(2), 163–183 (2012)

105. Kim, J., Feng, D.D., Cai, T.W., Eberl, S.: Integrated multimedia medical data agent in e-health. In: Proceedings of the Pan-Sydney area Workshop on Visual Information Processing, vol. 11, pp. 11–15 (2001)

106. Kiourtis, A., Mavrogiorgou, A., Kyriazis, D., Graziani, A., Torelli, F.: Improving health information exchange through wireless communication protocols, pp. 32–39 (2020). https://doi.org/10.1109/WiMob50308.2020.9253374

107. Kiruba, W.M., Vijayalakshmi, M.: Implementation and analysis of data security in a real time IoT based healthcare application, pp. 1460–1465 (2018)

108. Ko, J., Lu, C., Srivastava, M.B., Stankovic, J.A., Terzis, A., Welsh, M.: Wireless sensor networks for healthcare. Proc. IEEE **98**(11), 1947–1960 (2010)

109. Kondawar, S.S., Gawali, D.H.: Security algorithms for wireless medical data, pp. 1–6 (2016)

110. Krishna, R., Kelleher, K., Stahlberg, E.: Patient confidentiality in the research use of clinical medical databases. Am. J. Public Health **97**(4), 654–658 (2007)
111. Krombholz, K., Busse, K., Pfeffer, K., Smith, M., von Zezschwitz, E.: "If https Were Secure, i Wouldn't need 2fa"-end User and Administrator Mental Models of https, pp. 246–263 (2019)
112. Kumar, M., Chand, S.: Medhypchain: a patient-centered interoperability hyperledger-based medical healthcare system: regulation in covid-19 pandemic. J. Netw. Comput. Appl. **179**, 102975 (2021)
113. Kumar, S., Namdeo, V.: Enabling privacy and security of healthcare-related data in the cloud
114. Kumar, V.N., Rochan, M., Hariharan, S., Rajamani, K.: Data hiding scheme for medical images using lossless code for mobile HIMS, pp. 1–4 (2011)
115. Kuo, M.H., Chrimes, D., Moa, B., Hu, W.: Design and construction of a big data analytics framework for health applications, pp. 631–636 (2015)
116. Lee, C.Y., Ibrahim, H., Othman, M., Yaakob, R.: Reconciling semantic conflicts in electronic patient data exchange, pp. 390–394 (2009)
117. Lees, P.J., Chronaki, C.E., Simantirakis, E.N., Kostomanolakis, S.G., Orphanoudakis, S.C., Vardas, P.E.: Remote access to medical records via the internet: feasibility, security and multilingual considerations, pp. 89–92 (1999). https://doi.org/10.1109/CIC.1999.825913
118. Li, P., Xu, C., Luo, Y., Cao, Y., Mathew, J., Ma, Y.: Carenet: building regulation-compliant home-based healthcare services with software-defined infrastructure, pp. 373–382 (2017)
119. Li, X., Huang, X., Li, C., Yu, R., Shu, L.: Edgecare: leveraging edge computing for collaborative data management in mobile healthcare systems. IEEE Access **7**, 22011–22025 (2019)
120. Liu, H., Kadir, A., Liu, J.: Color pathological image encryption algorithm using arithmetic over galois field and coupled hyper chaotic system. Opt. Lasers Eng. **122**, 123–133 (2019)
121. Lohiya, S., Ragha, L.: Privacy preserving in data mining using hybrid approach, pp. 743–746 (2012). https://doi.org/10.1109/CICN.2012.166
122. Lomotey, R.K., Pry, J., Sriramoju, S.: Wearable IoT data stream traceability in a distributed health information system. Pervasive Mob. Comput. **40**, 692–707 (2017)
123. Jones, J.M., Duezguen, R., Mayer, P., Volkamer, M., Das, S.: A literature review on virtual reality authentication. In: Furnell, S., Clarke, N. (eds.) HAISA 2021. IAICT, vol. 613, pp. 189–198. Springer, Cham (2021). https://doi.org/10.1007/978-3-030-81111-2_16
124. Mahima, K.T.Y., Ginige, T.: A secured healthcare system using blockchain and graph theory (2020). https://doi.org/10.1145/3440084.3441217
125. Majam, T., Theron, F.: The purpose and relevance of a scientific literature review: a holistic approach to research. J. Public Adm. **41**(3), 603–615 (2006)
126. Maji, A.K., et al.: Security analysis and implementation of web-based telemedicine services with a four-tier architecture, pp. 46–54 (2008)
127. Majumdar, R., Das, S.: Sok: an evaluation of quantum authentication through systematic literature review. In: Proceedings of the Workshop on Usable Security and Privacy (USEC) (2021)
128. Mashima, D., Ahamad, M.: Enhancing accountability of electronic health record usage via patient-centric monitoring (2012). https://doi.org/10.1145/2110363.2110410

129. Masood, I., Wang, Y., Daud, A., Aljohani, N.R., Dawood, H.: Privacy management of patient physiological parameters. Telematics Inf. **35**(4), 677–701 (2018)

130. Masood, I., Wang, Y., Daud, A., Aljohani, N.R., Dawood, H.: Towards smart healthcare: patient data privacy and security in sensor-cloud infrastructure. Wirel. Commun. Mob. Comput. **2018** (2018)

131. Mbonihankuye, S., Nkunzimana, A., Ndagijimana, A.: Healthcare data security technology: hipaa compliance. Wirel. Commun. Mob. Comput. **2019** (2019)

132. McLeod, A., Dolezel, D.: Cyber-analytics: modeling factors associated with healthcare data breaches. Decis. Support Syst. **108**, 57–68 (2018)

133. Melchiorre, M.G., Papa, R., Rijken, M., van Ginneken, E., Hujala, A., Barbabella, F.: eHealth in integrated care programs for people with multimorbidity in Europe: insights from the ICARE4EU project. Health Policy **122**(1), 53–63 (2018)

134. Miah, S.J., Hasan, J., Gammack, J.G.: On-cloud healthcare clinic: an e-health consultancy approach for remote communities in a developing country. Telematics Inf. **34**(1), 311–322 (2017)

135. Mirto, M., Cafaro, M., Aloisio, G.: Peer-to-peer data discovery in health centers, pp. 343–348 (2013)

136. Mounia, B., Habiba, C.: Big data privacy in healthcare Moroccan context. Procedia Comput. Sci. **63**, 575–580 (2015)

137. Naseem, M.T., Qureshi, I.M., Muzaffar, M.Z., et al.: Robust watermarking for medical images resistant to geometric attacks, pp. 224–228 (2012). https://doi.org/10.1109/INMIC.2012.6511496

138. Nausheen, F., Begum, S.H.: Healthcare IoT: benefits, vulnerabilities and solutions, pp. 517–522 (2018)

139. Noah, N., Das, S.: Exploring evolution of augmented and virtual reality education space in 2020 through systematic literature review. Comput. Animation Virtual Worlds e2020 (2021)

140. Noel, K., Yagudayev, S., Messina, C., Schoenfeld, E., Hou, W., Kelly, G.: Tele-transitions of care. a 12-month, parallel-group, superiority randomized controlled trial protocol, evaluating the use of telehealth versus standard transitions of care in the prevention of avoidable hospital readmissions. Contemp. Clin. Trials Commun. **12**, 9–16 (2018)

141. Nofer, M., Gomber, P., Hinz, O., Schiereck, D.: Blockchain Bus. Inf. Syst. Eng. **59**(3), 183–187 (2017)

142. Olaronke, I., Oluwaseun, O.: Big data in healthcare: Prospects, challenges and resolutions, pp. 1152–1157 (2016)

143. Pai, R.R., Alathur, S.: Determinants of mobile health application awareness and use in India: an empirical analysis, pp. 576–584 (2020)

144. Paksuniemi, M., Sorvoja, H., Alasaarela, E., Myllyla, R.: Wireless sensor and data transmission needs and technologies for patient monitoring in the operating room and intensive care unit, pp. 5182–5185 (2006)

145. Palta, J.R., Frouhar, V.A., Dempsey, J.F.: Web-based submission, archive, and review of radiotherapy data for clinical quality assurance: a new paradigm. Int. J. Radiat. Oncol.* Biol.* Phys. **57**(5), 1427–1436 (2003)

146. Pandey, A.K., et al.: Key issues in healthcare data integrity: analysis and recommendations. IEEE Access **8**, 40612–40628 (2020)

147. Pandey, H.M.: Secure medical data transmission using a fusion of bit mask oriented genetic algorithm, encryption and steganography. Future Gener. Comput. Syst. **111**, 213–225 (2020)

148. Parameswari, R., Latha, R.: Analysis of wavelet transform approach for healthcare data security in cloud framework. Int. J. Sci. Res. Sci. Eng. Technol. **2**, 241–246 (2016)

149. Parmar, M., Shah, S.: Reinforcing security of medical data using blockchain, pp. 1233–1239 (2019). https://doi.org/10.1109/ICCS45141.2019.9065830

150. Perumal, A.M., Nadar, E.R.S.: Architectural framework of a group key management system for enhancing e-healthcare data security. Healthcare Technol. Lett. **7**(1), 13–17 (2020)

151. Petković, M.: Remote patient monitoring: Information reliability challenges, pp. 295–301 (2009)

152. Pirbhulal, S., Samuel, O.W., Wu, W., Sangaiah, A.K., Li, G.: A joint resource-aware and medical data security framework for wearable healthcare systems. Future Gener. Comput. Syst. **95**, 382–391 (2019)

153. Pirbhulal, S., Shang, P., Wu, W., Sangaiah, A.K., Samuel, O.W., Li, G.: Fuzzy vault-based biometric security method for tele-health monitoring systems. Comput. Electr. Eng. **71**, 546–557 (2018)

154. Połap, D., Srivastava, G., Yu, K.: Agent architecture of an intelligent medical system based on federated learning and blockchain technology. J. Inf. Secur. Appl. **58**, 102748 (2021)

155. Połap, D., Srivastava, G., Jolfaei, A., Parizi, R.M.: Blockchain technology and neural networks for the internet of medical things, pp. 508–513 (2020). https://doi.org/10.1109/INFOCOMWKSHPS50562.2020.9162735

156. PraveenKumar, R., Divya, P.: Medical data processing and prediction of future health condition using sensors data mining techniques and r programming. Int. J. Sci. Res. Eng. Dev. **3**(4) (2020)

157. Psarra, E., Patiniotakis, I., Verginadis, Y., Apostolou, D., Mentzas, G.: Securing access to healthcare data with context-aware policies, pp. 1–6 (2020)

158. Qazi, U., Haq, M., Rashad, N., Rashid, K., Ullah, S., Raza, U.: Availability and use of in-patient electronic health records in low resource setting. Comput. Methods Program. Biomed. **164**, 23–29 (2018)

159. Rajagopalan, S., Dhamodaran, B., Ramji, A., Francis, C., Venkatraman, S., Amirtharajan, R.: Confusion and diffusion on FPGA-Onchip solution for medical image security, pp. 1–6 (2017)

160. Reni, G., Molteni, M., Arlotti, S., Pinciroli, F.: Chief medical officer actions on information security in an Italian rehabilitation centre. Int. J. Med. Inf. **73**(3), 271–279 (2004)

161. del Rey, A.M., Pastora, J.H., Sánchez, G.R.: 3d medical data security protection. Exp. Syst. Appl. **54**, 379–386 (2016)

162. Richardson, J.E., Ancker, J.S.: Public perspectives of mobile phones' effects on healthcare quality and medical data security and privacy: A 2-year nationwide survey, vol. 2015, p. 1076 (2015)

163. Rocha, A., et al.: Innovations in health care services: the caalyx system. Int. J. Med. Inf. **82**(11), e307–e320 (2013)

164. Rodrigues, H.A.M., Antunes, L., Correia, M.E.: Proposal of a secure electronic prescription system, pp. 165–168 (2013)

165. Rodriguez-Colin, R., Claudia, F.D.J., Trinidad-Blas, G.: Data hiding scheme for medical images, pp. 32–32 (2007). https://doi.org/10.1109/CONIELECOMP.2007.14

166. Safkhani, M., Rostampour, S., Bendavid, Y., Bagheri, N.: IoT in medical & pharmaceutical: designing lightweight RFID security protocols for ensuring supply chain integrity. Comput. Netw. **181**, 107558 (2020)

167. Sammoud, A., Chalouf, M.A., Hamdi, O., Montavont, N., Bouallegue, A.: A new biometrics-based key establishment protocol in Wban: Energy efficiency and security robustness analysis. Comput. Secur. **96**, 101838 (2020)

168. Sartipi, K., Yarmand, M.H., Down, D.G.: Mined-knowledge and decision support services in electronic health, pp. 1–6 (2007)

169. Schmeelk, S.: Where is the risk? analysis of government reported patient medical data breaches, pp. 269–272 (2019)

170. Shaarani, I., et al.: Attitudes of patients towards digital information retrieval by their physician at point of care in an ambulatory setting. Int. J. Med. Inf. **130**, 103936 (2019)

171. Shahbaz, S., Mahmood, A., Anwar, Z.: Soad: securing oncology EMR by anonymizing DICOM images, pp. 125–130 (2013). https://doi.org/10.1109/FIT. 2013.30

172. Shakil, K.A., Zareen, F.J., Alam, M., Jabin, S.: Bamhealthcloud: a biometric authentication and data management system for healthcare data in cloud. J. King Saud Univ. Comput. Inf. Sci. **32**(1), 57–64 (2020)

173. Shen, H., et al.: Miaps: a web-based system for remotely accessing and presenting medical images. Comput. Methods Program. Biomed. **113**(1), 266–283 (2014)

174. Shere, A.R., Nurse, J.R., Flechais, I.: Security should be there by default: investigating how journalists perceive and respond to risks from the internet of things, pp. 240–249 (2020)

175. Shi, W., Dustdar, S.: The promise of edge computing. Computer **49**(5), 78–81 (2016)

176. Shrivastava, S., Srikanth, T., VS, D.: e-Governance for healthcare service delivery in India: challenges and opportunities in security and privacy, pp. 180–183 (2020)

177. Shrivastava, U., Song, J., Han, B.T., Dietzman, D.: Do data security measures, privacy regulations, and communication standards impact the interoperability of patient health information? a cross-country investigation. Int. J. Med. Inf. **148**, 104401 (2021)

178. da Silva Etges, A.P.B., et al.: Development of an enterprise risk inventory for healthcare. BMC Health Serv. Res. **18**(1), 1–16 (2018)

179. Simões, A., et al.: Participatory implementation of an antibiotic stewardship programme supported by an innovative surveillance and clinical decision-support system. J. Hosp. Infect. **100**(3), 257–264 (2018)

180. Simplicio, M.A., Iwaya, L.H., Barros, B.M., Carvalho, T.C., Näslund, M.: Secourhealth: a delay-tolerant security framework for mobile health data collection. IEEE J. Biomed. Health Inf. **19**(2), 761–772 (2014)

181. Sosu, R.N.A., Quist-Aphetsi, K., Nana, L.: A decentralized cryptographic blockchain approach for health information system, pp. 120–1204 (2019). https:// doi.org/10.1109/ICCMA.2019.00027

182. Soualmi, A., Alti, A., Laouamer, L.: A blind image watermarking method for personal medical data security, pp. 1–5 (2019). https://doi.org/10.1109/ICNAS. 2019.8807442

183. Sreeji, S., Shiji, S., Vysagh, M., Amma, T.A.: Security and privacy preserving deep learning framework that protect healthcare data breaches. Int. J. Res. Eng. Sci. Manage. **3**(7), 148–152 (2020)

184. Stobert, E., Barrera, D., Homier, V., Kollek, D.: Understanding cybersecurity practices in emergency departments, pp. 1–8 (2020)

185. Stowell, E., et al.: Designing and evaluating mhealth interventions for vulnerable populations: a systematic review, pp. 1–17 (2018)

186. Sudha, G., Ganesan, R.: Secure transmission medical data for pervasive healthcare system using android, pp. 433–436 (2013)

187. Sutton, L.N.: PACS and diagnostic imaging service delivery-A UK perspective. Eur. J. Radiol. **78**(2), 243–249 (2011)

188. Tan, C.C., Wang, H., Zhong, S., Li, Q.: Body sensor network security: an identity-based cryptography approach, pp. 148–153 (2008)

189. Tan, C.C., Wang, H., Zhong, S., Li, Q.: Ibe-lite: a lightweight identity-based cryptography for body sensor networks. IEEE Trans. Inf. Technol. Biomed. **13**(6), 926–932 (2009)

190. Thamilarasu, G., Lakin, C.: A security framework for mobile health applications, pp. 221–226 (2017). https://doi.org/10.1109/FiCloudW.2017.96

191. Tian, Y., et al.: Popcorn: a web service for individual prognosis prediction based on multi-center clinical data collaboration without patient-level data sharing. J. Biomed. Inf. **86**, 1–14 (2018)

192. Tolba, A., Al-Makhadmeh, Z.: Predictive data analysis approach for securing medical data in smart grid healthcare systems. Future Gener. Comput. Syst. **117**, 87–96 (2021)

193. Tyler, J.L.: The healthcare information technology context: a framework for viewing legal aspects of telemedicine and teleradiology, pp. 1–10 (2001)

194. U.S. Department of Health & Human Services: Anthem pays OCR $16 Million in record HIPAA settlement following largest health data breach in history, 15 Oct 2018. https://www.hhs.gov/hipaa/for-professionals/compliance-enforcement/agreements/anthem/index.html

195. Usman, M.A., Usman, M.R.: Using image steganography for providing enhanced medical data security, pp. 1–4 (2018). https://doi.org/10.1109/CCNC.2018.8319263

196. Uy, R.C.Y., Kury, F.S., Fontelo, P.: Wireless networks, physician handhelds use, and medical devices in us hospitals, pp. 1–6 (2015)

197. Vallathan, G., Rajamani, V., Harinee, M.P.: Enhanced medical data security and perceptual quality for healthcare services, pp. 1–6 (2020). https://doi.org/10.1109/ICSCAN49426.2020.9262309

198. Vassis, D., Belsis, P., Skourlas, C.: Secure management of medical data in wireless environments, pp. 427–432 (2012)

199. Véliz, C.: Not the doctor's business: privacy, personal responsibility and data rights in medical settings. Bioethics **34**(7), 712–718 (2020)

200. Vidya, M., Padmaja, K.: Enhancing security of electronic patient record using watermarking technique. Mater. Today Proc. **5**(4), 10660–10664 (2018)

201. Vijayalakshmi, A.V., Arockiam, L.: Hybrid security techniques to protect sensitive data in e-healthcare systems, pp. 39–43 (2018)

202. Wagner, P.: Third party breaches-a survey of threats and recommendations, SSRN 3782822 (2021)

203. Walker-Roberts, S., Hammoudeh, M., Dehghantanha, A.: A systematic review of the availability and efficacy of countermeasures to internal threats in healthcare critical infrastructure. IEEE Access **6**, 25167–25177 (2018)

204. Wang, C.X.: Security issues to tele-medicine system design, pp. 106–109 (1999)

205. Wang, D., Kale, S.D., O'Neill, J.: Please call the specialism: Using wechat to support patient care in china, pp. 1–13 (2020)

206. Wang, D., Huang, Q., Chen, X., Ji, L.: Location of three-dimensional movement for a human using a wearable multi-node instrument implemented by wireless body area networks. Comput. Commun. **153**, 34–41 (2020)

207. Weaver, A.C., et al.: Federated, secure trust networks for distributed healthcare it services, pp. 162–169 (2003). https://doi.org/10.1109/INDIN.2003.1300264

208. Yaghmai, V., Salehi, S.A., Kuppuswami, S., Berlin, J.W.: Rapid wireless transmission of head CT images to a personal digital assistant for remote consultation1. Acad. Radiol. **11**(11), 1291–1293 (2004)

209. Yang, W., et al.: Securing mobile healthcare data: a smart card based cancelable finger-vein bio-cryptosystem. IEEE Access **6**, 36939–36947 (2018)

210. Yang, Y., Xiao, X., Cai, X., Zhang, W.: A secure and high visual-quality framework for medical images by contrast-enhancement reversible data hiding and homomorphic encryption. IEEE Access **7**, 96900–96911 (2019)

211. Yang, Y., Xiao, X., Cai, X., Zhang, W.: A secure and high visual-quality framework for medical images by contrast-enhancement reversible data hiding and homomorphic encryption. IEEE Access **7**, 96900–96911 (2019). https://doi.org/10.1109/ACCESS.2019.2929298

212. Yesmin, T., Carter, M.W.: Evaluation framework for automatic privacy auditing tools for hospital data breach detections: a case study. Int. J. Med. Inf. **138**, 104123 (2020)

213. Zatout, Y., Campo, E., Llibre, J.F.: Toward hybrid WSN architectures for monitoring people at home, pp. 308–314 (2009). https://doi.org/10.1145/1643823.1643880

214. Zhang, B., Chen, S., Nichols, E., D'Souza, W., Prado, K., Yi, B.: A practical cyberattack contingency plan for radiation oncology. J. Appl. Clin. Med. Phys. **21**(7), 181–186 (2020)

Work in Progress: Can Johnny Encrypt E-Mails on Smartphones?

Katharina Schiller[(✉)] and Florian Adamsky

Institute of Information Systems (iisys), Hof University of Applied Sciences,
Hof, Germany
{katharina.schiller,florian.adamsky}@hof-university.de

Abstract. E-mail is nearly 50 years old and is still one of the most used communication protocols nowadays. However, it has no support for End-to-end encryption (E2EE) by default, which makes it inappropriate for sending sensitive information. This is why two e-mail encryption standards have been developed—namely, Secure/Multipurpose Internet Mail Extensions (S/MIME) and OpenPGP. Previous studies found that bad usability of encryption software can lead to software that is incorrectly used or not at all. Both consequences have a fatal impact on users' security and privacy. In recent years, the number of e-mails that are read and written on mobile devices has increased drastically. In this paper, we conduct to the best of our knowledge, the first usability study of e-mail encryption apps on smartphones. We tested two mobile apps, one uses OpenPGP on Android and one uses S/MIME on iOS. In our usability study, we tested both apps with eleven participants and evaluated the usability with the System Usability Scale (SUS) and the Short Version of User Experience Questionnaire (UEQ-S). Our study shows that both apps have several usability issues which partly led to unencrypted e-mails and participants sending their passphrase instead of their public key.

1 Introduction

As a saying goes, *there is life in the old dog yet* and this is particularly true for e-mail. Numerous articles, e.g. [3,4,9], have predicted the end of e-mail in the last years. It has been nearly 50 years [23] since the first e-mail was sent and it is still one of the most used communication medium nowadays with over 3.9 billion [7] users worldwide. Despite the increasing usage of social media, Instant Messaging (IM), and communication tools such as Slack and Microsoft Teams—the latter ones require a valid e-mail address—the worldwide e-mail usage continues to grow. According to a forecast from the Radicati Group [7], the number of e-mail users will increase by 3% every year.

However, there is one major change in our e-mail usage: an increasing number of e-mails are read and written on mobile devices such as smartphones and tablets. According to a report from IBM [10], 49.1% of all e-mails worldwide are read on mobile devices. In some regions, these numbers vary, e.g. in the United Kingdom and Ireland 62.9%, and in Europe 38.6% are read on mobile devices.

© Springer Nature Switzerland AG 2022
S. Parkin and L. Viganò (Eds.): STAST 2021, LNCS 13176, pp. 182–193, 2022.
https://doi.org/10.1007/978-3-031-10183-0_9

A big problem with e-mail is the lack of End-to-end encryption (E2EE) by default. To solve this problem, the two e-mail standards, Secure/Multipurpose Internet Mail Extensions (S/MIME) and OpenPGP [6], have been developed. To encrypt e-mails with one of those standards, additional software is needed. The research community conducted various usability studies [8,18,19,24] of these encryption software and concluded that the bad usability is partly responsible why e-mail encryption is rarely used. Since nearly half of all e-mails are now read and written on mobile devices, how is the usability of encryption software on mobile devices? To the best of our knowledge, this paper provides the first usability study of e-mail encryption software on mobile devices. We selected two apps, one was on iOS using S/MIME and the second on Android with OpenPGP. We conducted our study with the following Research Questions (RQs) in mind:

RQ1 Are users able to encrypt e-mails with a smartphone without critical mistakes?

RQ2 Are the apps usable according to the usability questionnaires?

Our work makes the following contributions. We *(1)* conducted a usability study with eleven participants at a German university testing two mobile e-mail encryption apps; *(2)* evaluated the usability of both apps with the Short Version of User Experience Questionnaire (UEQ-S) [20] and the System Usability Scale (SUS) [15]; *(3)* show that both apps have several usability issues which resulted in sending unencrypted e-mails and accidentally sending the passphrase instead of the public key.

2   Related Work

An early usability study of e-mail encryption was conducted by Whitten and Tygar [24] about Pretty Good Privacy (PGP) 5.0 with 12 participants. Four of them fulfilled the given sign and encryption tasks correctly, the others failed.

PGP has undergone major changes in the upcoming years, including usability issues. Eight years after their first study, Sheng et al. [22] did another research at the current at that time version of PGP 9 with even worse results. None of the participants was able to complete the tasks to verify keys and sign or encrypt an e-mail, although there have been improvements through automatic encryption.

Other approaches to the topic followed. One of them is Private Webmail (Pwm), a tool that integrates into existing webmail services and provides encryption functions as an overlay and supports automatic key management and encryption. In their study, Ruoti et al. [16] compared Pwm with a standalone tool that required manual interaction with ciphertext and discovered that for that reason users trust the standalone tool more.

In another study Ruoti et al. [17] compared two revised versions of Pwm in an A/B testing scenario regarding their level of automation to discover the impact on the understanding of encryption processes and how it helps users to avoid mistakes. Both versions received a SUS score of around 80 that is known as the highest score for secure e-mail tools at this time. The results show that automatic encryption or manual encryption does not affect how well users understand the process.

Atwater et al. [1] checked in their study three tools on their trustworthiness, according to the level of transparency of encryption processes and the level of integration. They found that especially integrated tools can provide good usability and the majority had no preferences according to the trustworthiness, even though some of them thought standalone tools are more secure since they are an "offline" tool installed locally on their device.

Nevertheless, the existing solutions are still not widely adopted. Another research from 2015 [19] regarding one of the integrated PGP tools from the previous study shows again a poor usability by testing it with groups of participants. It shows that after decades of studies and improvement, PGP is still not user-friendly enough to be used by the masses. Ruoti et al. [18] conducted another study on three different secure e-mail tools including Pwm with pairs of acquainted participants. Their conclusions are similar to previous studies, adding that both participants acted more naturally, because they were novice and familiar with each other.

However, we did not found studies that cover e-mail encryption software on mobile devices.

3   Background

In this section, we provide a brief overview of the two encryption standards OpenPGP and S/MIME.

OpenPGP is according to the website[1] the most widely used e-mail encryption standard and is defined by the OpenPGP Working Group in RFC 4880 [6]. It is based on PGP version 5 encryption concept developed by Phil Zimmermann [13]. In OpenPGP there is no central trust entity, instead it is based on a web of trust in which participants sign keys of each other and therefore verify their identity. The public keys are often on keyservers and can easily be retrieved by other participants. Public keys also serve as a signature which also confirms the authenticity of the e-mail. The signature can be checked by comparing hash values.

S/MIME has, in comparison to OpenPGP, a central trust entity called Certification Authority (CA). One generates a public key and the CA signs the public keys and generates a certificate. The certificates are assigned to different classes and sometimes cost money. Free certificates have to be checked again after a certain period. There is no key server on which the public keys are located, so users have to request them by letting the contact send a signed e-mail. This signed e-mail contains the public key and simultaneously confirms authenticity.

---

[1] https://www.openpgp.org/.

4   Study Methods

In this section, we describe our usability study method in detail.

4.1   App Selection

We intended to test OpenPGP and S/MIME on iOS and Android. To make a selection of which apps should be tested, 18 apps were investigated, 6 from the iOS AppStore, 10 from the Android PlayStore and 2 for both. According to studies [22, 24], users prefer to use their existing e-mail account. Therefore, we excluded all apps that require the creation of a new account, only offer secure communication with other users of the same app, or are not free. It turned out that none of the PGP apps for iPhone worked without errors on the test device iPhone 6s with iOS 13, and no S/MIME app on the Android device Samsung Galaxy S7 Edge.

iOS Mail App is the standard e-mail app for the iPhone and supports only S/MIME. It can be enabled in the settings menu. However, a certificate in the Public-Key Cryptography Standards (PKCS) #12 format is required. This certificate must then be installed and activated for the respective e-mail account. In preparation, we applied for the certificate, changed the format from CER to PKCS #12 format, and transferred it to the iPhone with a cable. The participants would take too long for this process and a computer is required.

FlowCrypt is a third-party app that supports OpenPGP and was selected for Android. The number of installations is according to the PlayStore over 10,000 [14]. FlowCrypt[2] is also available for GMail as a browser extension for Firefox and Chrome. At the time of the study, an app for iOS was in an early testing and evaluation phase but was not available on the app store. To use the app, the user has to login with an existing e-mail address. The app automatically generates a key pair and publishes the public key on a keyserver. After setting up a new account FlowCrypt sends a backup of the private key via e-mail, protected with the used passphrase, and a first encrypted e-mail, that informs about the app and explains basic elements.

4.2   Overview of Our Usability Study

The usability tests were carried out at our university of applied sciences in Germany in January 2020. For this reason, all questionnaires, task sheets, and interviews were in German. The smartphones used for the study are an iPhone 6s with iOS 13 and a Samsung Galaxy S7 Edge with Android Version 8. We did not observe any negative influences in our study from the Operating System (OS), although the smartphones were not the latest models. We configured the devices such that only the relevant apps could be found on the start screen. The

---

[2] https://flowcrypt.com/.

participants used an prepared Gmail account for this study and did not have to enter any private data. We planned a time frame of 45 min to 60 min per attendee. An overview of the procedure model we used is presented in Fig. 1.

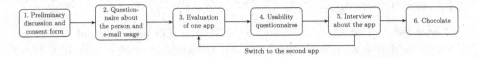

Fig. 1. Procedure model for our usability study for every participant.

Participants and Pre-questionnaire. We asked in university courses for participants and contacted some others directly. Eleven volunteers participated in our study, of which seven were males and four females. The majority with seven participants was between 21–30 years old. Two participants were in the age group 31–40, and two were over 60 years old. Seven out of eleven participants work in IT, including six students. The other four participants had no former background in IT. Two of them were students of business law.

After a short introduction, the participants were told that they want to communicate with a friend John Doe about something private and therefore have to encrypt their e-mails. The participants used the e-mail address from Max Anderson. Both, the given e-mail address, including password, and the e-mail address of the contact was specified on the task sheets so that no one had to use private accounts.

Furthermore, the pre-questionnaires include questions about their smartphone usage and general questions about e-mail and encryption. The majority which includes 64% of the participants write an e-mail with their smartphone once per month. In these e-mails, 82% considered the content-sensitive. Surprisingly, it is important for all participants that strangers cannot read their e-mails. However, 82% of all participants had already heard that e-mails can be encrypted, but only one of them encrypts e-mails or has done it in the past with PGP.

Usability Tests. In our usability study, we used the thinking-aloud method [11]. The tasks for both apps include subtasks for checking key management, sending encrypted e-mails, and how participants recognize encrypted e-mails because previous studies [1,8,19,24] have rated these tasks as prone to problems. We decided to include the set-up processes in the usability test by giving the participants clear instructions on the required settings.

Six participants started with the iOS Mail app and five with FlowCrypt on the Android smartphone. All responses from the e-mail contact were prepared and sent by the study coordinator during the test. The usability test for the iOS

Mail app first asks participants to add a new account in the settings with the given credentials and enable S/MIME in the settings menu.

After that, they should open the Mail app and read a signed e-mail from the contact, which tells them that there is a key included. At this point, they should discover and install the sender's public key, because in the next step they are prompted to send an encrypted e-mail back to the sender. If the participants skipped this task, the app shows a warning dialog that the e-mail they want to send to the contact is not encrypted. However, they could skip this warning as well and send the e-mail unencrypted. In the last subtask, the participants received a reply from the contact and they should recognize that this e-mail is encrypted.

With FlowCrypt, the participants first had to set up the app with the given e-mail address and a given passphrase. In the next step, they had to send an e-mail to the given recipient and attach their public key.

If they did this incorrectly, they received an auto-generated e-mail from FlowCrypt that gave them further instructions and helped to send the correct key to the recipient. Finally, the participants received a reply and must recognized that it is encrypted.

Usability Questionnaires. After the test, the participants immediately filled out two usability questionnaires. We decided to use the SUS [5] to compare the results with other studies [1,16–19]. Additionally, we use the UEQ-S [21], which includes hedonic quality. Since we conducted the usability study in German, we used the translated version for SUS from the SAP User Experience Community [15] and replaced the term *system* with *app*. For UEQ-S we used the translation from the official website [20]. All answers from the questionnaires were given in the form of a Likert scale [12].

Interview. The interview finalised the usability test and the questionnaires. Both apps contained query dialogues about key management. Key management was part of a subtask, however, the question is whether the participants understood why they need to do this.

Regarding the iOS Mail App, we asked questions about the certificate and whether the participants would request one and if so, how much they would be willing to pay. Furthermore, we asked the participants what they would improve, if they would use the apps. If they did not mention the aspects we noticed during the usability test, we tried to refer to this and in most cases received explanations of things that the participants were not aware of.

5   Evaluation of the Usability Study

This section shows the results for the iOS mail app and then the results for FlowCrypt. We itemise the results by first showing the results of SUS and UEQ-S, then the observational results of the usability tests and finally the results of the interview.

5.1   Results for iOS Mail App

Usability. The average SUS score for the iOS Mail App is 42.04, which is rated between *poor* and *ok* on the Bangor's scale [2]. For better comparison, we marked this value on more a human-readable scale in Fig. 3. On the acceptability scale from Fig. 3, it is classified as not acceptable. Figure 2a shows the result for the UEQ-S. The chart shows the individual mean values for *Pragmatic Quality* with −0.57, *Hedonic Quality* with 0.25, and the *Overall* result −0.16. All results are classified as *bad* that can be interpreted as in the range of the 25% worst results.

Observational Results. The first general problem we noticed was during enabling S/MIME. Nine out of the eleven participants forgot to confirm the settings for S/MIME, due to the placement of the finish button on the previous view and they switched directly to the e-mail app using the home button. The study coordinator informed the participants about this mistake, since otherwise the encryption function would not work. In general, many participants complained about the setup process. For instance, one of them said: *"To set everything up, I think I would need someone who already uses the app."*

While all participants successfully opened the Mail app and read the received e-mail, the next problems occurred during writing an encrypted e-mail. Eight participants had difficulties finding the public key of the recipient. Two of these participants sent an unencrypted e-mail and ignored the warning dialog. One of them thought the open lock means the e-mail is encrypted. Through a hint, they found the certificate with the public key and installed it. The e-mail encryption itself takes place automatically and was no problem for the participants.

The last task asked to explain how to recognize that the e-mail is encrypted. Ten participants correctly identified the lock icon next to the sender's e-mail address as a sign for an encrypted e-mail. One of them additionally selected the e-mail address and received more information about the certificate, including the encryption status.

Interview Results. In the interview, seven participants could describe the encryption process, because they already had previous knowledge due to their employment. The other participants suspected that the installation of the certificate had something to do with the encryption process. One of them mentioned: *"I couldn't send an encrypted e-mail before I installed the certificate, so I think it's for the encryption process"*. Some participants assumed the public key was a normal e-mail attachment, but it was hidden behind the sender's e-mail address. They suggested to show the certificate in a more obvious way or show a pop-up message, if an e-mail is signed and the certificate is not installed yet. All participants were sure that the certificate with the private key should not be transferred to the smartphone by sending an unencrypted email.

With eight participants, the majority would not request a certificate for private reasons. The rest could imagine doing it, if there is a reason to do so. One of them said: *"I don't think someone is interested in my private e-mails"*. Therefore, only two participants could imagine paying for a certificate.

Five participants answered yes to the question of whether they would use the app, while two did not answer, and one participant could imagine using it for business purposes only. One participant mentioned: *"The biggest problem would be to find a recipient that uses encryption as well."*

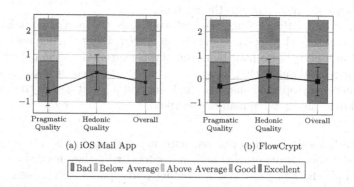

(a) iOS Mail App   (b) FlowCrypt

| ∎Bad ∎Below Average ∎Above Average ∎Good ∎Excellent |

Fig. 2. UEQ-S results for the iOS Mail app (a) and the Android app FlowCrypt (b) with the mean values for pragmatic quality, Hedonic quality, and the overall result. The error bars show the confidence intervals ($p = 0.05$) per scale with $N = 11$.

5.2   Results for Android App FlowCrypt

Usability. The app reached an average SUS score of 53.41. On the Bangor's scale, this is rated between *ok* and *good* and *Marginal Low* on the acceptability scale. Again, for better comparison, we marked this value on a more human-readable scale in Fig. 3. The average *Overall* result of the UEQ-S is -0.08, with a *Pragmatic Quality* of -0.29 and a *Hedonic Quality* of 0.14, which can be seen in Fig. 2b. All results are in the area *bad*.

Observational Results. During the setup process, we could not notice special occurrences, with the exception of a few typing errors in the passphrase that prevented the sign in. The study coordinator informed the participants if they did not notice the mistake themselves. In general, one participant described the setup as *nice and simple*. After the participants had access to the account, only one opened the information e-mail from FlowCrypt. The remaining participants ignored this e-mail or did not notice it.

For the first task, the participants had to send an encrypted e-mail with their public key attached. Seven participants performed this task correctly. One of them was still unsure, if the sent e-mail was encrypted because it was not necessary to select this as an option. Although the app shows a caption that the e-mail is encrypted, he or she did not recognize this. Out of the remaining participants, three did not find the key. One of them thought the passphrase is the public key and sent it in an encrypted e-mail to the contact. Another participant suspected the app always automatically attaches the public key to an e-mail and therefore did not attach it manually.

In all these cases, the participants received an e-mail with instructions from the app on how to proceed. All of them could follow these instructions and correctly sent the public key to the contact.

Similar to the iPhone app, the last task asks the participants to explain how they can tell whether an e-mail is encrypted. Eight participants correctly identified an encrypted e-mail based on the background or the colour scheme. One participant thought that an e-mail is only encrypted, if a key is attached and another one suspected that the word *encryption* that was in the recipient's e-mail address meant the e-mail is encrypted.

Interview Results. All seven participants working in the IT sector could describe the encryption process and understood why they needed to send the public key to the recipient. The remaining participants were unsure about it. One said: *"It's not secure to send the [public] key in the attachment."* The question of whether they would use FlowCrypt was answered by two with yes, seven with no and one did not give an answer. One who answered with no explained: *"The app should visually look more like an e-mail app. [...] it's a mixture of e-mail app and messenger app."* Another participant explained that he or she would only use it for business purposes but not for private ones.

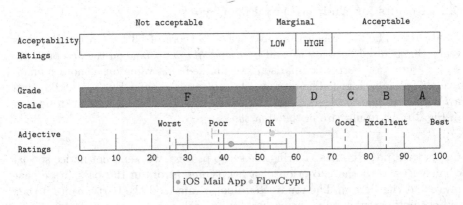

Fig. 3. The bangor's scale associates the SUS scale with more human-readable scales based on [2]. The error bars show the confidence intervals ($p = 0.05$) per scale with $N = 11$.

6   Discussion and Comparison of Our Results

Based on the evaluation of the usability tests, we can clarify RQ1 and RQ2 raised in Sect. 1. Regarding RQ1, we come to the conclusion that in our tests the participants were not able to encrypt e-mails on smartphones without critical mistakes. Most participants had difficulty sending an encrypted e-mail using the iOS Mail App. Despite a warning, some sent an unencrypted e-mail because they did not know how to proceed and could not find a solution on their own. Furthermore, participants mentioned that they would have problems to find the correct settings to activate S/MIME without help. FlowCrypt automatically encrypts e-mails, therefore less participants had difficulties with this task. The problem with this app is that the encryption process is too opaque. If users had to take care of key management, this led to a very critical mistake in one case, where the participant sent the passphrase as the public key.

Regarding RQ2, both apps are not usable according to the usability questionnaires. Even if the SUS scale for FlowCrypt is slightly over the *OK* area, the results of the UEQ-S are in the area *bad* on the benchmark chart. Apart from the usability questionnaires, more participants answered that they could imagine using the iOS Mail App for private purposes. Several participants mentioned that the setup process is too cumbersome, which could lead to a lower rate on both usability questionnaires, although the usability of the actual encryption and decryption process may be suitable.

7   Conclusion and Future Work

In this study, we analysed two e-mail encryption apps on smartphones according to the usability of their provided encryption functions, to detect if they are usable without critical mistakes. Since nearly half of all e-mails are read on mobile devices and other communication methods like messenger apps use E2EE by default, it was questionable why e-mail encryption on smartphones is not widespread. This study with eleven participants showed according to the usability questionnaires similar results as previous studies on desktop tools and indicated several usability issues. Many participants criticised a complex setup process for S/MIME and declared that they see no requirement to request a certificate for private purposes. Another problem was the participants' lack of understanding for key management, where especially S/MIME requires basic knowledge and the iOS Mail App needed manual user intervention. The results of the Android app FlowCrypt showed that too opaque handling of encryption leads to uncertainty amongst some participants because they were not sure if e-mails were encrypted.

In future work, we would like to repeat our study with more participants who better reflect the general public and have less technical background. Since the devices we used for our study were not recent ones, we would like to use current devices and use more email encryption apps, including paid apps to make more generic conclusions. We are also planning to let the participants request certificates themselves, transfer them to the smartphone and set them up independently. Another point should be the cross-use of email encryption on mobile devices and desktop devices. We want to check whether it is possible to read encrypted e-mails and to send encrypted e-mails on all devices used, in order to prevent that users can read the same encrypted message on the smartphone but not on the computer.

Acknowledgements. We thank Zinaida Benenson for the discussion and comments that greatly improved the manuscript.

References

1. Atwater, E., et al.: Leading Johnny to water: designing for usability and trust. In: Proceedings of the 11th Symposium On Usable Privacy and Security (SOUPS), p. 20 (2015). https://doi.org/10.5555/3235866.3235873
2. Bangor, A., Kortum, P., Miller, J.: Determining what individual SUS scores mean: adding an adjective rating scale. J. Usability Stud. **4**(3), 10 (2009)
3. Brandon, J.: It's 2018 and email is already dead. here's who zapped it into extinction (2018). https://www.inc.com/john-brandon/its-2018-email-is-already-dead-heres-who-zapped-it-into-extinction.html. Accessed 19 Jul 2021
4. Brandon, J.: Why email will be obsolete by 2020. Library Catalog: www.inc.com Section: Vision 2020 (2015). https://www.inc.com/john-brandon/why-email-will-be-obsolete-by-2020.html. Accessed 20 May 2020
5. Brooke, J.: SUS - a quick and dirty usability scale. Technical Report, p. 7 (1996)
6. Callas, J., et al.: OpenPGP message format. RFC 4880. RFC Editor, Nov 2007. http://www.rfc-editor.org/rfc/rfc4880.txt
7. Email Statistics Report, 2019–2023. Technical Report, The Radicati Group, Inc., (2019). https://www.radicati.com/wp/wp-content/uploads/2018/12/Email-Statistics-Report-2019-2023-Executive-Summary.pdf
8. Garfinkel, S.L.: Johnny 2: a user test of key continuity management with S/MIME and outlook express. In: Proceedings of the 1st Symposium On Usable Privacy and Security (SOUPS), pp. 13–24 (2005)
9. Haselton, T.: Personal email is dead - but I still can't quit it (2018). https://www.cnbc.com/2018/05/16/personal-email-is-dead-but-i-still-cant-quit-it.html. Accessed 19 Jul 2021
10. IBM Watson marketing. marketing benchmark report: email and mobile metrics for smarter marketing (2018). https://www.ibm.com/downloads/cas/L2VNQYQ0. Accessed 29 Apr 2020
11. Lewis, C.: Using the "Thinking-aloud" method in cognitive interface design. Technical Report, IBM Thomas J. Watson Research Center, p. 6, Feb 1982. Accessed 24 May 2020
12. Likert, R.: A technique for the measurement of attitudes. Archi. Psychol. **22**, 5–55 (1932). https://legacy.voteview.com/pdf/Likert_1932.pdf. Accessed 29 May 05 2020
13. Orman, H.: Encrypted Email. SCS, Springer, Cham (2015). https://doi.org/10.1007/978-3-319-21344-6
14. PlayStore: FlowCrypt: encrypted email with PGP (2018). https://play.google.com/store/apps/details?id=com.flowcrypt.email. Accessed 13 Jul 2020
15. Rummel, B.: System usability scale - jetzt auch auf Deutsch (2015). https://experience.sap.com/skillup/system-usability-scale-jetzt-auch-auf-deutsch/. Accessed 29 May 2020

16. Ruoti, S., et al.: Confused Johnny: when automatic encryption leads to confusion and mistakes. In: Proceedings of the 9th Symposium on Usable Privacy and Security (SOUPS) (2013). https://doi.org/10.1145/2501604.2501609. Accessed 01 May 2020

17. Ruoti, S., et al.: Private webmail 2.0: simple and easy-to-use secure email. In: Proceedings of the 29th Annual Symposium on User Interface Software and Technology (2016). https://doi.org/10.1145/2984511.2984580

18. Ruoti, S., et al.: We're on the same page: a usability study of secure email using pairs of novice users. In: Proceedings of the 2016 CHI Conference on Human Factors in Computing Systems (CHI 16) (2016). https://doi.org/10.1145/2858036.2858400

19. Ruoti, S., et al.: Why Johnny still, still can't encrypt: evaluating the usability of a modern PGP Client. (2015). arXiv: 1510.08555 [cs.CR]

20. Schrepp, M.: UEQ - user experience questionnaire (2018). https://www.ueq-online.org/. Accessed 29 May 2020

21. Schrepp, M., Hinderks, A., Thomaschewski, J.: Design and evaluation of a short version of the user experience questionnaire (UEQS). Int. J. Interact. Multimedia Artif. Intell. 4, 103 (2017). https://doi.org/10.9781/ijimai.2017.09.001

22. Sheng, S., et al.: Why johnny still can't encrypt: evaluating the usability of email encryption software. In: 2006 Symposium On Usable Privacy and Security - Poster Session (2006)

23. Tomlinson, R.: The first email. http://openmap.bbn.com/~tomlinso/ray/firstemailframe.html. Accessed 04 Jun 2020

24. Whitten, A., Tygar, J.D.: Why Johnny can't encrypt: a usability evaluation of PGP 5.0. In: In Proceedings of the 8th USENIX Security Symposium (1999)

Towards Detection of AI-Generated Texts and Misinformation

Ahmad Najee-Ullah$^{(\boxtimes)}$, Luis Landeros , Yaroslav Balytskyi ,
and Sang-Yoon Chang

University of Colorado Colorado Springs, Colorado Springs, CO 80918, USA
{anajeeul,llandero,ybalytsk,schang2}@uccs.edu

Abstract. Artificial Intelligence (AI) in the form of social text bots has emerged online in social media platforms such as Reddit, Facebook, Twitter, and Instagram. The increased cultural dependency on information and online interaction has given rise to bad actors who use text bots to generate and post texts on these platforms. Using the influence of social media, these actors are able to quickly disseminate misinformation and disinformation to change public perception on controversial political, economic, and social issues. To detect such AI-bot-based mis-information, we build a machine-learning-based algorithm and test it against the popular text generation algorithm, Generative Pre-trained Transformer (GPT), to show its effectiveness for distinguishing between AI-generated and human generated texts. Using a Neural Network with three hidden layers and Small BERT, we achieve a high accuracy performance between 97% and 99% depending on the loss function utilized for detection classification. This paper aims to facilitate future research in text bot detection in order to defend against misinformation and explore future research directions.

Keywords: Misinformation detection · Bot detection · Artificial intelligence · Generative Pre-trained Transformer (GPT) · Natural language processing · Machine learning · Neural networks · Bidirectional Encoder Representations from Transformers (BERT)

1 Introduction and Background

Popular social networks like Facebook, Twitter, Reddit, and others are targeted by text bots generating human-sounding texts. In this example, text bots refer to any algorithm that can quickly generate text that, to the average reader, would sound like a human had written it. These text bots can be highly effective in pretending to be humans online, spreading misinformation and disinformation, spreading false narratives, and pushing perspectives to change a readers perception on an issue [1]. As discussed in [1], text generation algorithms like OpenAI's third iteration of the Generative Pre-Trained Transformer (GPT-3) and its predecessor, GPT-2, have become very efficient at generating text that is difficult to identify as AI-generated and distinguish from those written by

© Springer Nature Switzerland AG 2022
S. Parkin and L. Viganò (Eds.): STAST 2021, LNCS 13176, pp. 194–205, 2022.
https://doi.org/10.1007/978-3-031-10183-0_10

humans. For example, in a viral AI-authored blog post in 2020, not only did the GPT-3-generated posts read like a human author, it also fooled the readers of Hacker News and was voted as the number one blog post [2]. This highlights how human readers have already begun to interact with artificially generated text and how susceptible they can be to the social influence exerted.

The impact of AI generated text has major security implications if used for malice. On platforms like Twitter, Facebook, and Reddit, posts criticizing big ticket issues like climate change and US international affairs pose a major cybersecurity risk if bad actors are successful in altering public opinions. This is especially concerning when looking at the rise of political extremists in the United States, claims of foreign election influence, as well as the riots, protests, and other public backlash seen as a result. Further research into the use of GPT-3 has revealed its efficiency in creating propaganda used to radicalize civilians outside and within the United States [3]. This has amplified the need to detect the use of algorithms like GPT-3 in attempts to disseminate misinformation and disinformation amongst the public and condemn the bad actors behind said attempts.

In this paper, we build a machine-learning-based detection algorithm to distinguish between AI-generated and human-generated texts in order to enable the defense against AI text bots and its use for spreading misinformation. For testing the detection algorithm, we generate the AI text passages from a popular text generation engine, GPT, and collect human-generated posts from Reddit. Our detection prototype provides an accuracy of 98.8% with the categorical cross-entropy-based and mean squared error-based algorithms. Since we already achieve high accuracy performance, we leave further optimization as well as adding greater sophistication and complexity on the detection as future work. We discuss even more future directions in order to facilitate greater research in addressing the important issue of misinformation.

2   Related Work

Online Bots and Text Generation: There have been instances of bots being utilized to fill online forms, provide services online, and attempt to impersonate humans on social platforms. However, a growing concern is the use of bots for text generation that could assist in swaying political elections or push anti-vaccine conspiracy theories as discussed in [4] and [5]. While these texts provide insight into the detection of per-account social bot detection, we focus on the ability to differentiate human and AI generated text anonymously. The spread of misinformation and disinformation can take many forms and bad actors can implement a multi-account approach to dissemination. Therefore, it is important to be able to detect AI text generations regardless of account associativity.

Previous research into the efficiency of text generation algorithms such as GPT has highlighted the use cases for maliciously generated texts. As seen in [3], the efficiency of GPT-3 generated texts that could be used for the mass spread of propaganda poses a significant threat to the public. Although the efficiency of GPT-3 has been proven, we elected to use its predecessor, GPT-2 because of the increased risk it poses by being readily available to bad actors (GPT-3 code is currently under research/API access). By choosing to create an algorithm to detect GPT-2 we provide insight into the detection of sophisticated text generation algorithms that are more easily accessible. Furthermore, we design and build a detection scheme which could be adapted for GPT-3 based text generations and detection upon its full release.

Detection Methods: This section highlights previous research in detection algorithms and approaches with a focus on those relevant to our problem statement of text-based detection. There are many paths to take when working towards detection. For example, in [6], it is mentioned that early detection, detection by multi-modal data fusion, and explanatory detection can be used for improving the detection performances. There are also directions such as GLTR [7] which can detect fake text with an accuracy of 72% in pre-training. Other detection methods include using Bidirectional long short-term memory (BiLSTM) and developing a Recurrent Neural Network (RNN) to detect human and spam-bot accounts on twitter [8]. Another method in previous research is the use of deep neural networks based on contextual long short-term memory (LSTM) [4]. There are others who also used the BERT model to detect fake news on Twitter [9]. When compared to these other methods, our research is different in the way that we use BERT to perform binary classification on text generated by either humans or AI. For this, we use GPT-2 to generate the AI data then crawl and collect the human data from Reddit posts.

3   Our Detection Scheme and Approach

We build our scheme to detect the AI-generated texts and distinguish it from the human-generated texts using machine learning. To validate and test our scheme, we gather GPT-generated texts and collect human-generated texts from Reddit (see Sect. 4).

Our detection algorithm makes a binary decision to classify whether a text passage is from either an AI/machine ("1") or a human author ("0"). We use a Neural Network based on the Small BERT model because BERT has proven to be a state-of-the-art model and can operate at high efficiency for many natural language processing problems. We also use mean squared error (MSE) and categorical cross-entropy (CE) as loss functions for the accuracy performances.

Binary Classification: During this experiment, we observed a binary classification in differentiating between human and AI generated texts. We encoded the human data as "0" and the AI generated data as "1", a human classification representing the negative case and an AI classification representing the positive case. Considering the task of determining whether a text was written by a human or GPT author, there are only two options for classification. Therefore, the use of a binary "yes/1" or "no/0" classification is sufficient for this problem.

Sequential Neural Network: We utilized a Sequential Neural Network in Keras that has three hidden layers. For each of the layers, the dot product is performed on the input and weights are added that correspond to each following layer. We then pass this through an activation function of our choosing. The 3-Layer Sequential Neural Network is a popular starting point for many natural language processing problems due to its retaliative simplicity and ease of use. This network provided a suitable starting point to determine a baseline for accuracy performances.

Bidirectional Encoder Representations from Transformers (BERT): This model is designed to pre-train deep bidirectional representations from unlabeled text by jointly conditioning on both the left and right context. By having bi-directional understanding of a sentence, the model is able to better grasp context in language. BERT was selected as the natural language model of choice due to its efficiency and popularity as a state-of-the-art model. Additionally, it proved to be 7% to 10% more accurate in classifying human and AI generated text when compared to the 3-layer Sequential Neural Network.

We used the Small BERT model [10] pre-trained for English on the Wikipedia and BooksCorpus data set. Small BERT, as the name implies, is designed to be simple and more lightweight than the other BERT models. We encoded the binary classification as mentioned in the previous section as the labels in training. For the visualization of data integrity and accuracy, we used UMAP [11].

Loss Function: In our models, we used two loss functions, one based on the mean squared error (MSE) and another based on the categorical cross-entropy (CE). Both MSE and CE are standard and appropriate for loss functions, as they increase with greater differences between the truth vs. the algorithm output decision. CE in particular increases as there is smaller dependency between the truth vs. the algorithm decision, e.g., CE = 0 if they are the same/completely dependent. CE is defined as:

$$\text{CE} = -\sum_{i=1}^{N} y_i \ln(\hat{y}_i) \tag{1}$$

where y_i is the true value at the i-th instance, i.e., $y_i \in \{0, 1\}$ where 0 corresponds to human and 1 corresponds to AI, and $\hat{y}_i$ is the algorithm decision value, i.e., $\hat{y}_i$ can be any value between 0 and 1 and $\hat{y}_i \in [0, 1]$.

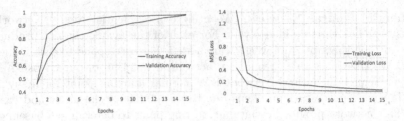

Fig. 1. Accuracy and MSE loss as the training progresses.

4   Data Collection for Testing

4.1   Generating and Collecting Text Data

AI Data: Since GPT has already proven itself to be capable of fooling the average reader into thinking its a human writer [2], the use of OpenAI's easily accessible GPT-2 is sufficient for the task of gathering AI generated text. The data generated by our GPT-2 prototype was designed to mimic online posts from human authors. Although we previously discussed the efficiency of GPT-3 in the creation of human-sounding text generations, the technology is not openly available to the public. Therefore, the use of GPT-2 provides a more realistic look into what current day bad actors have access to (i.e., readily accessible in open source) and the harm they could inflict on social media.

Human Data: In recent years, we have seen the increased popularity and influence that social media platforms can impose on various industries. Reddit, with over 50 million users engaging in daily text-based conversations, has already made headlines in the financial sector with the WallStreetBets subredddit. A large community of investors were able to raise GameStop stocks from $48 to $480 during a "short squeeze" that caused major losses throughout the industry to those who weren't involved [12]. Imagine the potential damage that could be caused by a similar group empowered by bad actors utilizing AI to spread misinformation and influence public opinion.

Reddit provides an ideal environment for bad actors to employ AI generated language. Considering that GPT-2 was trained utilizing vast amounts of text data from Reddit, it also serves as a sufficient environment for collecting human data. In order to collect human texts similar to the data used to train the GPT algorithm, we gathered human data by scraping the top unique posts on Reddit and each comment from their respective comment forests. By pulling only the top posts, we ensure that initial posts and their comments have been curated by humans through the use of an up-vote.

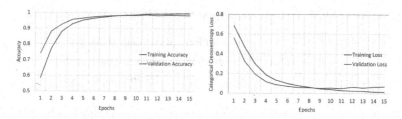

Fig. 2. Accuracy and CE loss as the training progresses.

5 Evaluation Results

5.1 Training Analyses in Processing

In machine learning, the model learns the relevant features rather than memorizing the training samples. The model processes the data to extract the relevant features for the classification process to generalize the classification, i.e., it can classify the new input data not used/seen in training. To achieve such feat, we introduce the dropout layer. In this section, we vary the training overhead in the number of epochs; increasing epochs increases the processing and, more specifically, the back-propagation rounds. Beyond this section, we fix the training to use fifteen epochs by default.

Figure 1 and Fig. 2 show the accuracy/loss performances as we progress and vary the number of training epochs. Figure 1 uses MSE as the loss function while Fig. 2 uses CE. In both loss-function cases, the accuracy gain difference decreases as we increase the number of epochs for training, i.e., there are diminishing accuracy gains as we progress in training. For example, in Fig. 2 using the CE-based loss function (which has better performance than when using MSE-based loss function), from one epoch to two epochs, the accuracy increases by 0.185 from 0.585 to 0.770; this gain difference is greater than both that from two epochs to three (accuracy increases by 0.109 from 0.770 to 0.879) and that from three epochs to fifteen epochs (the accuracy increases by 0.117 from 0.879 to 0.996). In addition, our model saturates the training curve after around fifteen epochs, i.e., the accuracy does not improve after increasing the number of epochs past this point. When the saturation is reached, the loss curve varies by less than 1%. Therefore, we train our algorithm for fifteen epochs to avoid overfitting and to make the training economical (more epochs require greater processing), and ensuring that the model learns the relevant features rather than memorizing the data. We observe that the CE training curve saturates faster than the MSE, as shown in Figs. 1 and 2, and results in higher accuracy.

5.2 Testing Accuracy Performance

Based on the trained model using fifteen epochs (we study training in Sect. 5.1), we test the detection performance of our scheme, where the testing data and the training data do not overlap. In the case that AI texts are predicted to

Table 1. Correlation table with the MSE loss function.

	Classified human	Classified AI
True human	$97.52 \pm 0.94\%$	$2.48 \pm 0.94\%$
True AI	$2.14 \pm 1.44\%$	$97.86 \pm 1.44\%$

Table 2. Correlation table with the categorical cross-entropy loss function.

	Classified human	Classified AI
True human	$99.06 \pm 0.54\%$	$0.94 \pm 0.54\%$
True AI	$2.94 \pm 1.35\%$	$97.06 \pm 1.35\%$

be AI generated, we have an occurrence of a true-positive (TP). Conversely, a true-negative (TN) represents the detection of a human author when the text was indeed written by a human. Thus P represents the total occurrences of AI generated texts (positive occurrences), and N represents the total occurrences of human written texts (negative occurrences).

We use the standard definition of Accuracy (ρ), i.e., $\rho = \frac{TP+TN}{P+N}$ to calculate the efficiency of correctly classifying negative and positive predictions.

Since the accuracy performances depend on the loss function, we indicate the loss function in the subscript, e.g., ρ_{MSE}, the accuracy performance of the detection algorithm when minimizing the mean squared error (MSE).

We observe that the classification of human text when using categorical cross-entropy (CE) as its loss function provides better accuracy performance than when using MSE. The accuracy based on minimizing MSE is 97.52% and the accuracy based on minimizing the categorical cross-entropy is 99.06%. Additionally, we observe that the classification of AI text provides slightly better performance when utilizing MSE rather than CE, at 97.86% and 97.06% respectively. Thus, we report a conservative estimate of 98.8% detection accuracy. We generated the uncertainty bands by the batch method with 5 runs of the model, took the mean value and set the uncertainty as one standard deviation, σ.

$$\rho_{MSE\text{-}Human} = 97.52 \pm 0.94\% \quad \rho_{CE\text{-}Human} = 99.06 \pm 0.54\%$$

Additionally, we observe the chance of our algorithm generating false-positives (FP) and false-negatives (FN) by calculating the false-postive and false-negative rates. The former represented by human authored texts classified as AI-generated and the latter being AI-generated texts being classified as human written. We use the definition of the False Positive Rate (α), where $\alpha = \frac{FP}{FP+TN}$ and the False Negative Rate (β), where $\beta = \frac{FN}{FN+TP}$.

We determine the chance of providing a FP and FN by observing the loss function in both MSE and CE. When reviewing the false-positive rate, minimiz-

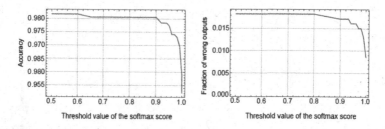

Fig. 3. Model accuracy and fraction of wrong outputs by softmax threshold.

ing based on the CE had a lower chance of occurrence at 0.94%. Meanwhile the occurrence of a false-negative was lower utilizing MSE with 2.14%.

$$\alpha_{\text{MSE}} = 2.48 \pm 0.94\% \quad \alpha_{\text{CE}} = 0.94 \pm 0.54\%$$

$$\beta_{\text{MSE}} = 2.14 \pm 1.44\% \quad \beta_{\text{CE}} = 2.94 \pm 1.35\%$$

The correlation Tables 1 and 2 provide the percentage of TP, TN, FP, and FN identified in our data set. The training loss and accuracy are as function of the epochs are represented in Figs. 1 and 2. The overlap of classified texts as a function of the softmax score is represented in Fig. 4, and one can observe that BERT separates human and AI samples with high confidence.

When considering the FP and FN rates, its important to recognize the importance of these figures in relation to security. The situation created by a 2.14% false-negative rate or "miss rate" highlights the 2% chance of the algorithm classifying text as human written when it was actually AI-generated. This poses a larger security risk in comparison to a false-positive scenario as it providing validation to a post that could be spreading misinformation through the use of AI. Fortunately, 2% is relatively low, however efforts to decrease this number will lower the risk related to security implications.

5.3 Model Validation

When implementing a neural network, the confidence interval in which classifications are made is important to determining a models reliability. To better understand the confidence threshold in the algorithm, we observe the accuracy in relation to the softmax threshold (see Fig. 3). The threshold determines which outputs from the algorithm are classified as human or AI. We can see that the accuracy is not significantly affected until a threshold greater than 0.9 is implemented (Fig. 3 left). Similarly, the chances of incorrectly classifying an output improves after a threshold of 0.9 (Fig. 3 right). Figure 4 (left) highlights the distinct classification of human and AI texts with no overlap with "0" representing human texts and "1" representing AI texts. Figure 4 (right) further illustrates the accuracy of detecting human and AI generations in relation to the softmax score.

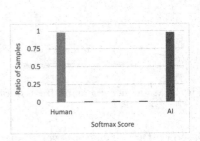

Fig. 4. Classification results visualized by UMAP [11].

6 Future Directions and Discussion

Other AI Engines: This paper focuses on the detection of text generated by the GPT-2 algorithm. While GPT is considered to be one of the best easily accessible text generation tools for imitating human text, other algorithms exist for this task. For example, it would be beneficial to investigate other tools for generating text in mass and adapt a Neural Network to detect the text generated by different natural language algorithms.

We recognize that our research generalizes AI text generation through the use of GPT, which has its own limitations. For example, when generating longer texts, GPT-2 tends to go off topic and requires more human monitoring. If the focus of text bot detection shifts from social media platforms to long form blog posts and articles, methods for detection may need to change. If a GPT instance, or a different algorithm all together, is trained to generate longer articles with little human intervention, it may possess different features in its generation that are needed for detection.

Open Set Recognition: Open Set Recognition (OSR) solves a classification problem when there is data with unknown classes. OSR is commonly used in the training and testing phases of natural language processing problems. The introduction of unknown or never seen before data can introduce higher rates in errors/false-positives. However, the ideas discussed and approach taken in the OSR techniques and Entropic Open Set Loss function [13,14] serve as proof in the ability to increase the accuracy of algorithms when handling unknowns.

Taking a similar approach to these previous research directions, utilizing an Entropic Open Set Loss function can increase accuracy and reduce errors in the detection of AI generated texts, since the errors (especially with false-negatives) can have a critical impact on AI-based misinformation detection. As previously discussed, the result of detection in our algorithm is more concerned with the rate of false-negatives than the rate of false-positives due to the potential security implications (see Sect. 5.2). Therefore, OSR and Entropic Open Set Loss function could aid in reducing the chance of a false-positive when differentiating between text generations from multiple algorithms and human authored texts.

Furthermore, in the case of our research, in addition to providing the algorithm with different data for training and testing, we could utilize OSR to detect texts generated by AI engines beyond GPT. It would be interesting to see how the algorithm would handle the classification of AI and human written texts when more than one engine is producing said text. This is important because GPT produces features within its generations that the algorithm is able to use for classification. Alternative text generation engines may possess different features. Therefore, ensuring that a detection algorithm can identify and correctly classify multiple different engines as AI is important for our overall objective.

Expanding the Data Set: Expanding the number of recognizable characters to the algorithm would also be beneficial in improving detection accuracy. We realize the absence of emoticon recognition in our current algorithm and data set. The concept of emoji2vec introduced in [15] provides a valuable contribution for detection. Emojis are used extensively on social media platforms. Therefore, having an algorithm that is accurately able to interpret them would be important in its implementation.

Different Detection Algorithms: Upon realization of results achieved on a simple 3-Layer Neural Network on Keras and the smaller BERT model, expanding to bigger models may yield better results. The details behind the state-of-the-art success in the performance of BERT is not yet completely understood [16,17]. Nonetheless, the smaller model utilizing less stacked encoder blocks provided the 97% to 99% accuracy figures for human detection (recognizing the difference in MSE and CE) and the 97% accuracy for AI detection. Implementing the larger BERT algorithm with more encoder blocks may prove to increase accuracy and decrease the false-negative rate.

Alternatively, there is the option of creating our own detection model based on the features gathered from GPT text generation. BERT and 3-layer Sequential Neural Networks are efficient in solving a multitude of natural language processing problems. However, designing an algorithm specifically for detection may prove to be more accurate and efficient for this task. Detection algorithms such as [7] prove to be successful on the smaller 117M parameter model of GPT. However, when using more complex architecture, it becomes less accurate in detection. It is important to improve the detection accuracy on texts generated from the bigger models to better capture what may be used by bad actors.

Active Measures Our work focuses on building the detection intelligence (passive measure) which enables the active measures based on such intelligence. Future research can build on our work to create active defense against misinformation distribution, including the text-post revocation, the network-layer filtering of the misinformation, and the filtering based on the identification of the malicious or compromised accounts.

7   Conclusion

With an increase in AI generated text, the spread of misinformation has become a greater threat. Social media platforms are being targeted by mass misinformation campaigns using AI text generation. Being able to detect if text was written by humans or AI is crucial in preventing the spread of misinformation from altering public perception on political, economic, and social issues.

Our classification uses a Neural Network and Small BERT to determine if a text has been written by an AI or a human. When classifying samples, it is always important to think about the possibility of false-positives and false-negatives. In this case, a false-negative represents the classification of a text sample as human when in reality it was generated by an AI. This possibility poses a greater security risk because by classifying the text as human generated, it creates an opportunity to continue the spread of misinformation.

We design and build our detection classification and collect data to train and test our scheme. Our data collection includes both the generation of AI texts using GPT and crawling/collecting the human texts from Reddit. Our experimental results give an accuracy performance of 98.8% and a 2.14% chance of a false-negative as opposed to a 2.48% chance of getting a false-positive. Table 1 Having a false negative is a more dangerous outcome, therefore it is important to highlight that during testing, the probability of this occurring was the lowest.

Despite the simplicity of the algorithmic design of our scheme (selecting algorithms known to be efficient and using and small number of layers), we provide strong accuracy performances in detecting AI-generated texts. We include discussions for potential future directions, including more sophisticated design/techniques and active measures beyond intelligence building, to facilitate further research to secure the social networking against AI-generated misinformation.

Acknowledgment. This material is based upon work supported by the National Science Foundation under Grant No. 1922410.

References

1. Knight, W.: Ai can write disinformation now-and dupe human readers, Wired, May 2021
2. Lyons, K.: A college student used GPT-3 to write fake blog posts and ended up at the top of hacker news, The Verge, August 2020
3. McGuffie, K., Newhouse, A.: The radicalization risks of GPT-3 and advanced neural language models, arXiv preprint arXiv:2009.06807 (2020)
4. Kudugunta, S., Ferrara, E.: Deep neural networks for bot detection. Inf. Sci. **467**, 312–322 (2018)

5. Efthimion, P.G., Payne, S., Proferes, N.: Supervised machine learning bot detection techniques to identify social twitter bots. SMU Data Sci. Rev. **1**(2), 5 (2018)
6. Guo, B., Ding, Y., Yao, L., Liang, Y., Yu, Z.: The future of misinformation detection: new perspectives and trends, arXiv preprint arXiv:1909.03654 (2019)
7. Gehrmann, S., Strobelt, H., Rush, A.M.: Gltr: Statistical detection and visualization of generated text (2019)
8. Wei, F., Nguyen, U.T.: Twitter bot detection using bidirectional long short-term memory neural networks and word embeddings. In: 2019 First IEEE International Conference on Trust, Privacy and Security in Intelligent Systems and Applications (TPS-ISA), pp. 101–109 (2019)
9. Dukić, D., Keča, D., Stipić, D.: Are you human? detecting bots on twitter using bert. In: 2020 IEEE 7th International Conference on Data Science and Advanced Analytics (DSAA), pp. 631–636. IEEE (2020)
10. Devlin, J., Chang, M.-W., Lee, K., Toutanova, K.: Bert: pre-training of deep bidirectional transformers for language understanding, arXiv preprint arXiv:1810.04805 (2018)
11. McInnes, L., Healy, J., Melville, J.: Umap: uniform manifold approximation and projection for dimension reduction, arXiv preprint arXiv:1802.03426 (2018)
12. Yarovaya, L.: Gamestop: Wallstreetbets trader army is back for a second share rally - here's how to make sense of it, The Conversation, February 2021
13. Dhamija, A.R., Günther, M., Boult, T.E.: Reducing network agnostophobia, arXiv preprint arXiv:1811.04110 (2018)
14. Song, L., Sehwag, V., Bhagoji, A.N., Mittal, P.: A critical evaluation of open-world machine learning, arXiv preprint arXiv:2007.04391 (2020)
15. Eisner, B., Rocktäschel, T., Augenstein, I., Bošnjak, M., Riedel, S.: emoji2vec: Learning emoji representations from their description, arXiv preprint arXiv:1609.08359 (2016)
16. Kovaleva, O., Romanov, A., Rogers, A., Rumshisky, A.: Revealing the dark secrets of bert, arXiv preprint arXiv:1908.08593 (2019)
17. Clark, K., Khandelwal, U., Levy, O., Manning, C.D.: What does bert look at? an analysis of bert's attention, arXiv preprint arXiv:1906.04341 (2019)

Author Index

printed in the United States
by Baker & Taylor Publisher Services

Printed in the United States
by Baker & Taylor Publisher Services